D1195533

THE MANAGEMENT
OF CAPITAL PROJECTS

THE MANAGEMENT
OF CAPITAL PROJECTS

STUDIES IN THE COAL, TRANSPORT
AND ELECTRICITY SUPPLY INDUSTRIES

BY

R. J. S. BAKER

THE LONDON SCHOOL OF ECONOMICS
AND POLITICAL SCIENCE
(*University of London*)

G. BELL AND SONS LTD
LONDON . W.C.2

TO MY WIFE

Printed in Great Britain by Richard Clay and Company, Ltd.,
Bungay, Suffolk

PREFACE

I have to thank a great many people and institutions for enabling me to write this book, first the London School of Economics and the Passfield Trustees for the facilities I enjoyed under the Webb Research Fellowship from October 1958 to February 1960 and also for arranging publication.

The ideas and questions on which these studies were based, however, go back a good deal further. During the period 1951–58 I had the experience, as Head of the Buildings Branch at Post Office Headquarters, of controlling individual building schemes and annual building programmes—which increased gradually from £3½ million to £11 million a year—and of co-ordinating them with our very much larger engineering programmes. I owe an enormous amount to my chiefs and colleagues within the Department, who set me such challenging problems during this time, and supported me towards their solution. After I had published an account [1] of the building programme system which we devised, the *Architects' Journal* commented as follows:[2]

> Two generations of under-investment have left us with colossal arrears of obsolescence in houses, schools, hospitals, roads and other things. Expansion, rebuilding and replacement cannot, obviously, be done all at once or even over a short period. Hence the need for selection and for programmes of work to be started in a given period. Curiously, the methods of selection and the procedure of drawing up investment programmes for the public services have received little examination or explanation in public.
>
> This essay is . . . therefore welcome as one of the few documents which are available to would-be students of this administrative problem.

Shortly afterwards I took up the L.S.E. Fellowship in order to study how some other public industries and services tackled their capital development programmes and projects. Again I

[1] R. J. S. Baker, 'Post Office Building Programmes', *Public Administration*, Summer 1958. (Awarded the Haldane Medal of the Royal Institute of Public Administration, for 1958.)
[2] 7th August 1958.

must thank the Post Office for granting me sabbatical leave for this purpose.

I soon found myself not only tackling bigger subjects but doing so over a wider field, not only the planning, controlling and seeing through to completion of large projects and programmes but also the building up of groups of specialists and management structures within each organisation to deal with these tasks. Yet despite this extension into new fields, I soon felt that most of the people in the organisations I was studying spoke much the same language as I did. Of course I could not range over all the public services, and I soon found that I would be fully occupied for over a year if I concentrated on the National Coal Board, the various different Electricity Boards and London Transport. (I also visited the L.C.C. and the United Steel Companies for comparison, contrast and background; but I found in the end that an account of either would not easily fit within the scope of this book.) I am deeply grateful to a number of very busy people in all these organisations, Board Chairmen, Chief Officers and others, for their time and trouble in talking to me, letting me visit their various Headquarters, planning offices, works and construction sites, and see, and publish, many internal documents.

I must, however, emphasise the limitations of time on the number of visits that I could make within each organisation, or type of organisation. In the National Coal Board, London Transport and the Central Electricity Generating Board I was able to visit all the Headquarter Departments and offices concerned with my subject, but with their organisations outside London, I had to be selective. In the Coal Board I visited the West Midlands Divisional Headquarters and the North-East No. 3 and North Staffordshire Areas; in the C.E.G.B. the Southern Project Group and the London Region Headquarters. I had to be more selective still with Area Electricity Boards. There are twelve of these in England and Wales independent of one another, and I was only able to visit five of them, London, Southern, South-Western, Yorkshire and North-Western and certain Sub-areas and District Headquarters. I also went to the Headquarters of the South of Scotland Electricity Board (and also its Edinburgh Area) and of the North of Scotland Hydro-Electric Board, but the latter could only arrange one interview. Hence in all these industries, despite my efforts to see representative places and to supplement my visits by reading and discussion, I may well have failed to get a truly representative picture on certain points. In particular, I cannot be certain that what I have said about Area Electricity Boards in general applies to the seven out of twelve Boards to whom I made no approaches.

I must also make another important qualification. I finished compiling my information in January 1960, and shortly after returned to the Post Office. Since then I have in my spare time made various revisions in the form and arrangement of the manuscript—which have gone hand-in-hand with various ideas about publication. I could not, however, attempt to keep up-to-date with the internal workings of each industry described, and I have done no more than add one or two footnotes on particularly important points which have come to my notice from Annual Reports and other publications. The whole of the main text of this book, therefore, should be taken as an account of the situation as I was able to discover it by the end of 1959. Yet I would claim that the great bulk is still up-to-date and has not been superseded by any other publication.

The penetrating study by Dr. Tibor Barna of the National Institute of Social and Economic Research *Investment and Growth Policies of British Industrial Firms* (1962) throws a flood of light on problems somewhat similar to those which I have discussed but in the very different field of the food-processing and electrical manufacturing industries. It appeared after my manuscript went to press, so I have only been able to refer to two of its most striking conclusions in footnotes (pp. 245, 252).

I am deeply grateful to all those who have either given me information, ideas or criticisms themselves or introduced me to others who did so. There were a great many such people within the organisations I have studied, as well as colleagues in the Civil Service. It is difficult to single out individuals, and I hope that all these serving public servants will accept the thanks I now offer collectively and anonymously, yet very warmly. Among others, however, I must mention, at the London School of Economics the Director, Sir Sydney Caine, Professor W. A. Robson (then Professor of Public Administration, under whose auspices I worked), Professor R. S. Edwards (former

Professor of Economics and now Chairman of the Electricity
Council) and Professor Sir Arnold Plant (Professor of Commerce); at the Post Office Sir Gordon Radley (former Director
General) and Mr. J. K. Horsefield (former Director of Finance
and Accounts and now with the International Monetary Fund);
at the Royal Institute of Public Administration Mr. Raymond
Nottage, the Director.

I must, of course, add that no one whom I have mentioned,
nor indeed any institution or person other than myself, bears
any responsibility for anything I have written or implied.

R. J. S. B.

CONTENTS

INTRODUCTION

Quite a lot of people nowadays—practical business men, trade unionists and political leaders, as well as economic theorists—are showing a great deal of interest in long-term economic planning—particularly the planning of capital development. Of course, different people have different ideas in mind when they use these phrases, whether in relation to this country, to other economically advanced countries or to the under-developed countries. Now any kind of planning involves a certain amount of hard thinking, including abstract thinking—it may even involve mathematics. But no kind of economic planning can get very far unless the people who are doing it understand, in practical concrete terms, what is the real nature of their subject matter and how their ideas can be carried into concrete achievements on the ground. However grand the architectural design may look, it cannot mean very much unless the architects really understand the nature of the materials they are using—the individual bricks and other things out of which their house is to be built. This is particularly true of such a large subject as the planning of capital development. 'Capital development' can mean, in practice, so many different things—either the purchase of a wheelbarrow from a local shop or the construction of a nuclear power station, which will not only involve years of design, followed by years of construction, but also an earlier period still in which large numbers of people will have to be trained to do the designing. Many other things which go under the name of 'capital development' are nearly as complex to plan and design and get carried out as nuclear power stations, even though they may sound more familiar to most people. A modern coal mine, for instance, is both in its construction and in its subsequent working a vast collective enterprise of miners, mining engineers, mechanical, civil and electrical engineers, backed up by the efforts of a great variety of people, varying from the economists and geologists, on the one hand, to solicitors and accountants, on the other. A modern coal mine, during the course of its construction, looks more like the site of a complete new town than any single

1

industrial project.   It may be ten years from the time that the idea of having such a new mine is first conceived in outline in somebody's mind to the time when the whole project has reached its maximum level of production.   Coal mines and nuclear power stations are not exceptional.   Very similar remarks could be made about chemical plants, railway electrification projects and many other things—although there are, of course, quite another set of projects, very important in any general schemes of capital development, which can be brought into use in very much shorter periods.   The point is that if we are talking in general terms about capital development, all the things necessary to sustain and develop the life of a modern community, we must know something about the nature and size of these projects, and the time they take to develop, before we can really talk usefully about any forms of economic planning.

Furthermore, the very word 'planning' needs to be used with care.   It must not, for instance, be confused with 'forecasting'.   Planning involves decisions about what to do by somebody who has power to carry out these decisions.   Forecasting, on the other hand, is the uncertain art of trying to predict what other people will do—or, indeed, how *things* or the forces of nature will behave.   Planning, of course, is dependent on forecasting on the basis of the most reliable information available.   The planning of capital development involves a proper knowledge of those factors which are under one's own control and those which are not.   It involves understanding the physical nature and composition of the particular capital projects concerned—what is involved in their construction, how both the raw materials and the manufactured components and apparatus will behave, and above all, knowledge about the many different groups of people involved in the processes of design and construction, and how far the activities of such groups of people can be influenced or controlled.   Anyone who has had any practical experience of the construction of even a small building, let alone any large industrial project, knows that it is very likely to be delayed both in its starting and completion, and that it will probably cost in the end a good deal more than the estimate.   In sound planning or forecasting it is necessary to try to understand some of the factors that cause these delays—whether they are the responsibility of the architect, the contractor, the sub-contractors, the various groups of tradesmen or the weather, or the possibly varying demands of the people who have commissioned the building, or whatever the project may be. It is seldom possible to understand these things without spending a good deal of time actually looking round the construction site and the planning offices. It is necessary, however, to come back to this question of how the person or organisation which commissioned the project in the first instance arrives at the decision and formulates the requirements in detail—whether this process is done at the right time and with sufficient clarity and understanding, and what is implied in terms of time and cost and the risks involved.

This consideration takes us back again one stage farther to a consideration of the many different purposes for which people plan many different types of project, all of which are sometimes lumped together under the general term 'capital development'. On the one hand, there may be some completely new development, the settlement of virtually undeveloped territory with the laying out of roads and other communications, electric power supplies and other public services. There may, on the other hand, simply be an expansion of such services or of manufacturing or extractive industries in an already developed country, such as the United Kingdom. For instance, telephone exchanges are being built in order to provide telephone service for people who have not had it at all before. Similarly, there has been some development in the electricity supply industry to serve the needs of country people who previously had no electricity at all. Many developments of public services in this country, however (as distinct from manufacturing industry), have been to maintain or expand services to existing consumers. The great bulk of the very extensive developments of the electricity supply industry have been designed largely to cater for such increased use by existing consumers. There is, however, both in electricity and in other public services, an element of replacement of old equipment by more modern equipment, either because the former was physically worn out or more often because it was considered to be uneconomic. In some types of project, both in manufacturing and extractive industries, and in the public services, it is very important, but also very difficult, to distinguish between the elements of re-placement and of provision for expansion. The same project will cater for both purposes, and only a very careful economic study will distinguish which is predominant. Special problems arise in connection with certain industries. In electricity there is the question of the pattern of demand—'peak loads' and 'base loads' for which different types of plant may be suitable. In coal mining there is a very intricate and complex connection between provision for expansion and provision for replacing outworn capital equipment, and the carrying on of current operations. The very term 'capital development' is extremely difficult to define in the coal-mining industry. Much of the capital consists in the last analysis of empty spaces in the ground. There are main tunnels and shafts which may be considered as essential parts of more or less permanent capital projects—and there are further extensions of the tunnels which are simply expendable parts of current operations. Further-more, the whole process of extending the semi-permanent capital construction is mixed up with the day-to-day operations and there can be mutual interference between the two types of activity.

This brings us to another aspect of the processes of capital development planning and execution which may be of par-ticular interest at the present time—the way in which the working of these processes illustrates, and indeed influences, the general structure and techniques of management in large organisations. In the very largest concerns, such as the National Coal Board and the Central Electricity Generating Board, new capital development is such a major part of the functions of management at all levels that it calls for the creation of new and quite separate departments and organs of manage-ment and the working out of special relationships between these departments and other parts of the management structure. Such problems of inter-relationship arise also even in concerns where new capital development takes a relatively small place in the whole of management activity. Moreover, there are many different ways in which these relationships can be worked out. The predominating influence may be exercised by technical departments; or financial and commercial depart-ments may take a very important, if not quite an equal, share.

In any case there will be complex problems of communication and co-ordination between departments of these sorts and other departments—for instance, those concerned with forecasting, with training and provision of specialised staff, with marketing and with research. The process of planning and then carrying out capital projects also provides fascinating examples of different methods of tackling the perennial problems of centralisation and decentralisation and of the relationship between different professional hierarchies. Again there is a further set of problems in the relationships of the planning and using organisation, on the one hand, and manufacturers, contractors and consultants, on the other. There are, indeed, important problems as to whether particular parts of the process of planning and carrying out capital projects should be given to internal staff or to these outside concerns. Among the different organisations described in this book we shall find examples of varying methods of tackling all these problems, and will be able to discuss, on the basis of a certain amount of factual detail, the techniques and the standard working arrangements which have been employed. Perhaps the factual material produced in the course of these discussions may be of interest to those concerned with the more general study of management structures and management techniques.

In describing all these different aspects of the problems of capital development we shall take as examples two major public services, the electricity supply industry and London Transport, and one extractive industry, the coal industry. With some reference in each case to the management organisation concerned, we shall look at the reasons why in recent years this industry or service has needed new capital equipment, of what the capital equipment has consisted and what, in detail, is involved in the process of getting such equipment provided—including the processes of looking back at the end and checking how far the achievement compares with the original plan. In the case of electricity supply we shall study separately the two very different sides of that industry, generation and distribution, with a briefer look at the main transmission system which connects the two.

These studies are based, not on any economic judgements as to the policies of the industries concerned, but rather on investigations into the practical processes of carrying them out. The writer, who has had some experience of responsibility for similar activities in another public service, has worked on material obtained in discussions with the people concerned with getting the various parts of the job done in the various sides of the organisations concerned—all the way from the national headquarters to the construction sites. In presenting and analysing this material he is not claiming to present any comprehensive theory, but merely to provide a number of thoughts and considerations, and, it is hoped, some useful raw material from which others can develop more general studies.

CHAPTER I

THE COAL INDUSTRY (I)

(a) *Purposes and Forms of Capital Development*

The National Coal Board has by law the duty, and the monopoly, of 'working and getting the coal in Great Britain', and from selling coal it got 88 per cent of its income in 1958. It also makes much of the nation's coke—from which it got 5 per cent of its income in 1958 or £48·7 million—and certain manufactured fuels, gas, chemical by-products and bricks. The type, quality and quantities of coal obtainable by a given amount of mining effort depend on geography, geology and mining methods. The suitability of coal for different markets is also affected by its preparation after mining—and, of course, the markets for coal have themselves varied in recent years. So have the markets for coke. All these factors affect the Coal Board's decisions about adding to, extending or adapting its capital equipment. This equipment includes not only coal mines and coal carbonisation and other manufacturing plants but also a number of other things subsidiary to these, offices and research laboratories, Area stores and workshops and houses for miners.

Table I shows the additions made to fixed assets during 1958. This gives an idea of the types of assets most important in current capital programmes.

From these and other post-war figures of capital investment the broad picture emerges of very high and continuing investment of new capital in collieries—high in proportion to capital already invested and putting collieries in a somewhat more preponderating position among the industry's assets even than they were in 1947. By contrast we see the capital connected with subsidiary activities, including carbonisation, taking a proportionately lesser place. The only other proportionately increasing group of capital assets is the 'central services', which in fact means Area workshops and stores and research establishments, all largely existing to serve colliery activities.

The natural resources of the British coal-mining industry

extend over much wider areas than those of the individual collieries.   They consist of a series of more or less horizontal seams, some near or actually touching the surface, but the bulk at depths of 1,000, 2,000 or 3,000 feet or more.   These seams

TABLE I [1]

ADDITIONS TO FIXED ASSETS DURING 1958

Type of Asset	Value £m.	Percentage of total
Collieries (including coal preparation plants) . . .	89·79	86·21
Opencast working (mainly equipment) . . .	1·14	1·09
Coal selling depots	0·10	0·10
Coke ovens	4·41	4·23
Secondary by-product plants	0·04	0·04
Manufactured fuel and briquetting plants . . .	0·06	0·06
Brickworks and tileworks	0·11	0·11
Houses	0·80	0·77
Estates and farms	0·19	0·18
Central services (largely Area Workshops and Stores; also Research Establishments)	6·82	6·55
Other assets	0·69	0·66
TOTAL .	104·15	100·00

may stretch over a score of miles or even over two or three counties.   The coalfields are the areas within each of which various coal seams are at present known to exist at workable depths.   A coal mine is simply a section of a coalfield worked as a convenient unit.   It is not necessarily even a unit worked from a single pair of shafts, because additional shafts may be added to old collieries, and workings from different shafts may inter-connect below ground.   Normally, however, we can think of the basic elements of a colliery as being a pair of shafts[2] penetrating one, two or up to about six seams, and tunnels for the working of these seams extending horizontally over areas up to three or four miles in one or a number of directions from the shaft bottom.   There can also be opencast workings, and drift mines (not very common in Britain), where seams fairly near the surface are approached by sloping tunnels.

The sinking of the shaft is about the second largest and the most expensive single element in the long chain of processes

[1] N.C.B. *Annual Report and Accounts* for 1958.   Vol. II, p. 14.
[2] In deep mines there must be at least two shafts for ventilation and safety.

which comprise the development of a colliery. It may take over a year and cost over half a million pounds, and is an extremely specialised operation. There was very little new shaft-sinking in this country between the Wars, and indeed only a limited amount till recently. A large proportion of the Coal Board's capital expenditure has gone on 'reconstruction' schemes not involving new shafts. There is in fact a good deal more recent experience of shaft sinking, particularly at very great depths, in the coal-mining industries of the Continent of Europe and in the gold-mining industry of South Africa. No machine has so far been produced which will carry out the whole or the bulk of the shaft-sinking operation. The normal process is to drill a number of holes in the rock with mechanically worked but hand-held drills, fire explosives in the holes, remove the debris to the top of the shaft and then line the shaft with reinforced concrete.[3] The Coal Board is most concerned to reduce the time taken to sink the shaft, since obviously no other underground work can be started till it is complete. Speed depends not only on the amount of mechanical equipment but on manual, supervisory and managerial skill and effort. During 1958 significant advances in shaft-sinking techniques were made. Hand-loading of spoil in new shafts has been replaced entirely by mechanical methods which are twice as fast. The work is usually done by contractors (some from abroad), but sometimes by the Board's own labour.

When work is done by contract the terms are so arranged as to give a strong incentive for quick completion, and the contractor can make bonus payments to his employees accordingly. As the rate of shaft-sinking is so important, it is worth while for the Board to pay a higher price for quicker completion. The contractor needs special equipment, most of which would be unsuitable for most other civil engineering purposes, and only large contractors would be inclined to invest in it, and then only in the hope that they would be given similar work in the future. Possibly a separate contract will be placed for the preliminary site work and excavation until rock is reached, and another separate contract for a temporary winding engine for use during construction. Certainly the permanent headframe

---

[3] Where water is encountered special measures have to be taken to freeze it temporarily or to seal it off by injecting cement into the strata.

itself, with its tower, will be the subject of a separate contract, and the manufacture and supply of the winding engine another. All new collieries have electric winding engines, and very often a sound economic case can be made for the replacement of steam by electric engines at existing collieries. The main saving will be on man-power. The case may not always be straightforward, and will depend on such factors as how important it is to use the particular shaft to its maximum capacity; how old or unreliable the steam engine is; the net cost of electricity; and the value, quality and alternative marketability of the coal used in the steam engine. Steam or electric power at the pithead is also required for other purposes, particularly the making of compressed air, the working of conveyors and railways below ground (direct or by charging batteries), and for coal-preparation plant and the conveyors above ground. A decision to introduce an electrification scheme at a colliery will, therefore, involve very careful and critical consideration.

The largest single item of expenditure in a new colliery is the underground tunnelling. Before the time of mechanical conveyance the excavated seams themselves were used as tunnels, whatever their gradients, but the Reid Report of 1944[4] on the technical aspects of the British coal industry recommended the general introduction of 'horizon mining'—that is the driving of horizontal tunnels—quite level—from the pit bottom, ignoring any slopes, undulations or 'faults' in the seams—to convenient points where coal 'faces' can be developed. This is, of course, a very crude simplification. There are innumerable ways in which underground workings can be designed to take advantage of the great variety of geological conditions and the different kinds of mechanical equipment that are available. The point that concerns us here is that the major new development work underground in the sinking of a new colliery (or for that matter the extension of an old one) consists of the driving of fairly long level tunnels through rock and their equipping for the transport of coal, men and machinery to and from the coal face. The main underground tunnelling work in a new colliery would normally cost at least a million pounds, and possibly two or three million pounds or even more. The work might take two or three years or more and, of course, this would be one of the

[4] See below p. 20.

main factors affecting the time when the whole colliery could be brought into production. Rather similar considerations about methods of control of work and payment, therefore, arise in tunnelling as in shaft sinking. Although most tunnelling work has been done direct by the Board's own labour, there may in some circumstances be advantages in putting it out to contract, and this has in fact been done in a number of cases. Much may depend on how the new tunnelling work fits in with current production.

The mechanical and electrical equipment of a mine is, of course, very considerable, and has accounted for a greatly increased proportion of the total cost of new colliery schemes and extensions in recent years. Apart from ventilating and pumping equipment there may sometimes be moving band conveyors the whole way from the coal face to the pit bottom. More usually there will be locomotive-drawn cars—loaded by conveyors. How satisfactorily coal can be mechanically cut and also mechanically loaded depends on the width and nature of the seams, the type of coal and the layout of the underground workings. There are a dozen or so different types of coal-cutting machinery, most designed and developed by British manufacturers, some by overseas concerns and some by the Board's own staff. Although many machines work well and are economic, there are still important problems to be solved. Machines tend to produce too much small coal and dust. Some cutting machinery requires the preliminary use of explosives and some does not. Some machines—with a faint suggestion to the layman of the principle of a reaper and binder or combine harvester—cut the coal and simultaneously throw it on to a band conveyor which connects with other band conveyors. Such machines are known as power loaders and achieve much the greatest savings in man-power and money. They have, however, the greatest tendency to break coal too small. All the mechanical and electrical equipment below ground in a modern mine will generally cost over £1 million, frequently £2 million or more. Possibly between half and a third of this would go on cutting and loading equipment at the coal face—most of the rest on transport and conveyors and perhaps £100,000 or £200,000 on pumps, switchgear and miscellaneous equipment at the pit bottom.

At the surface there is a considerable array of buildings and other structures and a great expanse of railway lines, roads and bunkers for outdoor storage—occasionally wharves. The whole may well cover an area extending over a quarter or even half a mile in at least one direction.

Most large pits have their own coal-preparation plants, but sometimes one plant will serve two or three pits. Sometimes indeed it is found worthwhile to replace old and uneconomical preparation plants at, say, three pits by a single new plant. The preparation plant removes the dirt and stone from the coal by passing it through water (or other liquid). The grading is done by passing the coal over vibrating plates with holes (like a riddle). A coal-preparation plant, therefore, comprises a quantity of heavy mechanical equipment—including conveyors —but little building work in the traditional sense: it is primarily a mass of mechanical equipment supported on a steel or concrete framework with light cladding at appropriate places. A large plant may well cost up to half a million pounds or more. Its importance, however, for enabling the Coal Board to meet the demands of its customers economically is crucial.

We ought now to try to put together the various component parts of a whole new colliery scheme and get an idea of its magnitude in terms both of cost and the time taken to complete it. The difficulty is in defining a typical colliery. Average figures are certainly misleading. The average book value of the 800-odd existing collieries on the basis of the Board's accounts works out at only just over £600,000. This, however, includes over 150 collieries which go back over a hundred years or more. On the whole, modern collieries are tending to become much larger and costlier. Because of increased mechanisation below and above ground and the more general need for preparation plants—and because of working at greater depths—the cost of shafts, surface works and essential equipment at the top and bottom of the shaft has been increasing very considerably. As a result, it is often best to work a much more extensive system of underground tunnels from a single pair of shafts and to have fewer separate collieries working in a particular coalfield or series of seams. All this is a very broad generalisation and will depend on the geological and other conditions. The tendency, however, in recent years has been for the largest colliery schemes to be very much larger. Some costing over £10 million or even £15 million are now being planned or carried out.

The following are averages of the cost of the component parts of three schemes planned in recent years:

TABLE II

AVERAGE COSTS OF RECENT COLLIERY SCHEMES

Surface   £m.
  Site preparation, roads, sidings, etc. . . . . . . 0·8
  Coal-preparation plant . . . . 0·8
  Winders, fans and other surface plant and buildings . . . 2·5

                          Total surface works . . . . . 4·1

Underground
  Shaft sinking . . . . 1·2
  Underground mining work (tunnelling) . . . . . 2·2
  Underground plant and equipment . . . . . . 2·0

                          Total underground work . . . . 5·4

                                          TOTAL . . . 9·5
                                                    say 10·0

Schemes of this magnitude might involve over four or five years' work from first clearance of the site to the first substantial extraction of coal, and another one or two years or even more before the tunnels had been so extended as to allow maximum production. Allowing about two years for planning and design and ordering of equipment, it can thus well take *ten years or even more* from the time a large new colliery scheme is decided upon in principle to the time when it reaches full production. The Coal Board is now concentrating much effort on reducing these times, both by stepping up the physical work and shortening (by standardisation) the planning, authorising and design processes. Not all new colliery schemes are of this magnitude. They include a number of drift mines and smaller deep mines. Moreover, the bulk of the Board's capital expenditure on colliery schemes does not go on new collieries but on reorganisation and reconstruction schemes.

One difficulty in discussing the total costs of colliery schemes is to know what is meant by 'capital expenditure'. Other public authorities and private businesses make distinctions in various ways between expenditure required to renew existing assets, or improve or extend them, or to provide something quite new.   But coal is an asset which is wasting all the time, and a high proportion of capital expenditure is required simply to keep the same amount of assets in production—before any effective extension is obtained.   Moreover, it is unlikely that any one colliery exactly replaces another in total capacity, and it may well produce different types of coal.

The difference between the coal industry and other industries, however, is not simply that its assets have a high rate of depreciation, nor that they are replaced indirectly rather than directly.   There is in the coal industry a much narrower line of distinction between capital and revenue expenditure.   In farming the road or track which the farmer makes to his field is presumably capital (if he will keep it there for some years despite changes in the rotation of his crops).   Similarly, the furrow he ploughs across his field is revenue expenditure, because it serves only for this year's crop, and he will have to plough it again next year.   There is no chance of confusion between a road and a furrow.   But what about mine works which may last for varying periods of years—periods not always precisely foreseeable when they are dug?   The shaft itself and its equipment (as of course the permanent buildings and plant at the surface) are clearly capital: the actual excavation of the coal face (simply for the purpose of getting coal and not to make a permanent tunnel) is clearly revenue.   Other tunnelling, however, may produce coal but also serve to provide a semi-permanent means of access to large reserves of coal farther on.   The first clear distinction drawn was one agreed upon in the Coal Industry before the War.   Any works within the 'shaft pillar',[5] even if they result in the excavation of coal, count as capital.   In relatively small collieries, before the driving of permanent tunnels in rock or horizon mining was common, most or much working outside the shaft pillar was directly along coal seams and (especially if very long permanent tunnels were not intended and no elaborate equipment installed) the cost of much of it might reasonably be counted as revenue expenditure.   But nowadays, the cost of 'horizon' tunnels and other tunnelling of a permanent or semi-permanent

[5] The areas around the shaft where, for safety, no side tunnels are driven.

nature—required for main transport, ventilation and so forth—will generally be charged to capital account.

Quite distinct from all this is most of the capital equipment required for carbonisation. At a large combined carbonisation plant dealing with all types of secondary by-products the coal preparation, storage and transport arrangements have to be very extensive and must represent a high proportion of the cost of the whole plant. They also make it necessary to have a very large site. One such site comprises 188 acres and is some three-quarters of a mile in length. All this means that if the carbonisation processes for a considerable area are to be concentrated in one plant some distance from the various collieries, there will have to be a system of railway sidings, conveyors and various equipment for the preparation, crushing, blending and storage of coal. On the whole, this now tends to make it more economic to have carbonisation plants at pitheads directly adjacent to coal-preparation plant.

The plants vary greatly in size—both in the size of the batteries of coke ovens and the extent of the by-product plants. A new moderate-sized plant with equipment for primary by-products only might now cost between £2½ million and £3½ million—that is a plant with a 'throughput' of about 365,000 tons a year—though there are some plants with a 'throughput' of up to a million tons a year. Out of this total cost rather more than three-quarters would be required for the coke ovens and by-product plants themselves, and the rest would go on site preparation, transport, storage, boilers and other subsidiary services. The largest type of plant, producing a full range of secondary by-products, might cost up to £10 million.

The Coal Board is not the sole purchaser of most of the types of carbonisation equipment it uses. Not only do iron and steel firms and Gas Boards also have coke ovens of varying kinds but much of the by-product plant is not fundamentally different from plant used in the chemical and oil industries. Another important factor is that even at the height of its construction programme the Coal Board was only building a handful of carbonisation plants (and these of different sizes), in contrast to its hundreds of (basically similar) colliery projects. It is hard to say to what extent these or any other factors may have influenced the Board's policy not to undertake the complete design of carbonisation plants with its own staff, but to specify requirements, performance, output and so on, and to leave the bulk of the detailed design work to its contractors. There are in fact only about four large engineering firms in this country who can contract for all aspects of the design and construction of a complete carbonisation plant, and they sub-contract a large proportion of the work to firms of specialists in chemical and electrical engineering and so on. While the Board appoint site engineers to keep a close watch on progress, the major responsibility for progressing and co-ordinating the work can be undertaken by the main contractors. The Board will consult with contractors at an early stage in the planning of a new plant and subsequently invite two, three or four firms to tender with prices for the detailed design and erection of the complete plant—on the basis of a stated output capacity and a general performance specification. Sometimes the Board have invited only one firm to tender, on the ground that it had specialised knowledge or techniques or that it was able to carry out that particular job more promptly, economically and efficiently than any other. When plant has to be rebuilt the Board will usually ask the firm that built it originally to do the work. When contracts for new plants or reconstructions are placed without competitive tendering the price negotiated will be based on costs plus a fixed fee.

The Board's 150,000-odd houses are not only a legacy from the past but a factor which may affect present production, and any large-scale redeployments of men between different areas. Originally coal owners built houses because their collieries were in remote places, and they needed men. Sometimes such considerations still affect the Coal Board, but they usually themselves build their own houses only when sufficient Local Authority houses are not forthcoming at the right time and place. It is part of the Board's standard financial procedure to consider both at the outset and on final authorisation of any colliery project whether it is likely to give rise to housing expenditure. Such expenditure is taken fully into account in considering the profitability of the project.

Since the Board has set up nine Divisional and forty-eight Area offices, one might have expected much office building, but this has not in fact happened. In the Board's first five years building was restricted nationally, and office building, both public and private, was particularly discouraged. Important sections of the Press and public opinion were—and to some extent still are—especially critical of office building by public authorities. The Board took what offices they could get at collieries, converted country houses and so on, and this very often meant that different sections were separated by considerable distances from one another.

Despite the recommendations of the Fleck Committee,[6] the Board's 1957 Report showed only one new Area Office scheme and the 1958 Report three such schemes[7] costing over £250,000, with any expenditure falling within the year. In view of the size of the organisations, one would not normally expect to get a complete Divisional or Area office for less than that figure. The Board has, however, done more to implement the recommendations of the Fleck Report in the matter of central stores and workshops—large single-storey industrial-type buildings, which when combined together on one site might well cost half a million pounds with their fixed equipment.

Opencast mining involves the Coal Board in no permanent capital construction, and indeed in no major capital investment except the purchase of certain special plant. Opencast mines have been operated at up to a hundred sites throughout the coalfields since the beginning of the last War. In 1952 the Board took them over from the Ministry of Fuel and Power, and, like the Ministry, has worked them through civil engineering contractors (recently numbering about thirty). A significant proportion, about £5 million worth, of the capital equipment is owned by the Board and hired to the contractors. This enables more firms to compete for the work. Opencast mining is highly mechanised, and highly profitable. It has, however, been very controversial, owing to the temporary interference with farming and the appearance of the countryside, and it has also come under further attack from the National Union of Mineworkers in connection with the contraction of demand and the closing of pits.

[6] National Coal Board, *Report of Advisory Committee on Organization*, 1955, p. 39, para. 208. For the Fleck Report generally see p. 21 below.

[7] In neither case were there any new Divisional office schemes in hand. Area office buildings were combined with workshops, stores and/or laboratories.

From what we have already said about the coal industry three particular points emerge:

(a) Schemes for new pits, major colliery reconstructions and major carbonisation plants require the expenditure of quite exceptionally large blocks of capital. They are comparable only with the very largest capital construction projects of other industries—power stations, oil refineries, chemical plants and major railway schemes. Even central workshops and stores and middling-sized colliery reconstruction projects can rank with the major projects of most other industries. The responsibility for planning, authorising and controlling these schemes is, therefore, immense.

(b) When a major colliery scheme is first authorised it is most difficult to foresee what conditions will be in the coal industry and in the country as a whole when the scheme comes into full production. The same applies over a somewhat shorter time scale to carbonisation plants.

(c) Nearly all the component parts of colliery schemes are interdependent with one another, and sometimes with housing, carbonisation or other schemes, so that they involve the co-ordination of the work of a number of different groups of high-grade planning and supervising engineers both inside and outside the Coal Board, as well as the supply of a large number of different kinds of labour and equipment. Before considering how the Coal Board deal with these huge tasks of planning and co-ordination we must first mention briefly certain features of their internal organisation.

(b) *Elements in Management Structure Concerned with Capital Development*

The basic element in the management structure of the coal industry is the individual colliery under the control of a manager legally and personally responsible for all sides of activity (including safety) below ground and—in particular—for both current production and work on new development. Before 1947 there was little organisation in the coal industry extending

NATIONAL COAL BOARD ORGANISATION CHART

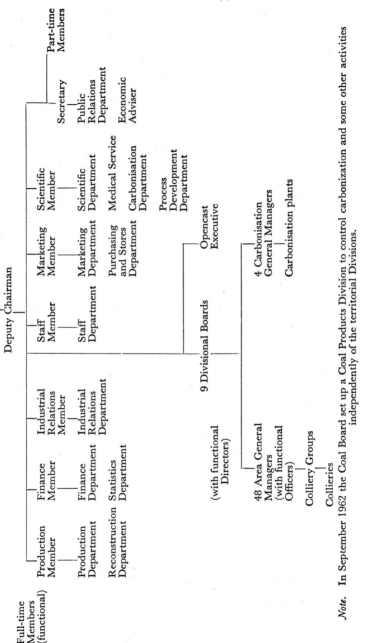

Note. In September 1962 the Coal Board set up a Coal Products Division to control carbonization and some other activities independently of the territorial Divisions.

beyond single collieries, but in 1944 the Reid Committee[8] (a body of technical experts within the coal industry appointed by the Coalition Government) recommended that it needed thorough technical re-organisation and re-equipment on the basis of 'horizon mining'. They said:

> an extensive and nationally co-ordinated programme of searching and boring for coal must be initiated and put into effect with all practicable speed.[9]

They criticised the lack of forward planning in the industry:

> The atmosphere of financial stringency and lack of broad vision which, it must be admitted, generally surrounded the British coal industry, provided the mining engineer with little encouragement to formulate broad schemes.[10]
>
> The great majority of undertakings have regarded a special Planning staff as unnecessary.[11]
>
> Mining engineering as a profession had become less attractive than in the past and so did not secure an adequate flow of young men of engineering ability.[12]

They said most units in the industry were too small for efficient organisation, for forward planning and for the establishment of the number of new collieries which were urgently required. They recommended the setting up of 'an Authority' to supervise the thorough re-organisation of the industry in a way that would enable problems to be examined 'on a coalfield basis rather than mine by mine'.[13]

The Coal Industry Nationalisation Act 1946 provided for the transfer of virtually all coal mines, and related concerns such as coke-ovens, to the National Coal Board, which was also given the duty and the monopoly of searching and boring for coal throughout Great Britain. The Act (unlike those for the nationalisation of other industries) left the Board free to settle the industry's geographical and internal management structure. The Board set up nine Divisions (broadly one for each coalfield) and forty-eight Areas. At each level there

---

[8] Ministry of Fuel and Power, *Coal Mining: Report by the Technical Advisory Committee*, March 1945, Cmd. 6610. The members of the Committee were all Managing Directors or Managers of large colliery companies and all but one mining engineers.

[9] *Ibid.*, p. 118, para. 700.   [10] *Ibid.*, p. 35, para. 199.

[11] *Ibid.*, p. 124, para. 731.   [12] *Ibid.*, p. 35, para. 200.

[13] *Ibid.*, p. 120, para. 706; p. 138, para. 760.

were various functional departments, those of Production and Finance being most important at first from the point of view of capital development. In 1955–56 certain changes in the departmental organisation were made mainly on the recommendations of the Fleck Committee.[14] The Committee made only one major recommendation about Headquarters Departments organisation directly affecting capital development. This was that a Department for purchasing and supplies should be set up separate from the Production Department, with which it was hitherto combined. They commented specifically on the need for better control and progressing of capital expenditure. The Committee made one important proposal for improving the structure of the organisation outside Headquarters to this end. They suggested that:

> as has already been done in some Areas, there should be appointed two Deputy Production Managers, one of whom would be responsible for operations and the other for planning.

As we shall see, the Deputy Area Production Manager (Planning) is the key man in the whole business of planning and controlling of capital expenditure. The Committee also commented on standardisation, control and housing of stores, planned maintenance of equipment and central workshops. The Board—reconstituted in February 1955—accepted all these recommendations.[15]

[14] National Coal Board. *Report of the Advisory Committee on Organization* 1955 (see especially p. 32, paras. 151–155, p. 47, paras. 252–254 and pp. 63–65, paras. 335–345). The Committee was appointed by the Board and consisted of leading businessmen and one trade unionist. Its chairman was Dr. (now Lord) Fleck, then Chairman of I.C.I. The general tenor of the Report and the subsequent reorganisation was to strengthen control from the centre—which was no doubt felt necessary because of the shortages of human and material resources at the time. It does not necessarily imply inconsistency of policy that the Board's 1961 *Report* says: 'In 1961 the Board reviewed the whole field of administration. They decided that there were many day-to-day administrative decisions which . . . could, with changing economic and commercial circumstances, be delegated. . . .'

[15] The Board's resultant directive on organisation and managerial principles was subsequently published in the Board's Annual Report for 1955 and also in *Public Administration*, Spring 1957, as an appendix to an article by Mr. C. A. Roberts, the Board's Secretary, on 'The National Coal Board and the Fleck Report'. He concluded:

> 'The whole tone of management has improved; questions that have agitated the minds of senior officials for years have been authoritatively answered; the General Directive of 1955 can serve as a Charter for management for years to come.'

We will mention only a few elements in the management structure which are particularly concerned with capital projects. In some large organisations in industry, commerce, the public services or the Armed Forces one will often find one department primarily responsible for making policy and directing the main operations—and other departments in varying degrees subordinate to it. Or there may be two or more major departments of more or less equal status, and coordinating direction may come only from the individual or Board at the head of the whole concern. In all kinds of civilian organisations, public or private, there are always finance or accounting departments—with functions and status varying between subservience and complete predominance.

In the Coal Board, at national and other levels, there is no question of a non-technical, commercial or finance department directing the operations of technical departments. Nor, on the other hand, is the Finance Department a purely advisory body or one confined to the technical operations of accounting. The prime job of the Coal Board is the getting of coal, and the methods of doing this are complex and technical. These methods are decided, and the operations directed, by the Production Department, which is headed and staffed largely, but not wholly, by engineers, the bulk of them mining engineers. The Finance Department has an important voice in policy at all stages and equal representation on the National Board itself with the Production Department. The same applies to the Reconstruction, Carbonisation, Marketing, Purchasing and Stores, Staff, and Industrial Relations Departments. None of these can be described as subordinate or advisory to the others. It is the Reconstruction, Production, Carbonisation, Finance, Marketing, and Purchasing and Stores Departments which concern us most.

It is perhaps surprising, however, that despite their concern about the control of new capital development and the overburdening of the Production Department, the Fleck Committee made no suggestion for a separate Reconstruction Department. This was set up in 1956 on the Board's own initiative.[16] Possibly in the industries of which the Fleck Com-

---

[16] The Board's *Report* for 1961, p. 26, para. 114, states that the amalgamation of the Reconstruction Department and the Production Department at Head-

mittee members had most experience the problems of new
capital development—although substantial—were different
from those of the Coal Board.   Some manufacturing industries
have capital development programmes consisting largely of a
relatively few really big separate projects, each of quite different types and presenting different kinds of problem.   Only a
few concerns, mainly but not wholly in the public sector, have
large capital programmes consisting of long runs of projects of
the same kind[17] requiring at least a similar organisation for
their design and control.   It may need a large, continuous,
long-term programme of this character to justify a special
Department concerned wholly with new capital developments.
The general experience seems to be that if there is major new
planning work to be done and if proper direction is to be exercised over such planning, it will not in fact get done quickly,
economically and efficiently unless there are enough responsible staff free to concentrate on it alone.   This may be done by
setting up special groups or project teams *ad hoc* for large individual projects, but where there is a continuous programme it
is desirable to accumulate the special type of experience required in a permanent staff.   It is not only a question of staff
time.   Problems of organising day-to-day production in any
industry or service are quite different from those of long-term
planning, and it is very difficult for senior staff to concentrate
their energies and drive on both.   It is indeed remarkable that
the Coal Board achieved so much before it had its separate
Reconstruction Department.   There was from the outset a
separate section of the Production Department concerned with
Planning and Reconstruction, but there was no separate
Director-General.

The Director-General, Reconstruction Department has four
Deputy Directors-General, a Chief Engineer and a Head of
Secretariat.   One Deputy Director-General deals with the
National Plan and progressing as a whole, while two others
(broadly surface and underground) deal with the planning and

---

quarters was begun in 1960 and completed in 1961 because the former 'had
largely completed the special tasks of expediting new collieries which it was set
. . . in 1956'.

[17] This is not to suggest that each colliery scheme does not present its designers
with completely new problems—but the purpose of them all is, at any rate, to get
up coal.

C

authorisation of individual schemes. A fourth is concerned with standardisation above and below ground. The Chief Engineer (Reconstruction) has a technical responsibility to the Director of Engineering, who also has staff in the Production Department. The terms of reference of the Reconstruction Department have been laid down by the Board as follows:

1. The Reconstruction Department's main objective is the implementation of the National Plan[18] with the speed necessary to ensure that the programme of reconstruction and new sinkings is achieved, and, if possible, improved upon. The Plan itself is kept under continuous review by the Department and, as it becomes necessary, recommendations are made to the Board for its revision.

2. The Department is responsible for guiding and assisting Divisions in the planning of colliery projects costing more than £250,000; for submitting projects to the Finance Committee at the various stages; for watching and stimulating the progress of such projects and advising Divisions on their execution; and for submitting completion reports to the Finance Committee in due course. The Department is also available to give advice to Divisions on the planning of other colliery projects.

The bulk of the Board's Headquarters engineering staff dealing with mechanical, electrical, ventilating and tunnelling questions are in the Production Department; while the Reconstruction Department has all the civil engineers and the Chief Geologist. The latter is responsible to the Deputy Director-General concerned with the National Plan. The Reconstruction Department are concerned with all major reconstruction and new colliery projects, but proposals requiring Headquarters' authority for new machinery not connected with a major reconstruction project go to the Production Department. Putting it another way, the Production Department gives policy guidance on mechanisation schemes at existing coal faces; but if new coal faces are to be opened up that involves new main tunnelling, and hence a 'reconstruction' scheme, which will be the concern of the Reconstruction Department. However, even on such schemes the Production Department will also be consulted.

[18] See below, pp. 33–40.

The Production Department receives each year from Divisions proposed programmes for purchase of mechanical equipment, and, after discussion, it authorises such Divisional purchases within a total annual figure. The Production Department is indeed the main Department concerned with the development and installation of new machinery. The Carbonisation Department, and not the Reconstruction Department, is the main Department concerned at Headquarters with new capital expenditure in carbonisation plants, and it is responsible to the Scientific Member of the Board, while the Production and Reconstruction Departments are responsible to the Production Member. No doubt this is convenient, because decisions as to manufacture of smokeless fuels and methods of carbonisation will depend largely on the results of research and development work. Opencast coal production has always been distinct from ordinary colliery organisation. The controversial nature of the work and the possible use of compulsory powers has involved special Headquarters control. An Opencast Executive operates independently of the Divisions and Areas through seven Regional General Managers.

The Finance Department lays down general instructions on the control of capital expenditure[19] at all levels and makes financial studies of particular capital projects. It does not itself submit such projects to the Board's Finance Committee, nor does it usually put up an independent written comment. A submission by the Department sponsoring the project—Reconstruction (for colliery schemes), Production (for machinery alone) or Carbonisation—must be fully discussed with the Finance Department and any other Departments concerned (e.g. Industrial Relations and Marketing). The final paper must bring out the views of all these Departments if, exceptionally, agreement on all points is not achieved between them. The Finance Member of the Board will, of course, be fully briefed by the Finance Department. A similar procedure obtains at Divisions. The Coal Board financial staff at all levels come into the discussion of projects at the earliest and most formative stages, working by constant oral discussion with

[19] Such instructions and compliance with standard financial procedures are enforced by the internal auditors, who operate at all levels and can report independently to higher levels.

other Departments, rather than as external critics. As a member of a Divisional Finance Department put it: 'You cannot really understand the financial basis of colliery working unless you are prepared to spend a great deal of time underground and get your face dirty.' (Metaphorically, getting one's face dirty might be a good motto for the financial advisers of any industrial organisation, public or private!) Many of the Board's finance staff have also worked in other industries or in commerce.

We have noted the quantity and variety of manufactured plant and equipment which goes into the Board's capital schemes and how far outside contractors are employed. Control of stores, purchasing and contracts is clearly, therefore, of the highest importance.

Accordingly, on the specific recommendation of the Fleck Committee, a separate Purchasing and Stores Department at Headquarters and equivalent organisations at Divisions and Areas were set up in 1955. The major changes in practice and policy which followed are of some interest to us as affecting the arrangements for manufacture and provision of capital equipment and its components and the need for stores buildings. They included:

(a) *Control of Ordering of Major Equipment.* Shortages of such things as coal-cutting machines, hydraulic pumps and electrical equipment could seriously delay colliery schemes. Until the new Department was set up there do not appear to have been adequate means for making the best of limited manufacturing resources. Orders for certain particular major items—varying from time to time—have to be placed through Headquarters, where the Purchasing and Stores Department can consult the Production and Reconstruction Departments about relative priorities, and, where the continuing demand is large enough, encourage additional firms to tender. These may include foreign firms. The Coal Board has never minded seeking tenders abroad when enough supplies at the right prices were not available at home, or when new and important technical developments were concerned.

(*b*) *Standardisation of Tendering and Contract Procedure*, including rules to ensure that the technical and the commercial discussions with contractors are not confused with one another, and that commitments to the detriment of sufficient competition are avoided.   Preliminary enquiries for estimates are controlled and replaced where possible by 'yardstick costs'.   The Purchasing and Stores Department (at Headquarters, Division or Area level, as the case may be) must be brought in at the earliest stages.   Certain non-standard types of contract must be submitted to Headquarters before discussion with contractors.

(*c*) *Physical Control of Stores*.   For some years before the setting up of the new Department it was the Board's policy to centralise storeholding and stores control at Areas in Area Central Stores.   The Purchasing and Stores Department have encouraged the acceleration of this process.[20]   They feel that a clearly visible orderly layout of stores in good accommodation is also a material factor in good stores control.

For further improvements in economy and speed of supply of plant and equipment, the Purchasing and Stores Department—in common with the Production and Reconstruction Departments—look to greater standardisation.   No one type of coal-cutter or power-loader or conveyor is suitable for every type of coal seam, but they think that the present variety could probably be reduced.   The same applies to various other equipment, including winding engines—which have hitherto usually been designed individually.

The Board's research, development and design activities comprise (for our purposes—excluding the human and medical side) :

(*a*) research into the location, quality, characteristics and uses of coal;

(*b*) research into coal-mining methods; and

(*c*) the development of mining machinery.

[20] In two places where collieries are closely concentrated there will now be Divisional instead of Area Stores.

The establishments concerned are under the control of different Departments. The analysis of coal deposits is the responsibility of the Coal Survey, an organisation taken over by the Board from the Department of Scientific and Industrial Research. The function of making borings and locating and plotting in detail particular coal deposits for the purpose of planning new or extended collieries is the responsibility of the Divisions and Areas. They have geologists on their planning staffs under the technical direction of a Chief Geologist in the Reconstruction Department at Headquarters. Boring is mainly controlled from Divisions, and when—as is usual—it is preliminary to a new colliery or reconstruction, its cost counts as capital expenditure. The Board had to institute a very extensive programme of boring and surveys in its early years before the National Plan could be drawn up. One of the main foundations of the Plan is a comprehensive survey of the location, quality, quantity and accessibility of the coal deposits of Great Britain. The Coal Survey and the Board's geologists collaborate with the Geological Survey—a Government organisation independent of the Board.

The Board's Coal Research Establishment studies types of coal and their potentialities—particularly for making coke, by-products and manufactured fuels—and the Board's Mining Research Establishment studies mining methods. Both these Establishments and the Coal Survey are responsible ultimately to the Scientific Member of the Board. The Central Engineering Establishment (at Bretby, Derbyshire) does development work and is under the control of the Board's Director of Engineering—an arrangement endorsed by the Fleck Committee. He provides services for both the Production and the Reconstruction Departments. Prototypes may be manufactured in the Establishment itself, or by manufacturers to the Establishment's detailed plans and specifications under development contracts. But it is the Board's policy not to have to rely substantially on manufacturers for the design of such equipment. After preliminary tests at Bretby some types of equipment need extensive tests in the mines. Priority has recently been given to power-loading and the development of a tunnelling machine. But many other projects are in hand on such subjects as roof supports, conveyors and coal-preparation plants. Bretby does

not deal at present with coke and by-product plant, for which
the Board has at present no large new construction programme
and for which it is not the sole British purchaser. Here the
Carbonisation Department's engineers normally issue performance specifications to manufacturers rather than detailed
designs. It would presumably not be economic for them to
duplicate the development work of the manufacturers (and
possibly that of the steel and gas industries).

Until 1955 there was no one Headquarters Department
responsible for recruitment, training, career planning, promotion and general organisation of managerial and professionally
qualified engineering staff. Personnel organisation is important to us because for so long capital development was held up
by lack of staff to plan and direct it. The Reid Report said:

> The atmosphere of financial stringency and lack of broad
> planning which, it must be admitted, generally surrounded the
> British coal industry provided the mining engineer with little
> encouragement to formulate bold schemes.[21]

It seems also to have provided young men with little encouragement to become mining engineers. The Fleck Report says:

> Between the wars much of the industry was depressed and lived
> in an atmosphere of poverty and unrest . . . failed for many years
> to get the share it ought to have had of the nation's brainpower
> and executive ability. For example at one University with a
> Mining Department the average yearly intake between 1924 and
> 1938 was five, but on average only three of this intake finally
> qualified. In the war years of 1939–45 the average intake
> increased to 12 with 7 finally qualifying. Since the war the
> intake has been 17 with 14 qualifying. The figures for recent
> years are nevertheless below the industry's requirements. We
> are told the facts about this particular Mining Department are
> typical of others.[22]

(There are in fact nine British Universities with Mining
Departments.) The Board's Report for 1953 said:

> One of the main obstacles to faster progress in capital develop-
> ment is the shortage of qualified planning staff. Some mining

[21] Reid Report (see p. 20 above), p. 35, para. 199.
[22] Fleck Report, p. 23, para. 108.

engineers are reluctant to transfer from operational work [that is current production] to planning. . . . The staffs supervising progress of the work (of reconstruction) also need strengthening.[23]

It added that there had been some improvement that year and some help from consulting civil engineers, although the usefulness of such consultations appears now to be regarded as very largely limited to surface work. The industry was still particularly short of civil, electrical and mechanical engineers. The Report for 1954 commented:

> The industry greatly needs more men with good technical qualifications. The object of the Board's Technical Scholarship Scheme is to increase the number of graduate engineers in the industry by giving the chance of university training both to promising young men in the industry and to Advanced Level school leavers. Most of the scholarships are in mining engineering, but some are in mechanical or electrical engineering and in fuel technology, and, in 1954, the scheme was extended to men wishing to study chemical engineering. . . . A few conversion awards to enable science or engineering graduates to take mining engineering degrees are also made.[24]

The Fleck Committee said:

> At every level of the Board's organisation there is a serious shortage of able people equipped with the right qualifications and experience.[25]
> In the specialist branches of the Production Department the scarcity of able and experienced people is very serious. . . . The lack of people with experience in the planning and execution of large-scale schemes of reconstruction is putting a severe brake on the industry's progress. In the field of mechanical and electrical engineering the industry has relied too much in the past on people who have been long in the pit but have not got the right technical qualifications.[26]

The Fleck Committee therefore recommended, and the Board shortly afterwards established a strong new central Staff Department.

[23] Coal Board's Annual Report, 1953, para. 70.
[24] Coal Board's Annual Report, 1954, para. 168. (The scheme started in 1948 but in most years not all the scholarships offered have been taken up.)
[25] Fleck Report, para. 108.
[26] Fleck Report, para. 111.

The main channel through which the Board has obtained its qualified and senior engineers is the 'Directed Practical Training Scheme', which started as a scheme for further training of engineering *graduates* and was later extended to include non-graduates from within the industry with similar qualifications. It could not, therefore, get going till there was a sufficient supply of these people. In fact, it started in 1950. The training varies in length according to the previous experience, qualifications and aptitudes of the trainee, but before becoming eligible for a Colliery Manager's First Class Certificate a man must have worked underground for five years—or three years if he is a graduate. It was therefore not surprising that the Board were still complaining in 1953 that their development was being hampered by lack of engineers. Hardly any trainees were passing out till 1954, and for a year or two after that only a score or so. In 1952 the Board also started recruiting Arts graduates, and in 1956 they opened their College for management training.

How far and how soon did these and other measures overcome the shortages of planning and directing staff? The shortages now seem to be diminishing, although there is still some doubt whether there are enough experienced electrical, civil and mechanical—as distinct from mining—engineers. On present trends of recruitment and capital programming it looks as if the future situation would be satisfactory. But these answers remain in this tentative form until there has been a longer period of review with a Staff Department, equipped with the necessary statistics, in control. Until the new Staff Department was set up and the new organisation promulgated in November 1955 there were *no central records* of staff qualifications. Now it looks as if the means of solving the problem of numbers in the basic professional grades has been found just about the time this problem is in any case becoming less acute. But the Board, like any other large organisation, will clearly have a permanent problem of filling its managerial and technical posts without either excessive 'dilution' or 'hoarding' and under-employment of highly qualified staff. There is no evidence of the latter yet. Sometimes in large organisations promotion is too slow, sometimes it is too rapid—the Fleck Committee found signs of both troubles in the coal industry's past. It is extremely easy to swing from one tendency to another, and it is probably even more difficult to hit the target exactly in staff planning than in capital expenditure planning. And the effects of missing are probably worse, extending as they do to the morale both of people within the organisation and of potential recruits.   It is at least encouraging to know that the Coal Board, like many but perhaps not all other large organisations, is well aware that these problems exist.

In planning their capital expenditure the Coal Board need to know how much coal is required, of what kinds—and for what prices they can sell it.   It is one of the jobs of the Marketing Department (whose present organisation dates from 1953–54) to assess demands for coal and coke in both the short and the long term and help to plan how best to meet them.   These functions include not only pricing but also advising how coal production, preparation and carbonisation can best be planned to meet demand.   In fact, the Marketing Department need to be consulted—and it is laid down that they shall be consulted—at the earliest possible stage and at Area, Divisional and Headquarters levels—about production, reconstruction and new colliery and new carbonisation projects.   The points on which they may criticise a scheme will generally relate to the quality of coal to be produced, the degree of preparation required, prospects of sustained demand and the marketing advantages of alternative sources of production.   An otherwise sound colliery scheme might be turned down if the Marketing Department had serious doubts whether the kind of coal to be produced would be permanently saleable.

We need not discuss separately the departmental organisation at Divisional level—where it largely corresponds to that at Headquarters—except to say that at only two Divisions have quite separate Reconstruction Departments been set up.   The effect of the general changes in organisation since the Fleck Report has been to group the various specialists in the Production Department at Area under one or other of the Production Manager's three immediate subordinates, the Deputy Area Production Manager (Operations), the Deputy Area Production Manager (Planning) and the Chief Engineer.   Below this level there has not been complete standardisation of the structure—largely no doubt because of the varying balance of work in the different Areas. Some Areas have many millions of pounds' worth of new collieries or reconstructions in course of planning, while others have very little. The volume and nature of problems of current production differ also. Moreover, despite the Fleck Committee's emphasis on uniformity, some allowance no doubt has to be made in practice for different individuals' methods of working. The chief principle, however, is that each D.A.P.M. (Planning) has under his control teams of project planners, each team grouped generally on the basis of a large project or a series of projects. The groups may be territorial. They include site engineers for particular schemes, and usually a special engineer or group concerned with timetables, progressing and phasing. There may be mining engineers not allocated to particular projects or groups of projects but specialising on certain types of work, notably shaft sinking. Similarly, the mechanical, electrical and civil engineers, under the Area Chief Engineer, will be a separate group for the whole Area—so will be the Chief Surveyor, and the Mineral Estates Manager and the Geologist. The Senior Architect will generally report to the Area Civil Engineer.

Whenever there is a substantial volume of new capital work there is a 'Capital Expenditure Officer', with no other duties, working physically and organisationally in close, continuous contact with the planning engineers, but responsible to the Area Chief Accountant. He is part of the team of the D.A.P.M. (Planning), although his job is to form an independent critical view from the financial angle. He is consulted informally by the planners from the earliest possible stages.

(c) *Nationwide and Long-term Planning*

This book is primarily a study of the arrangements for dealing with individual capital projects, and we can only refer to overall industry-wide planning in so far as it forms an essential part of these arrangements. In the coal industry, for the reasons laid down by the Reid Committee, it certainly does. Capital development in the coal industry is, first, the strategy of exploiting the coalfields of the country as a whole, and only after that the tactics of developing particular mines. The National Coal Board always had the planning of major new development as one of its prime objectives. The scale of the redevelopment and the degree of systematisation of the arrangements for planning have increased from year to year. But the need for a total national plan has always been recognised. Individual schemes, though at first planned piecemeal, were always regarded as within the context of such a national plan. While it was clear that this planning of major redevelopment was one of the Board's first tasks, it was also clear that they had on their hands the even more immediate task of maintaining and increasing current production of coal—in addition to the problems of setting up their own organisation. The inter-connection of these dual responsibilities of current production and development has been one of the Board's basic and continuing problems. The Board inherited various capital schemes, but only from the largest colliery companies—and mostly in outline only. The small size of most colliery undertakings, the financial difficulties before the War, the shortages and the difficulties of wartime and uncertainties about the future had largely prevented the undertaking of any large-scale redevelopment planning such as that recommended in the Reid Report.

The essential basis of proper colliery development is a thorough and accurate geological survey. This should be based on information from current and past working, on a sufficient number of test borings and on a careful appraisal of the mining problems involved. This must be followed by detailed estimates of the worthwhileness of particular schemes in terms of quantities of coal production, demand for particular types of coal and finance. All this involves time and the building up of considerable specialised staffs. But the Coal Board clearly made considerable efforts to get started on this job as soon as possible, particularly on parts which would produce the earliest results. In their second Report (for 1947) they said (para. 192):

> After reviewing existing plans, Area offices turned to preparing additional plans of their own. In some instances where the setting up of Area planning staffs was delayed, much of this detailed work was in fact done at Divisional Headquarters. These co-ordinated Area plans and decided on their relative urgency. Towards the end of the year planning work was

sufficiently well advanced for Headquarters to call for an account of what was being done in each Division to enable work on the first National Plan to be started.

It involved finding out which Areas should be expanded and which contracted—how much capital was required in total and how it should be shared out. Such planning, the Report said, involved consultation with the Minister of Fuel and Power, because the development of the coal industry was basic to the whole national economy and because of the statutory requirement that the Board should obtain the Minister's approval for the lines on which their programmes of reorganisation and development were framed. The Report said such a National Plan was necessary to give the Divisions and Areas the framework within which to make their own plans.

In 1948 the Board called for specific contributions from its Divisions and Areas to a National Plan. This was the Plan that was eventually published in October 1950 in outline form under the title *Plan for Coal* and which received the Government's approval. Much has changed since those days, but the way in which the Board tackled their first comprehensive plan is still interesting, and the basic planning principles still hold.

Plan for Coal was a 15-year programme expressed in terms of:

(*a*) planned output of coal;
(*b*) man-power required to achieve that output; and
(*c*) capital expenditure.

Capital expenditure was broadly allocated between:

(i) new collieries (deep mines);
(ii) new surface mines;
(iii) major reconstructions; and
(iv) minor reconstructions.

The different figures were broken down in some detail geographically, with separate targets under all the above heads for each Division and each 'Planning Area'. These were based on Divisions' appraisals of the potentialities of every colliery, but the Plan did not include a final decision on each, and it was also somewhat less definite as to the phasing of the expenditure over the different years. It gave it, in fact, in five-year periods.

Plan for Coal says the Board in its first four years planned to tackle the 'hard core' of new mining projects which would un- doubtedly be required, if only to maintain output. All pro- jects then (in 1950) being undertaken were within this hard core. The Board now had to decide in general terms between coalfields producing different types of coal, with different labour conditions and differently placed in relation to markets:

> A National Plan is needed to decide between the claims of the coalfields for capital, and to some extent for manpower. The need is urgent. Schemes have to be drawn up today, capital finance obtained, and arrangements made to recruit, train and house the men required, so that the industry will be able to meet its obligations *ten or fifteen years from now.* (My italics.)

Great emphasis was placed on the point that, on looking so far ahead, the plan had to be flexible and subject to revision later on. It was assumed that the latest known and best new tech- nical developments would be applied as part of the Plan, but no assumptions were based on the introduction of further improved techniques which had not yet been developed.

The new policy would concentrate production through a smaller number of shafts, use horizon mining with locomotive haulage, power-loading and 'skip-winding', and improve methods of coal preparation. However, detailed surveys had indicated that the greater part of future production must come from Areas already explored and worked in the past. Con- siderations of mining and of marketing must be balanced. Labour supply was discussed. Some coalfields would have to expand and others contract. The Plan included a review of the prospects and proposals for each particular coalfield. The whole Plan was based on an estimate of demand. The Board said they had considered and rejected a method of forecasting based simply upon an analysis and projection of past trends of consumption in relation to the index of industrial production of the Central Statistical Office. Of *inland* demand they said:

> Analysis of past trends is thus inconclusive. Projecting the pre-war trends gives an inland demand in the long run of not more than 190 m. tons. The short-term trend, however, indi-

cates a demand of about 215 m. tons. The true estimate probably lies somewhere between the two figures.

In making these estimates the Board have had the trends of the past as a background, but they have also taken into account the known or probable developments of the main industries.

These included iron and steel, railways, electricity and gas supply. Forecasts also covered the geographical distribution of demand. The British Electricity Authority estimated demand in power stations in detail up to 1955 and broadly thereafter. Forecasts for exports and ships' bunkers brought total demand to 230–250 million tons in 1961–5. Account had to be taken of increasing difficulties and costs of mining certain types of coal.

Planning on this assumption will have the effect of a policy of conserving special coals for posterity, but it will also mean a policy for meeting the current demands of users at the lowest cost.

Certain assumptions were also made about wages.

The Board then described how the Plan had been worked out in detail on the basis of all these assumptions, and they pointed out how enormous this task was, involving detailed reviews on the engineering, financial and commercial sides in each Area. They concluded by emphasising how flexible the Plan must remain and that as now presented it is 'one of a series of successive approximations'. Capital expenditure, although set out like man-power and output, with separate tables for each Division and Area, was not broken down by years, and a total programme for 1950–65 was given, divided broadly between collieries and other activities. Each Division and each coalfield was allotted a certain number of colliery schemes. The Plan includes very interesting technical appendices on the reserves of coal in particular coalfields, thicknesses of seams, types of coal, with percentages of ash, etc., and an outline of the main lines of technical progress proposed—also plans for expenditure in successive years for establishing central workshops.

Plan for Coal was a projection into the future of an enormous capital programme quite without precedent in the mining industry in this country. It therefore had to be made without the benefit of practical experience of similar operations in the past. (There had been no large-scale expansion between the Wars, and in the period of expansion before 1914 conditions— particularly with the absence of mechanisation—had been wholly different.) After five years, therefore, the Coal Board undertook a major review of *Plan for Coal*. Although the Plan was under continuous review at all levels, some years' experience was needed before it was really possible to take stock of the position. All very large capital programmes are open to this difficulty. The period of building up the successive stages of a programme is so long—with financial approval, staff recruitment, surveying, planning, contract work and so on —that it may be a very long time before there are any concrete results sufficient for a full review. For major new colliery schemes the time scale, however, is probably longer than for any other type of capital development, including power stations. It is not surprising, therefore, that a complete review (with important revisions) of *Plan for Coal* had to wait till 1955, when the Coal Board's booklet *Investing in Coal* was published.

The aim of *Plan for Coal* was 240 million tons a year or thereabouts from 1961–65 onwards. *Investing in Coal* reduced this by 4 per cent, that is to 230 million tons in 1965, and said that 240 million tons could not be reached until 1970. The estimates for the resources required to produce this output, however, were more substantially revised, and it was admitted frankly that:

> The difficulties involved in creating a healthy coal industry were much greater than was thought at the time.
> The material and intellectual resources had first to be assessed and this required action in many fields at once, in recruitment, staffing, training, education, welfare, research and engineering.

Moreover, productivity measured as 'output per man year' was now expected to be less than forecast. A rise in prices between mid-1949 (on which *Plan for Coal* was based) and mid-1955 had added £300 million to the original estimate. It was found necessary to add a number of major projects to compensate for the lower estimates of productivity. Other schemes were modified in course of construction, and it was found that the cost of certain schemes in the original Plan had been underestimated.

In October 1959 the Board published *Revised Plan for Coal* containing further revisions of its plans up to 1965. It said:

> Capital expenditure estimates have been rigorously pruned and they reflect the fact that output estimates are lower than they were in *Investing in Coal*. Moreover, with modern methods of shaft sinking and tunnelling, projects can be completed quicker than previously.

The new estimates were based on consultation with major users, including the Iron and Steel Board, the Gas Council, the Electricity Boards and the British Transport Commission. The Plan provides for a change in the balance of production between different parts of the country, arising partly from the change in the balance of demand. The capital expenditure on carbonisation in the next six years does not include any new plants, but 'is likely to be confined to necessary rebuilding of coke ovens and to modernisation of ancillary equipment at some plants'.

Within the general framework of these long-term plans annual capital programmes for each Area and Division are generally submitted by Areas in February or March and approved by the early summer—that is for the programme of work due to start in the immediately following calendar year. Most of the schemes in the programme will not only be included in outline in the long-term National Plan but will also have been planned up to 'Stage II'.[27] If the programme has to be cut, this can be done by the deferment of schemes due to start in the later part of the year in question or by the slowing down of projects. The whole exercise of approval of Area and Divisional plans depends on the Government's approval of the Coal Board's National Plan. Headquarters and Divisions have normally tended to defer schemes at Stage I or II rather than veto or cut them from the firm programme after they have been individually authorised. Where some authorised schemes have to be cut out of programmes because the total amount of money is not sufficient the non-colliery projects have usually been the first to suffer.

When the firm programmes are submitted in the spring for

[27] See pp. 45–46 below.

D

the immediately following calendar year, provisional pro-grammes are also submitted for the three succeeding years after that. These will not be finally approved at the time, but they will probably be given provisional approval or made the sub-ject of discussion, both between the Divisions and the Areas and between Divisions and Headquarters.

CHAPTER II

THE COAL INDUSTRY (II)

(a) *Detailed Planning and Control of Individual Colliery Schemes*

We have seen that a new colliery or reconstruction scheme is not a self-contained industrial project but essentially a part of the whole organisation for exploiting a coal seam, or series of coal seams, or indeed a whole coalfield. It may well result from a choice between a number of alternative methods of exploitation. It is a combination of underground tunnels and transport systems, shafts and winding gear and surface installations, and its planning is largely the tactics of combining these elements in the most effective and economical proportions.

We may quote as an example a model (imaginary) scheme circulated by N.C.B. Headquarters to indicate how the technical and financial case should be set out. This presumably typical project had as its stated objectives:

(*a*) to increase production from 2,000 to 5,000 saleable tons per day;

(*b*) to improve overall productivity from 25 to 37 cwt. per man shift; and

(*c*) to increase profitability from 10*s*. 3·3*d*. to 19*s*. 10·4*d*. per ton.

The main reasons for promoting the scheme were:

(i) to increase the availability of good quality carbonisation coal;

(ii) to utilise the man-power that would be available in the Division when two other collieries were closed.

The scheme involved:

(*a*) providing a new shaft;

(*b*) constructing a main cross-measure drift for locomotive haulage to enable reserves of coal beyond a certain geological fault to be exploited;

(*c*) complete mechanisation of the surface and underground transport and coal-handling systems;

(*d*) a new coal-preparation plant;
(*e*) electrification at the surface.

The cost would be £6·6 million with a return on capital of 17·1 per cent. The case as developed showed how the various parts of the scheme were interdependent. At present only 10 per cent of the colliery's output was mechanically cut and loaded, and this proportion could not be increased until the underground transport system had been improved, another shaft provided and the capacity of the coal-preparation plant increased. Alternatives had been considered—a completely new colliery or another auxiliary shaft at a different place. The former would have meant more capital expenditure, the latter less on the specific project, but a compensating additional amount to keep the other parts of the colliery up to a sufficient level of production. Either alternative would have meant considerable expenditure on surface railway lines. The scheme is described further in considerable detail, including the possible need to construct 500 additional miners' houses.

It is clear that the planning of many new colliery and reconstruction schemes involves a choice of methods, a choice which cannot be made finally until a good deal of detail has been worked out. Nevertheless, the broad strategy will have to be thought out in outline by mining engineers on the basis of their experience before investigation of particular projects can be worked out in detail. Sometimes the choice will be fairly evenly balanced. In other cases it will be reasonably clear to an experienced man that there is only one thing to do. In the coal industry, as in other industries, it is not possible to give a cut-and-dried answer to the question: 'Where do capital expenditure schemes ultimately originate?' They originate in someone's mind, someone who has already thought a good deal about the exploitation of the particular coalfield and probably discussed it with a good many other people. It may be a Deputy Area Production Manager (Planning), it may be an Area General Manager or a Divisional Board Member. Proposals for the improvement of particular parts of equipment or parts of a colliery may well come from a Colliery Manager. Ideas will take shape in the course of discussion of the National Plan and of the Divisional and Area parts when they are

periodically revised. It is within the framework of these discussions of general policy and strategy that the working out of
individual schemes must be considered. A great deal of
thought and discussion has to be put in before the preparation,
submission and approval of a particular project can proceed,
but when general ideas and broad planning for complete coalfields have been reduced to particular propositions there is a
standard drill in dealing with their submission and authorisation.

Colliery schemes costing over £250,000 require Headquarters' approval, and those over £50,000 normally require
Divisional approval. Every large organisation has problems of
centralisation and de-centralisation of financial and other
authority. In every large organisation there are probably
complaints, on the one hand, of delay, over-complication and
frustration by too many things having to be referred to a
central authority—and, on the other hand, of inadequate and
unrealistic planning when too much is left to local offices which
have insufficient staff and experience to plan major jobs real-
istically. The Fleck Committee considered complaints of
both kinds in relation to the Coal Board. It was seriously
concerned about lack of sufficient central control, while deciding that complaints of over-centralisation were almost entirely
unjustified. The problem of devolution in large organisations
is really not a simple one of how much authority to devolve
(measuring everything by one financial yardstick), but which
kind of work is best done at one point and which best at another.
In the Coal Board it has been decided and confirmed after
experience, and with the approval of the Fleck Committee,
that the planning of individual schemes should be carried out
primarily in the Area office, not at higher levels,[1] nor, on the

---

[1] Divisional Headquarters, however, do take a substantial part in forward
planning, and may originate new colliery or reconstruction proposals from time to
time. Moreover, this arrangement for making Area Headquarters the basic
planning unit does not seem to have been fully standardised until fairly recently.
Writing a chapter (along with others contributed by various Members and senior
officers of the Board) in a book entitled *National Coal Board: The first ten years*,
published in 1957 by the Colliery Guardian Co., Mr. B. L. Metcalf, the Board's
Director of Engineering, said:

'No uniform pattern has been adopted as to the administrative level at which
reconstruction work should be carried out, as it depends very much on the

other hand, by the Colliery Manager, who is fully occupied with day-to-day responsibilities. It has also been decided that approval of major schemes must be given at the centre where control of the whole Plan is exercised and where the fullest information about new equipment and techniques and about marketing is available.

The Coal Board, therefore, has a problem similar to that of other large organisations. If planning is done in one place and approval in another will not an enormous lot of time and technical resources be wasted if and when plans are disapproved? Moreover, will this not create frustration and cynicism which will seep through to all sorts of other parts of the organisation and cause untold damage? The problem is to allow Headquarters to know what is going on and to be able to prevent planning time being wasted on things which it will turn down—without its getting involved in too much detail. The first instrument for this purpose is the National Plan itself. If a project is already in the Divisional and Area section of that Plan in outline it is reasonable to assume prima facie that it will be welcome to Headquarters, provided conditions have not changed, and provided it is still possible to predict a similar net output for the cost originally envisaged. The task of Divisional and National Headquarters, as well as that of the Areas, is thus very much eased. Particular schemes need not be looked at in a vacuum, but in relation to the Plan as a whole. There will, however, be many cases where departures from the Plan or basically different alternative ways of carrying it out have to be considered at an early stage, and there thus remains the problem of avoiding abortive planning. The Coal Board appear to have tackled this problem more systematically than many other organisations. They have issued very detailed, but clear, instructions to Divisions and Areas about the submission of all kinds of capital projects for approval. The present version of these instructions is dated June 1957, but the essential elements were embodied in the earlier version issued

---

volume of work to be done. In large Areas with a number of new projects on hand, it will be economic to accumulate the necessary staff in the Area Office to do the work, but where the total reconstruction is scattered among a number of different Areas in a Division it will be preferable for a team of people to be concentrated at Division to organise the work from there.'

in 1952. (The first outline instructions on the subject were issued in much briefer form in April 1948.)

There are three stages for the submission of each scheme, and at Stage I sufficient information only is put forward to initiate discussions about the broad outline and justification of the scheme; and whether it is worth while deploying a considerable amount of staff time on its preparation. Indeed, it is laid down that 'no formal submission' is required before these discussions begin, and they may, therefore, be initiated entirely orally or by informal notes. Discussions usually start with a number of people from the Area visiting the Division, or vice versa, followed by another discussion between Division and National Headquarters with Area officials present. It will normally take only a few weeks to arrange and complete such discussions, although there may before this be a period of several months, in the case of a large scheme, for preliminary consideration of planning—that is the period from the date when the scheme is first conceived to the date when the Area is ready to discuss it with the Division.

The Instructions cover all types of project, but we will deal for the moment only with colliery projects, although some of the points are general. At Stage I schemes have to be stated sufficiently clearly to be understood in relation to the National Plan. Stage I clearance is clearly accepted on both sides to involve no commitment but merely to avoid waste in abortive planning. Nevertheless, the informality is not to result in schemes being considered without sufficient authority at any level, and the instructions particularly provide that Divisional Boards must be kept in touch with Stage I discussions. There are tables showing the heads under which information must be submitted at each Stage. For Stage I for a colliery the main points to be covered are:

(*a*) reserves of workable coal and means of access to them;
(*b*) output from the colliery;
(*c*) main operating principles;
(*d*) marketing prospects (the Marketing Department must be consulted at each level);
(*e*) man-power availability (including any need for housing);
(*f*) broad costs and economic appraisal.

Draft plans of the underground development will be prepared before the discussions actually take place.

The effective authorisation of a colliery project is at Stage II when details have been prepared, including details of cost. These details are as precise and accurate as they can be made without obtaining firm tenders or quotations from manufacturers and contractors. The submission prepared by the Area will be formal, preceded by a narrative including:

(a) the objective of the scheme (e.g. whether to increase productivity or efficiency, to maintain output, etc.);

(b) the main grounds on which the promotion of the scheme is based (e.g. market demands, coal reserves, manpower availability, existing level of productivity and profits or losses);

(c) relationship of the present project to the National Plan.

(d) main technical features;

(e) cost and estimated return.

The summary is supplemented by plans and tables of figures, going into detail on all the above points. For instance, the calculation of workable reserves has to be made in a table listing the various seams, with thickness and level, and quoting the sources of information in each case. In another table the total workable tonnage of coal is estimated, showing the depths where it is to be found and an analysis of the content of ash, sulphur and volatile matter. The whole present capital equipment of the colliery above and below ground is analysed (with the age and condition of each part stated) in comparison with the additional equipment it is proposed to provide. There is also an analysis of the underground capital work to be carried out (tunnels, etc.) and the equipment required for it. Under the description of marketing proposals there has to be reference to the method of disposal, including transport, and the methods of coal preparation. If improvement, replacements or additions of coal-preparation plant have to be included in the scheme this is discussed in detail similar to that for the colliery equipment. Man-power requirements and availability are discussed in relation both to past experience and to the way in which recruitment might be affected by other mining commitments or developments in other industries in the locality from which labour could be expected to come. If it is necessary to attract additional labour from other localities, then methods of doing so have to be stated, including any need to provide housing or subsidised transport. Detailed progress schedules are also attached showing the time scale for the whole operation and indicating for each section of the work against each year in appropriate columns:

(*a*) planning period;
(*b*) tendering period;
(*c*) Stage III period;[2]
(*d*) manufacturing period;
(*e*) construction period.

Another table shows the phasing of the expenditure over successive years on both capital and revenue account, with the cumulative capital expenditure each year and the interest incurred thereon. Finally, a full estimate of the profitability of the project is made, with a statement of the operating costs both when the scheme is complete and also at the stage of 'interim production'. This is based, among other things, on estimates of physical output (analysed by the types of coal and estimates of wages, cost and productivity).

Despite the detail, the Board's instructions also contain a very important paragraph introducing a note of realism which might well be adopted, where it does not find a place at present, by all private and public organisations responsible for authorising large capital expenditure:

> In the case of many projects, and mining projects in particular, the results are likely to be speculative. In some cases the unknown factors will be much greater than in others, but it is important that each project should give an indication of the approximate margin of error to which the estimates are subject.

All in all, the Stage II submissions for a major colliery project will comprise a pretty thick file containing, as well as the narrative, detailed underground and surface plans and some dozen or more tables of detailed figures—although the whole will be summarised in much shorter papers for the Divisional and National Boards.

[2] Final approval on the basis of any revisions of cost as a result of tendering. See p. 49 below.

The Coal Board do not have standard periods for the various Stages of planning and approval of capital schemes. These schemes differ very substantially in size, nature and degree of complexity. Broadly, however, a Stage II application might take six to twelve months to prepare and then two to three months from the time it left the Area Headquarters to the time when the Area received it back with Divisional and Headquarters' approval. In a Division where there is a sizeable flow of capital schemes, officers at Area and Divisional Headquarters, both technical and financial, will be in the closest touch from the very outset of Stage I planning. As the staff have gained experience a definite speeding up and improvement of the work has resulted. In addition to discussions between various officers in the Finance, Marketing, Production (or Reconstruction), Labour Relations and other Departments at Area, Division and Headquarters, the capital schemes are submitted to and discussed by Divisional Boards and by the Finance Committee of the National Board (which includes most of the full-time members and two of the part-time members). Authorisations by Divisions under delegated powers (for schemes costing between £50,000 and £250,000) are subsequently reported to National Headquarters.

On all these processes the Fleck Committee commented:[3]

> Some members of Divisional Boards and some Area General Managers have expressed to us the view that the present procedure for the submission of large capital schemes to Headquarters imposes a serious burden upon them. The fact is that the preparation and submission of these schemes ought to be a serious burden on the lower formations. The officials there have a heavy responsibility in this regard and ought to spend a great deal of time, thought and research on the working out of a project, otherwise capital monies will be wasted . . . in our opinion major capital projects, far from being held too long for examination by Headquarters, do not get enough scrutiny there. With such large sums involved the schemes should have the thorough sifting and testing to which they would be subjected by a commercial concern in private industry.

In fact, the Divisional Board's authority to spend £250,000 on colliery projects (increased from £100,000 in 1951) appears to

[3] Fleck Report (p. 21 above), p. 64, para. 338.

be more than double that of any subordinate formation of any other nationalised industry except the Central Electricity Generating Board. In Imperial Chemical Industries any capital expenditure over £50,000[4] requires the sanction of the full top-level Board. It would be interesting—and surprising —to know if any other industrial, commercial or banking organisation has made any larger delegation of its powers to authorise or finance capital expenditure. On the other hand, by the device of the Board's National Plan, and successive revisions thereof, the National Coal Board have a means of keeping a watch on the whole capital expenditure of the Divisions and Areas. The reporting to Headquarters of authorisations by Divisions also contributes to this end.

Stage III constitutes the final authority to place contracts and firm orders and to let work go ahead. Divisional Boards have authority to approve Stage III applications from Areas without reference to Headquarters unless a substantial change is proposed, either technical or financial, in the scheme as approved at Stage II. Stage III estimates of cost must be based on firm tenders or quotations when outside contractors or manufacturers are involved, and in any case on detailed bills of quantities so far as surface building and civil engineering work is concerned. Whether or not Headquarters financial approval is required for a scheme at Stage III, the appropriate Headquarter Department's technical approval is required, prior to this Stage, for the plans of a considerable number of specific items in colliery and other projects, ranging from locomotives, pit-bottom drivages, fans and fan drives, power and compression equipment, to buildings for power houses, offices, workshops, stores, baths, canteens, medical centres and so forth. In all these cases there is an exception where a Headquarters' approved standard design is being used.

This process of standardisation of designs is going forward over a wide field. It already covers various items of mechanical equipment, and may eventually cover considerably more. Instructions were issued early in 1959 on standard layouts for surface buildings at collieries. They prescribe the various types of accommodation, including the use of individual rooms;

[4] G. E. Milward, *Large Scale Organization*, 1950, p. 150, quotes £20,000, but I.C.I. informed me in 1959 that this had since been revised to £50,000.

but after doing so they do not precisely lay down the area of each room for so many staff or units of work.   Dimensions are indicated broadly by scale plans, but a great deal of the emphasis in the text, and by implication in the drawings, is on certain basic principles of organisation in the *grouping* of different types of accommodation.   The object of this is apparently two-fold:

(*a*) efficiency of colliery operation; and
(*b*) economy in building (including roadway construction).

(It was indeed by close attention to the *grouping* of different parts of schools that the Ministry of Education achieved some of their most striking and well-known building economies.) The Coal Board standards include four alternative layout plans of colliery surface buildings, with the room layouts where appropriate, and there are more detailed plans of each block. All the plans are based on a colliery with a saleable output of 4,000 tons per day and a labour force of about 2,000 and require to be adapted for different-sized collieries.   There are six blocks—planned separately so as to avoid having to under-build on sloping ground, to give additional flexibility of grouping and to meet the requirements of restricted sites.   In addition to the plans and notes describing in detail the different types of accommodation and site works and their grouping, there are tables with precise standards of construction and finishes for roofs, floors, partitions, stairways, etc.   The instructions conclude with tables showing the total areas normally to be provided for each block and 'yardstick' costs for each per square foot—indicating precisely how far these include fittings and equipment.   There is, of course, a warning that each estimate of cost must take account of the site conditions and local factors affecting the supply of labour and materials. It is too early to see the effect of these new standards on the speed and cost of colliery surface building.   However, in view of its size and high cost and of the experience of other organisations who have introduced building standards, one would expect the economies to be considerable.

There are, of course, many grounds on which schemes submitted to Divisions or Headquarters may be turned down, questioned, deferred or amended.   Headquarters may know more about such matters as demand and alternative prospects of meeting it by other schemes, and in other coalfields.   Mr. (now Sir Joseph) Latham, the Deputy Chairman of the National Coal Board, was closely questioned by the Select Committee on Nationalised Industries in February 1958 as to how far his Board applied a yardstick of profitability to capital schemes.   He first explained the distinction between, on the one hand, expenditure which created new capacity and, on the other, mere replacement of exhausted assets.   All the Coal Board's figures of capital expenditure are gross and not net. They cannot make as clear a distinction as some other industries between the creation of completely new capacity and the renewal of plant which has reached the end of its economic life. The major assets are wasting all the time at a high rate. Mr. Latham said that his Board would not undertake new development—that is the sinking of a new colliery, or a major reconstruction scheme opening up considerable new capacity—unless it was going to show a profit.   He added, however:

> We have a good many pits where a small loss is being incurred. We have an established pit, we have substantial coal reserves, but we cannot see any way of spending capital in a way which would give us a yield.   Either we have got to shut up that pit or keep it going at the present rather poor results.   Now, in doing that, inevitably we have to replace assets.   We may have to replace the winding engine or some other asset.   I am simply restricting myself to that kind of replacement of assets as they wear out.[5]

He then went on to point out that with between 800 and 900 collieries, physical conditions, and therefore the production costs, must vary widely, and: 'It would not be practicable to have a separate price structure for each separate colliery.'

How far the closing of unprofitable collieries should go, or how far capital expenditure should be concentrated in the places where the greatest profit could be made, has depended on the general economic situation in which the Board has been working from year to year, and level of demand for coal.   Up till about 1956 the Board was not able to produce all the coal required to meet the national demand, and the total volume of production was evidently the major consideration.   Since then,

[5] House of Commons, *Report of Select Committee on the Nationalised Industries,* April 1958, Evidence Q540.

however, the Board has been able to produce as much coal as was required, and subsequently more, while its own overall financial position has somewhat worsened. Emphasis on profitability has, therefore, steadily increased. The situation is, however, different for different types of coal. Large coal remained scarce longer, and certain types of coal and coke are of particular importance to the export industries.

Mr. Latham said:

> We have got to fulfil the demand for coal. Therefore, we should continue to replace the assets until we have reached a very extreme point in losses, unless we can find some alternative. Our severest losses, I suppose, have been in the anthracite district in South Wales, where we have to meet the demand for anthracite. Conditions are very difficult indeed and we have some pits with heavy losses. We are investing in two big pits there which we hope will enable us to eliminate those losing collieries, but meantime we are carrying them on because we can see no alternative way of filling the country's need for anthracite.[6]

It is necessary, however, to get this in perspective. As the larger new collieries and reconstruction schemes started since the War now begin to come into full production, it is possible to rely less and less on the unprofitable pits, and in particular to restrict the capital expenditure required to keep such pits going. A larger proportion of new capital expenditure is, therefore, going into profitable, and in some cases highly profitable, projects. In recent years the level of profitability expected from pits where new work was being authorised and started has steadily increased.

(b) *Planning and Authorisation of Other Projects*

The same basic principles (and, indeed, to a large extent the same detailed directives) as those described in relation to collieries are applied in the planning, authorisation and control of all the Board's major capital projects—particularly the system of Stage I, II and III submissions, the estimating of profitability wherever possible, the phasing of expenditure and the submission of completion reports.[7] For some projects, workshops, stores, offices and laboratories, profitability cannot

---

[6] *Op. cit.*, Q545.
[7] For completion reports see section (*c*) below.

be directly assessed, but the directives call for the maximum amount of information to build up a cost assessment of any such proposal, together with counter-balancing savings and gains.

For carbonisation projects there are very detailed instructions and forms of report with tables. The Carbonisation Department at Headquarters must be provided with the Stage I information in advance of Stage I discussions. This includes:

(a) basic objective of the scheme—(to increase production or to replace obsolete plant);

(b) where a new coking plant is proposed to take output from a new or reconstructed colliery, the methods of synchronising the two projects;

(c) marketing prospects of all products of the plant, in particular gas;

(d) prospects of Town and Country Planning approval and such points as effluent disposal.

The appropriate Engineering Branch at Headquarters is to be consulted. Then at Stage II a detailed profitability statement is drawn up on the basis of cost assessments of staff and materials for each section of plant, the source of supply of coal and estimated reserves and the profitability of the collieries concerned. The technical economics of a carbonisation scheme have to be assessed in some detail. It has to be shown that the costs of the plant are in accordance with experience. The instructions add:

It should also be shown that the most economic use is made of energy in-put in the plant, and an energy balance will in general be required for comprehensive schemes. For rebuilds of ovens it will be necessary to demonstrate that the existing flow of energy distribution remains economic after the ovens have been rebuilt. Particulars should be submitted of engineering specifications and standards to which plant will be designed.

Man-power, marketing and housing factors are covered as in colliery projects. In assessing the costs of plant and material and labour requirements the plant is broken down into detailed sections, for instance, coal handling, coke ovens (with machinery and equipment in different sections), coke handling, the different by-product plants and effluent plant, etc.

The basic control and planning takes place in the offices of the Carbonisation General Managers whose status is comparable with Area General Managers.   Such an office has a standard drill—expressed in a chart—for the initiation and carrying through of capital-expenditure projects.   This covers both very large schemes requiring Headquarters' approval and relatively small additions to plant, and so forth, which can be authorised by the General Manager himself without going to higher authority.   The chart is somewhat elaborate, but the system can be fairly briefly described without reproducing it in full:

(a) *Initiation.* A proposal may come from any of the specialists in the Carbonisation General Manager's office— mechanical, civil or electrical engineers, Safety Officer, Scientific Officer, Purchasing and Stores, Marketing, or indeed Finance, Departments.   There is probably, on the carbonisation side, a greater variety of people who might initiate proposals for capital expenditure than on that of collieries.   The reason is that a large carbonisation plant contains so many different kinds of equipment, and improvements may be required for such reasons as controlling atmospheric pollution, producing new kinds of products or making products available for marketing more conveniently or economically.   These ideas will go to the General Manager, who will decide whether there is a prima facie case for the scheme, and if so initiate:

(b) *Stage I Discussion*—either between the General Manager and his own Departments if the scheme is within his own authority, or with Divisional Headquarters and if necessary the Carbonisation Department at National Headquarters, according to the size of the scheme—all broadly as in colliery projects.   A preliminary estimate will be made.   If no fundamental objection is seen there follows:

(c) *Stage II Application*—bringing in all the Departments in the General Manager's office.   For instance, the Finance Department will provide more detailed cost estimates, consult about depreciation and assess profitability.   Technical information will need to be provided by the various engineering specialists, and the appropriate branches will have to comment on safety, marketing and so on.   The Administrative Section will consider the prospects of purchasing any land needed and the prospects of Town Planning approval.   At a Carbonisation General Manager's office there is normally no section similar to that of the D.A.P.M. (Planning) at an Area concerned solely and permanently with new development.   Planning sections may be set up as required when there is much new development going on.   For a moderate-sized scheme, however, it is normal for the General Manager to appoint one of his engineers as a 'Development Officer' specifically to co-ordinate the planning on that job and to prepare, in agreement with the other Departments, the formal Stage II application.   This is submitted to the General Manager and by him to higher authority if necessary.

(d) *Stage III Application.*   If the scheme receives Stage II approval the Development Officer has to obtain final financial and other data and submit a Stage III application to or through the General Manager.

(e) *Project Control.*   After final approval the General Manager will appoint an officer (normally senior to the Development Officer) as 'Project Controller'.   He will be furnished with details of the proposals as authorised at Stage II and will have authority to tell all concerned what is required of them to enable the project to make satisfactory progress within the authorised expenditure.   Each Department will be required to co-operate with the Project Controller and provide particular staff to do so when necessary.   For instance, there may be an 'Assistant Engineer (Construction)' to control progress of the physical site work of each contract, and to prepare detailed programmes and progress records as required by Divisional and National Headquarters and by the Project Controller.   There may also be an 'Assistant Engineer (Planning)' to supervise the planning details of each project and a 'Capital Expenditure Officer' from the Finance Branch to fulfil functions similar to those of a Capital Expenditure Officer in an Area office.   How far these and other specialists may be taken off other work and devote their whole time to a particular capital project or to capital development generally may depend on the size and nature of the work.   On the whole there is much less allocation of full-time staff to capital work on the carbonisation than on the colliery side, but when a major new plant is being constructed there must undoubtedly be at least one or two staff on

E

planning and control work all the time the scheme is proceeding. The initiation of non-colliery projects has not become quite so much a matter of standard drill as that of colliery projects—or at least not until recently. Carbonisation projects have been fewer, rather less like one another and more dependent on outside planners (in the constructional and manufacturing firms).

Projects for central workshops, stores and offices normally comprise either replacement or improvement of existing facilities or the provision of new facilities which are expected to show certain advantages. A basic analysis of such schemes on these lines is required at Stage I. In particular, for workshops and stores there have to be details of the units now served and proposed to be served, present systems of planned maintenance and stores control and changes proposed, and in particular the current levels of stores holdings in the Area. Until recently more had been done in standardising the plans of workshops and stores than those of colliery projects. Where Headquarter standards cannot be adopted the reasons have to be given and details of the types of building proposed furnished at Stage II. For Stage II also it is laid down:

It is not practical to prepare a profitability statement quantifying all the advantages. The following information should be provided:

(a) for workshops, an estimate should be made of the annual revenue expenditure based on the workload information given in Appendix XXIII [not reproduced], the estimated materials required and the overheads of the workshops; details of any reduction in existing revenue expenditure as a result of the project should also be given;

(b) the estimated turnover in (a) should be roughly apportioned between:

(i) work transferred (from other existing workshops or sources),
(ii) work not now carried out.

(c) in the case of central stores, an estimate of the revenue costs of running the stores should be given, together with an estimate of any reduction in existing operating costs as a result of the project;

(d) any other financial information on benefits which will

arise from the proposals should be covered. This would include any reduction in the level of stocks of stores and spares, any reduction in the capital expenditure on other workshops and stores which would be necessary if the project were not carried out, as well as details of any buildings becoming available for sale or for other purposes.

Proposals for office projects are submitted on similar lines, although less technical detail and costing is possible. The basic principle is that the details of the existing areas and types of accommodation are reported, together with the present and future numbers and grades of staff and the long-term proposals for office organisation. On this basis, details of existing and future operating costs and interest and depreciation can be worked out.

There are separate and rather particularly thorough instructions about proposals for buying land and existing buildings. Photographs have to be submitted (preferably at Stage I), and information given, not only about the condition, use and value of the property, but also the town planning position. At Stage II a note has to be given of any arrears of repairs and their estimated cost.

(c) *Progressing and Completion Reports of Colliery Schemes*

We have seen that in a colliery scheme there are a great variety of types of direct labour and contract work, all interdependent physically and from the point of view of timetable. It is well known that the progress control on any ordinary large surface building scheme with a normal number of sub-contractors and work extending over eighteen months to two years is extremely difficult and complex. New colliery schemes may extend over six years or more and cost £5 million, £10 million or even £15 million each, and are among the most complex types of new construction to plan and co-ordinate.

It is not surprising that the Coal Board, like other organisations with large capital programmes, has had to struggle with the problem of work and expenditure falling behind schedule. This was a very serious problem until about 1955 or 1956. As we have seen, before then the Board on the whole had as much money as it could use, and the main restrictions were those of resources (particularly men) and in the mere time involved in getting a major programme and major individual projects planned and under way. Although, broadly, resources are now less scarce and money more restricted, the problem remains. Indeed, the greater the financial restriction, the more necessary it is to get the projects that are authorised completed to time and producing the results. It is also, of course, very important at such a time to be able to foresee any irrecoverable falling back of particular projects which cannot be made good, so that other projects can be brought forward in time. This was one of the few operational problems mentioned in the Fleck Committee's Report.[8]

> Although there is generally accurate information at all levels about the amount of capital expenditure incurred against authorisations and budgets, not enough attention is given to ensuring that the work of capital construction and development is being done on time. In other words we have not found a satisfactory system of progressing capital expenditure being generally applied in the industry. There is evidence that a good deal of capital work is not up to schedule and that projects are completed late.

They were referring here to the two parts of the problem— first, keeping track of the out-turn of expenditure and knowing whether or not it was falling behind or running ahead or likely to do so, and secondly, taking action to prevent or correct such deviations from the programme. They thought the first problem was well in hand, but not the second. Both problems are serious ones in large organisations, and the second cannot be properly approached till the first is solved. The first can be divided into two. It should not be difficult to devise an efficient system of reporting promptly, both in total and in detail, as soon as an underspending or an overspending has occurred. What is much more difficult is to get a regular, reliable system of forecasting, to report as soon as there is a *likelihood* of under- or overspending, in time for action to be taken to correct it or compensate for it in other parts of the programme.

The Coal Board has had a general system of progress reporting since its very early days. Both progress reports and completion reports (by Divisions to Headquarters) were first called for in 1948. A form of site progress record was recommended

---

[8] Fleck Report (see p. 21 above), p. 64, para 342.

by Headquarters as early as 1950, but other forms could be used if preferred. The Board's current instructions on 'The Submission of Capital Projects for Approval' say:

> The progress of physical work and expenditure must be adequately controlled by a suitable system of site records and reports from the site to Area, Division and Headquarters. Actual progress should be compared with the estimated progress set out and approved in the Stage II submission. A standard system of reporting on the progress of physical work and expenditure is set out in departmental instructions.

The prime responsibility for issuing such instructions lies with the Headquarters Reconstruction Department. The present version was issued in 1957, but it was an amplification of earlier directives. It is a very interesting example of a systematic attempt to deal with what throughout industry is a notoriously intractable problem, and extensive extracts are therefore reproduced in the Appendix (p. 68). The charts are too elaborate to reproduce, but they take the whole work in the same Sections as those given in the Stage II submission and record, against the forecasts then made, both the expenditure in money and the physical progress. There are section drawings of the shaft and plans of the underground workings coloured to show what is due to be completed and what has been completed in each quarter. Average advances achieved per week have to be shown in respect of the underground tunnelling and revised forecasts of the remainder of the work made. Departures from the timetable have to be analysed in terms of weeks lost or gained under the four headings—supplies, labour, mining and other causes. The same with the shaft work. The key documents are the progress control charts, with each item of work shown on a separate line and lateral bars drawn from this against a time scale. The bars indicate the amount of work which ought to have been done in each period, and as work progresses the bars are blacked-in to show how much in physical terms has in fact been done. As this is done periodically, a red vertical line is drawn at the date of report, and it is then possible to read the chart and assess progress quickly by noting which of the blacked-in bars extends up to or beyond the red line, and the extent to which other blacked-in bars fall short of it. There are two charts of this kind, one showing the current progress 'by months' with items of work in some detail, and the other 'the overall progress by years' with rather less subdivision of the work. The full tables and instructions take into account that the work on a major scheme may well extend over six years or more.

The crucial points in the whole system seem to be:

(a) The breaking-down of the expenditure and of the work into periods of time and physical parts *at the time when the scheme is authorised at Stage II.*

(b) The retention of this timetable as a point of reference for all subsequent reports unless specific Headquarters' permission has been given to vary it.

(c) Requirements for sending reports monthly to Division and quarterly to the National Headquarters.

These reports, however, are not used as a form of direct control of progress above Area Headquarters level. Divisions or National Headquarters receive the reports and enquire and intervene if something has gone wrong. If there has been serious delay with a large project Headquarters may call for reports monthly instead of quarterly. Neither Headquarters nor Divisions, however, hold regular progress meetings.

The main comprehensive control of progress of sizeable projects is exercised from the Area Office, although control of the work by N.C.B. labour is the responsibility of the Colliery Manager. The precise form of organisation and the extent to which special staff are appointed will vary from scheme to scheme and from Area to Area. For really large schemes— those broadly costing over £1 million—the Area will appoint a 'Site Engineer' or 'Project Engineer', who will spend all his time at the colliery and will be responsible for maintaining liaison between the various contractors and the Colliery Manager and his staff. There is, however, no rigid rule or entirely uniform practice about the appointment of Project Engineers. When none is appointed the Colliery Manager will be responsible for day-to-day working and co-ordination, but the forward planning and checking of progress and most of the dealings with the contractors will be carried out by the planning staff of the Area Production Department. Where the volume of work justifies it, this Department, in addition to its various specialists, will have planning engineers assigned to reconstruction work, each for a group of collieries, and they will spend a great deal of their time at these collieries. Where a Colliery Manager has a large volume of reconstruction or other special work on hand he may be given either additional Under-Managers and/or an Assistant Manager or Deputy Manager. Broadly, Under-Managers take charge of particular physical sections of work—for instance, one or more seams for current production or a reconstruction scheme, or part of it. An Assistant Manager will be able to help the Manager over a certain sphere of his work, particularly planning, but he is not in the line of command and does not carry the Manager's full authority in his absence. These functions would be fulfilled by a Deputy Manager, who would be appointed only for very large collieries or when very large reconstruction schemes were on hand. Whether or not any of these additional appointments are made, the Board's senior engineers consider that the personality and experience of the Colliery Manager himself will be one of the largest factors in ensuring that reconstruction schemes are carried out to schedule and economically and with as little disturbance as possible to current production.

Apart from day-to-day contacts at the colliery and between colliery, Area and Division, there are regular progress meetings at Area level. In one Area where a great deal of reconstruction has been going on, the Deputy Area Production Manager (Planning) holds two series of monthly meetings—one with his own Planning Engineers, the Project Engineer and the Colliery Managers, and another with all the Contractors. In addition to this, the Planning Engineers assigned to each Group of collieries visit the Group Managers and Colliery Managers weekly.

Progress reporting shows if the scheme is being completed in the time and at the cost originally estimated. It does not itself, however, constitute a check on whether the original case for the scheme was a sound one. This case would rest on an assumption of the quality and quantity of coal that could be got out of the pit, the cost of doing so, and hence the profitability of the scheme. Without a subsequent check on results actually achieved, calculations of profitability would have little value.

Results will not be achieved or expected immediately work is complete. A big new colliery or reconstruction scheme may take two or three years after that to get into full production. Until fairly recently the Board called for final completion reports (in some detail):

> when a reasonable period of not less than six months has elapsed after achieving planned results, or at the end of the year scheduled in the Stage II submission for the first full year during which results should have been obtained (whichever is the earlier).

These instructions, however, were amplified in 1958 to require an earlier report on results in the first completion report (at the stage when the scheme is 'substantially completed') in those cases where at that time it seemed unlikely that planned results can be achieved. In such cases:

> an estimate of the likely final results must be given, together with a full explanation of the circumstances which make it impossible to achieve the original aim. This appraisal should also include details of any further steps which might be taken to obtain the Stage II results.

The first completion report will in any case have included: 'an explanation of any technical changes in estimates, submissions, etc.' If the first completion report indicates that the scheme *is likely* to achieve the planned results the final completion report has to be submitted:

> . . . at the end of the year in which it was stated in the previous report that planned results should be obtained, or when these results are obtained, if earlier. This report should explain fully the reasons for any divergence between estimated results (adjusted for material changes in wages and price levels) and actual results.

There are tables which analyse results in some detail, with calculations of the net capital cost, operating costs and yield on both the new capital invested and the total invested in the colliery. Each item in the calculation has to be compared with the equivalent figure forecast at the Stage II submission.

Completion reports involve a good deal of labour at their preparation. The general view, however, among the Board's officers is that they are of the greatest value and indeed essential if the planning and authorisation of further projects is to go

ahead on a realistic basis.   To the outsider this would certainly
seem to be the right view, even if other large organisations do
not always follow it.   The beauty of the Coal Board's system is
that completion reports are a matter of routine, and, therefore,
it is not only the exceptionally good or bad cases that come to
notice, but the general run.   This, like any thorough system
of financial or efficiency control, necessarily involves a certain
amount of paper work.

(d) *Conclusions*

The Coal Board started with a very definite advantage in
having, in the Reid Report, an authoritative and full statement
of the need for major capital re-equipment and an indication
in some technical detail of the lines on which this ought to be
carried out.   Major redevelopment was accepted, therefore,
as a necessity from the outset and as a matter of national and,
therefore, Government concern.   Although in recent years the
Coal Board has suffered financial restrictions, on the whole and
particularly at the outset, it was one of those industries accepted
by successive Governments as requiring heavy and continuing
capital investment.   Planning could, therefore, start and continue on the assumption that substantial finance would be
available over a long period.

The Board did not need to feel, as some organisations may
have done in the post-war years, that major long-term planning
might be a futile exercise because of lack of any assurance about
financial or policy backing.   Admittedly it was between three
and four years after the setting up of the Board that *Plan for
Coal* was published, but the delay—if it can be called delay—
seems to have been due not to any policy hesitations but to all
that had to be done—geological surveying, engineering planning, consideration of markets and so on.   As we have seen,
Plan for Coal was revised in 1955 and again in 1959, and long-
term planning remains one of the Board's major activities.

Other circumstances which accompanied the setting-up of
the Board have been less favourable to such planning.   For
over ten years there was the even more pressing problem of
current production.   The whole British economy depended on
coal.   At the same time the Board had to create a completely
new organisation in an industry generally short of managerial

and technical personnel and composed of over 1,000 separate operating units.   Added to this, the Board inherited controversies of various kinds, notably in labour relations.   Nationalisation itself was controversial—not that there have been any subsequent projects for de-nationalisation.   The combining of a highly individualistic industry into one organisation was bound to involve some difficulties, and the Fleck Report shows that even in 1955 a number of responsible people in the industry felt strongly that there ought to have been far less centralisation.   The Fleck Committee forthrightly rejected such criticisms, and itself criticised the Board for not centralising more.   Whatever the merits of these arguments, it seems inescapable that whatever form the organisation of the industry had taken, there would surely have been difficulties and controversies and growing pains.

It is clearly difficult for even the ablest individual to keep his mind concentrated on more than two subjects at a time.   The same is no doubt true of organisations, because however much they may diffuse and devolve responsibility, it is bound ultimately to rest, if not on one individual, at least on a small group of individuals at the top.   Those responsible for directing the Coal Board's policies in its first ten, and in particular its first five years, had at least four major problems constantly on their hands—current production, re-organisation, labour relations and capital development.   Similar problems on a smaller scale would face all the Divisional Boards and all or nearly all the Area General Managers.   It would be very surprising if in such circumstances there was not a constant temptation to put off problems involving long-term planning until the others had been settled.

No complete relief from this burden on the highest levels of management could be given by the creation of separate planning departments.   Nevertheless, this was a most valuable development.   It is indeed under this head that the Coal Board has perhaps most to teach other organisations.   The first stage was clearly the creation of the separate Area Planning staffs.   The Reconstruction Departments at Headquarters and at two Divisions followed.   There are parallels in other organisations, but probably none, except the Central Electricity Generating Board, has done so much re-organisation specially for capital development as the Coal Board. Most have no doubt experienced the danger of new development getting thrust aside if it has to compete with current operations for the time and thought of over-burdened senior officers. The best way to get major capital works planned and carried out smoothly and promptly is to make them the sole responsibility of people at sufficiently high levels in an organisation to command the necessary resources and financial and other authority. The coal industry has no single member of the National Board solely responsible for new capital expenditure, but the Reconstruction Department is one of two Departments of equal status, responsible to the Production Member. The Finance Committee of the National Board, moreover, under the chairmanship of the Deputy Chairman, has a special responsibility for capital planning. At two Divisional Boards there is one full-time Board Member solely responsible for reconstruction.

Other features of the Coal Board set-up from which there seem to be most valuable lessons to learn are the systems of technical and financial authorisation and control, and progress and completion reporting. So often the greatest enemy of efficient progress in capital development is the atmosphere of frustration and cynicism surrounding very large projects which it is hard for anyone to believe will actually be carried out in their time. To avoid this it is essential to have control systems which create confidence. It is, of course, necessary to have a firm and effective system of critical control to get to the root of any proposals that are financially, technically or otherwise unsound. But it is equally important to exercise this control at the right stage. If schemes are criticised or turned down after many months or even years of work have been done the people putting them forward can so easily come to believe that the only purpose of the control system is to produce excuses for delay. It is here that the system of 'Stage I consultations' is so important. Other organisations from time to time consult informally at an early stage about major proposals for expenditure, but the Coal Board does this as a standard drill and a continuous process.

The system of progress reporting is also valuable in being a standard drill, with sufficiently frequent reports in sufficient detail to enable some grip to be kept on physical progress and expenditure before it runs away in terms of total cost or slides back excessively in terms of time.   Some kind of completion reports also seem manifestly essential for any large and complex projects, otherwise what check is there that the expectations on which financial proposals have been based will be fulfilled? But how many similar organisations (public and private) have a system so thorough and complete as that of the Coal Board?   Do all of them have a *system* at all?

Possibly more controversial is the centralised control of certain essential resources and processes, technical and other staff and certain types of equipment and stores and the placing of contracts.   The Board recognised from its very early days that shortages of technical man-power and of equipment were among the major obstacles to the achievement of its programmes.   Yet apart from the Directed Practical Training Scheme, these shortages hardly seem to have been dealt with centrally at all until the setting-up of the Purchasing and Stores Department and the Reconstruction Department—and the re-organisation and expansion of the Staff Department— after the Fleck Report.   The Purchasing and Stores Department claims to have achieved much by preventing overlapping and competition between Areas and Divisions in placing orders, and also waste and excess holdings of stores.   The Staff Department has only recently made a full assessment of the numbers of technical and other senior staff required to match up to the Board's programmes, and so possibly central staff planning has only become effective after the worst staff shortages have been at least within sight of solution.

Comparable with control of resources is standardisation of designs.   The Production, the Reconstruction and the Purchasing and Stores Departments are tackling this in various ways, and must have obviously done a great deal, but it would appear that they have an enormous field to cover.   With such a large and varied industry one would expect there to be considerable scope for standardisation—of types of machine needed in large numbers and buildings of basically similar form.   In any large and progressive industry there is bound to be a difference of approach between those who seek efficiency and economy through standardisation and mass-production, and those who fear that such measures will cramp initiative and improvements in design. There will probably be more to be learnt from the Coal Board's experience in these matters in the next few years, after its strengthened Headquarter Departments have been in operation longer. The system of requiring technical consultation with Headquarters on certain matters only when standard designs are not used would seem to give the necessary encouragement both to simplicity through standardisation and to innovation.

It is important to note the relationship between the coal industry and its suppliers and designers. In the colliery field the Coal Board is often the sole British purchaser of certain types of equipment. When the industry was in the hands of many separate companies design and research fell largely to the manufacturers, but once there was a single organisation in control it was natural that it should establish and extend its own research and development activities and rely less and less on outside research, designers and consultants. This did not happen all at once. At the times of the greatest shortages of technical staff the Board did rely partly on civil engineering and other consultants to ease its difficulties. For shaft-sinking and tunnelling there are still sometimes advantages in employing contractors. In opencast mining, where the work is all done by contract, the Board had to provide most of the equipment so as to allow more contractors to compete. On the carbonisation side, however, the Coal Board is not the sole purchaser of most of the types of equipment, and thus more of the design work is left to contractors.

To sum up—there is a very great deal to learn from the National Coal Board about the relationship between the cohesion of very large-scale organisations and the efficiency of capital development planning and execution. There is also, and will continue to be, much to be learnt about detailed systems and techniques of central control of such work, about standardisation of procedures and about centralisation and decentralisation. Clearly, the coal industry is a live, developing and changing organism, and each year may be expected to enable both those inside and outside the industry to draw new lessons from its experience.

APPENDIX

PROGRESS CONTROL

EXTRACTS FROM NATIONAL COAL BOARD
RECONSTRUCTION DEPARTMENT DIRECTIVES

1. The system described in this document should be used for reporting progress to Area, Division and Headquarters . . .

PART ONE

Control Chart

2. Since actual progress must be compared with the programme set out in the relevant appendices in the Stage II submission, these appendices form the basis of the progress system . . .

3. For each project a Control Chart . . . must be prepared, which will show the comprehensive and up to date physical and financial information essential to proper management control. It comes into operation as soon as the first expenditure is authorised.

6. In preparing the Chart the first operation is to set out the Overall Programme. For new projects this will be based on the information, as approved at Stage II . . . in the New Expenditure Schedule, the Sectional Progress Schedule and the Phasing of Expenditure Schedule.

7. There must be set out for each year:—

 (*a*) against each section the estimated cumulative expenditure for each year;

 (*b*) for all sections, other than General Expenses, the appropriate physical programme, and

 (*c*) for Shaft Sinking and Underground Drivages, the cumulative yardage performances in accordance with the approved Stage II programme.

Against 'Underground Equipment' the yearly production programme necessary to comply with the National Plan must be shown as the objective.

8. Preceding all these physical site programmes, the time allowed for the preliminaries of planning and design, invitation of tenders, Stage III applications and authorisation, and the manufacturing of equipment should be shown in accordance with the Sectional Progress Schedule.

10. The Current Programme is an expansion of the Overall Programme for the current twelve months (i.e. the standard accounting periods). In addition to the preliminary information of the Overall Programme it indicates the type of physical site progress involved. This necessitates detailed site charts for each current section, setting out the sequence in which its component items are to be carried out. Where work is to be carried out by contractors, at the times of tendering or ordering, these charts will be based on programmes prepared by the contractors to show how they propose to carry out their work in time to comply with the Overall Programme. N.C.B. personnel must deal similarly with sections which involve no outside general contractor.

.   .   .   .   .

Marking up the Chart

14. At the end of each . . . month each Control Chart must be brought up to date. This involves:—

  (i) marking up physical progress to date on the Current Programme by 'blacking' in the 'bars' over the physical programme chart in accordance with the progress shown on the relevant site charts. Progress is measured by the least advanced part of the Section or Sub-section;
  (ii) adding details of recent contracts satisfactorily placed;
  (iii) adjusting the Estimated Expenditure figures in keeping with each Stage III authorisation;
  (iv) filling in the actual expenditure figures up to the end of the *previous* month; and
  (v) filling in the total of N.C.B. man-power employed on both reconstruction and current production at the end of the current month.

.   .   .   .   .

Reading the Chart

17. By glancing down the red line on the current month column and noting its relationships to the ends of the 'blacked-in' 'bars' over the physical programmes, those concerned can immediately see the state of progress. By referring back along the expenditure figures it is possible to judge whether a section is gaining or losing ground, and by looking along the physical programmes it is possible to check forward planning. The Chart also enables an appraisal to be made of the current position with regard to expenditure, manpower and production.

18. The progress 'bars' do not show the percentage of work done;

they show how much each section is ahead or behind programme, early enough, in most cases, for appropriate action to be taken to keep the project on programme.

Revising the Chart

19. The programme as originally set out on the Control Chart must not be revised.   In exceptional cases, however, permission to do so may be given by Headquarters' Reconstruction Department.

Distribution of Chart

20. In addition to the copies of the Control Chart required on the site and at Area, prints must be sent by Area to Division each month and by Division to Headquarters each quarter together with the Reports and Charts required under Part Two for the Underground Construction.   Certain projects may have to be selected for special attention where Sections fall behind programme, in which case copies of the Control Chart may be required at Headquarters more frequently.

·   ·   ·   ·   ·

PART TWO

Underground Construction

23. In addition to the Control Chart, returns are required by which Area, Division and Headquarters can follow underground progress.   For this purpose all underground construction will be divided under the three sections Shaft Work, Pit Bottom Work, and Underground Drivages, and for each of these sections charts and report forms will be used to record progress.

·   ·   ·   ·   ·

Procedure

26. The following is the procedure for the submission of the charts and reports:—

(*a*) As soon as the first expenditure is authorised on a project the relevant charts must be prepared and copies sent to Area, Division and Headquarters.   These will be retained.

(*b*) In respect of items on which work has started report forms and charts (showing the progress to date) will be sent to Area and Division monthly, and to Headquarters on dates to be specified.   The reports will be retained, but the progress shown on the charts will be transcribed on to those submitted in accordance with (*a*) above and the second set of charts will be returned to be used as a shuttle copy at each subsequent reporting period.

(c) Where the start of work is delayed beyond the scheduled date, 'not started' reports should be submitted (on the standard form) for the period in which work was scheduled to start. If work begins ahead of schedule the implementation of the reporting procedure will be similarly advanced.

.   .   .   .   .

Notes on Reports

28. . . .

(b) The averages required against 'General work detail' in the shaft and underground drivage report forms must be calculated on time passed, not on time worked. Those receiving the reports will give weight to the entries according to the distribution of time lost, and according to the extent of 'intervening' works as illustrated on the charts, such as the construction of insets in shafts.

(c) Each report form has a section for the distribution of time lost or gained according to primary causes and for short explanations to be given. The intention is that the time given shall be cumulative and that

(i) against 'Supplies' will be entered the effect of availability of supplies and equipment (e.g. sinking winders in the case of shaft sinking reports);

(ii) against 'Labour' will be entered the effect of availability, suitability and turnover of labour and of trade disputes, attendance, etc.;

(iii) against 'Mining' will be entered the effect of unforeseen difficulties, such as exceptional flow of water, outbursts of gas, extremely hard ground, etc.; and

(iv) against 'Other Causes' will be entered other things which have an unpredictable effect on progress. For example, delayed administrative action, planning permission, etc. Only significant items should be entered and the causes should be defined under 'Remarks'.

F

CHAPTER III

LONDON TRANSPORT

(a) *Introduction*

London Transport provides all public road passenger services and some rail passenger services within *very roughly* the area from which people travel daily to work in Central London— excluding certain seaside places.   The broad long-term picture of traffic is of an increase between the Wars and since the last War up to 1948, followed by a decline—with both a relative and an absolute intensification of peak traffic (now a third higher than before the War).   London Transport has had special difficulties in coping with this changed pattern of traffic because of physical and financial limitations.   Road traffic congestion has intensified, tube tunnels and stations in central London are very difficult and expensive to build or extend, costs of all kinds have risen and there are special opportunities for natural resistance to increased charges to make itself felt.

London Transport contrasts strikingly with the coal industry; the Transport Act, 1947, introduced no change in its size as a unit of management, nor in its geographical and functional boundaries.   There were important changes in higher control and constitution, but few in internal departmental management.   We go back then to the Act of 1933 which created the London Passenger Transport Board; but the real roots of the present organisation stretch back farther still.   Large units of management controlling services very similar to those of the present Executive[1] had existed long before 1933—and had for a long time achieved a considerable degree of co-ordination with one another.   Moreover, throughout the successive changes many of the same people had remained in control. So the staff have been able to feel for a long while that they are working within well-established traditions.

---

[1] London Transport Executive, set up under the British Transport Commission in 1947, became the London Transport Board when the B.T.C. was dissolved in 1962.

Between the Wars there were great capital programmes of extension and modernisation. From the very early stages up till the 'thirties, amalgamations, working agreements and unification tended to go hand in hand with extensions of services and major capital development. The L.P.T.B.'s New Works programme 1935–40 included further integration of the various Underground lines with each other and with the suburban railways of the main-line companies. Its purpose was to meet the growth and spreading out of London's population. The majority of works were only partly completed at the beginning of the War. Some have since been or are now being completed, others were abandoned.

(b) *Types of Capital Projects*

Capital development in London Transport since the War has largely been a matter of renewal and modernisation. Trams have been replaced by oil buses, and the bus fleets by modern vehicles as the older vehicles reached the end of their economic lives. The various fleets of rail vehicles are also successively being replaced. There has been no major change of railway traction system since the War, except on two lines. The Central Line has been extended and electrified both eastwards and westwards, taking in, in places, former steam tracks of the old main-line railway companies. Sections of the Metropolitan Line are being widened and electrified. These projects make up the only really major post-War schemes of new permanent way and rail and signal construction, although very large signalling modernisation programmes have been carried out on existing lines. No completely new routes have been constructed since the War, though there is a proposal for a major new tube (the Victoria Line).[2] Certain large new buildings for both the road and rail services have been provided, but, apart from New Towns and railway extensions, these have been for rationalisation and economy rather than expansion.

In 1958 London Transport had 8,899 road vehicles, of which 6,389 were identical double-decker buses (the 56-seater 'R.T.s', brought into service in 1947–54 to replace the entire former bus

[2] In August 1962 the Government announced that they had agreed this scheme should now proceed.

fleet and the trams then remaining). The 1,536 trolleybuses were being replaced by double-decker buses in 1959–62. A new standard bus 'the Routemaster' (R.M.) (64 seats) is now coming into service—at first to replace trolleybuses. Apart from buses the capital equipment of a bus service consists of garages, accommodation for operating and controlling staff, and workshops for such repairs, overhauls and manufacture as the operating concern may decide to do for itself. The R.T. buses have a life of fourteen years for depreciation purposes, but are expected to be in service for a little longer. They are brought into the central works for complete overhaul every three and a half to four years. The road-vehicle maintenance and overhaul system is highly centralised, and the vehicles are highly standardised.[3] The local garages do little more than day-to-day maintenance and changing of units. All other repairs and overhauls are done on a standardised basis at the Central Works at Aldenham and Chiswick. All this makes for a centralised organisation. It also simplifies the problem of new design when a complete fleet of buses has to be replaced. Bodies and chassis generally are designed, down to detailed working drawings, by London Transport staff. Aldenham Works cost £4 million and took about four years to build. It occupies 54 acres. Besides Aldenham and Chiswick there are some 115 depots and garages, of varying sizes. They include canteens and offices, etc., for the bus crews and their controlling staff. Those recently erected in the New Towns have cost around £150,000 each, but much larger ones have been built nearer central London. London Transport try to site garages close to the routes they serve, but in practice their disposition very largely depends on the availability of land. In some places at some times vehicles are parked in the open for lack of garage space. Opinions seem to differ as to how uneconomic and inefficient such an arrangement is (balancing saving in building costs against quicker deterioration of vehicle bodywork). On the whole, London Transport is reasonably well provided with garages.

The railway side of London Transport has naturally much

---

[3] It seems, however, that a highly centralised maintenance and overhaul system could still be worked without such a large number of completely standardised identical vehicles.

more capital than the road side. It includes rolling stock, earthworks and structures, permanent way, stations, signalling systems and the extremely expensive tube tunnels. The rail system was substantially complete well before the War. Since the War investment has been mainly in renewal and modernisation. Resources were limited, and the needs of the road services were at first greater. Now, with its road fleets renewed, London Transport faces very heavy expenditures on railway rolling stock, and on the Amersham Line, electrification, additional tracks and new signalling (£4½ million). This will be the last electrification scheme and, although various other railway developments have been proposed, only one appears at all practicable in the next few years— the Victoria to Walthamstow tube (over £50 million). It is hard, therefore, to give typical costs. Any new deep tubes would cost between £1½ million and £2 million a mile for running tunnels and tracks alone, apart from stations and equipment. Even small extensions of platforms on the deep tubes in central London will often be virtually ruled out by the enormous cost of tunnelling, the complexity of the work and the extreme difficulty and expense of interfering with public and private property rights—but some platforms have been lengthened on the Bakerloo and Central Lines.

This very rigidity of the network of tracks, stations and tunnels has called forth every effort of adaptation and economy in design of new rolling stock. Major design efforts in recent years have concentrated on:

(a) reducing motive power cost by reducing the weight of trains;
(b) increasing the passenger space;
(c) increasing the door space for speedier movement of passengers into and out of the trains (this both reduces journey times and increases the number of trains per hour);
(d) securing a longer life from new rolling stock;
(e) reducing maintenance costs;
(f) improving signalling.

New rail cars are provided primarily:

(i) when the old cars have reached the end of their economic life—generally something over thirty years;

but also:

(ii) so that traffic may be carried more efficiently and/or economically—by providing more space, greater comfort and/or quicker and more convenient means of loading and discharge;

(iii) to improve reliability and safety.

Very broadly, each line has its own set of rolling stock (anything up to 800 cars), which is normally used on that line alone, and which, if possible, is renewed as a whole. A fleet of cars can be changed over between one tube line and another or between one 'surface' line and another (i.e. Circle, District and Metropolitan), but not between tube and surface lines (owing to the size of tunnels). Individual rail cars each now cost something over £10,000 for 'trailers' and over £20,000 for 'motor cars', and the renewal of a complete fleet will therefore cost over £10 million. That is why investment in railway rolling stock thus tends to go in large 'lumps'.

Most railway buildings—stations, signal boxes, electricity substations and so forth—are directly associated with the lines and, therefore, what we have said about the capital investment in the lines applies broadly to them also. There is, however, a system of workshops and depots centralised in a similar way to those on the road side—a large central repair and overhaul works at Acton and some nineteen other depots and sub-depots where rolling stock is housed and certain repairs as well as maintenance and cleaning done. Different groups of main and sub-depots serve the different lines. Only one new rail depot has been built since the War—at Upminster, to replace a depot at East Ham whose site was needed by British Railways. There has been little new capital development in the existing rail depots in recent years—only individual pieces of machinery, to save money or improve maintenance efficiency.

(c) *Elements in Management Structure Concerned with Capital Projects*

The London Transport management structure is shown on the chart on pp. 78 and 79. It can be seen that there are four separate Chief Engineers. Each is in full control of a section of engineering services, both for capital construction and for day-to-day running and maintenance, but his function is to provide services to meet the requirements of the Operating Managers. All these Chief Engineers and Operating Managers are co-equal, and none merely advisory or subservient to any of the others. Other officers directly responsible to Executive Members include the Chief Financial Officer, the Chief Supplies and Services Officer, the Architect and the Director of Research. Various of these and other officers meet on standing and co-ordinating Committees, but co-ordination between the different Departments, in the sense of direction to resolve differences, can come only from Executive Members. Moreover, on some subjects co-ordination can be exercised only by two or more Executive Members acting together, or by the Executive as a whole. All full-time Executive Members have long previous experience as officers of the L.T.E., L.P.T.B. and/or their predecessors. Major decisions are normally taken at meetings of the Executive or its sub-committees, and individual Members are told at a very early stage about new proposals, including capital projects of any size at all. The responsibilities of Executive Members are distributed on the basis of experience and convenience of sharing loads, and can readily be exchanged as the loads vary or individuals move. It is significant that L.T.E. is working within definite geographical and functional limits, that virtually the same Departments have had the same functions for practically a generation, and there is not much movement of senior staff into and out of the organisation.

London Transport's organisation has little geographical subdivision, and it would be hard to suggest any more that would be workable. The three Operating Managers—of Railways, Central Road Services and Country Buses and Coaches—are responsible for the provision of services for passengers, timing, routes and space in vehicles, subject to very close consultation with the Chief Engineers. Many questions, of course will

LONDON TRANSPORT EXECUTIVE CHART OF ORGANISATION

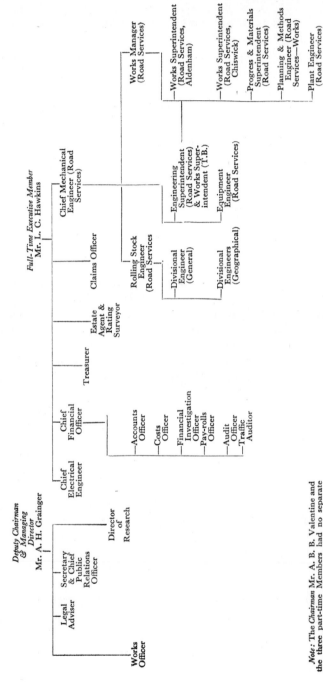

Note: The *Chairman* Mr. A. B. B. Valentine and the three part-time Members had no separate departmental responsibilities.

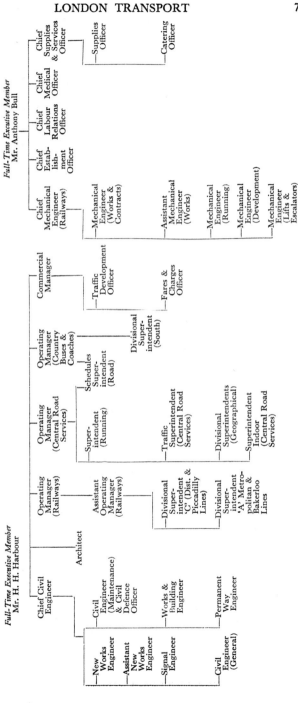

have to be dealt with jointly from the outset—for instance, the economics of speeding up the handling of passenger traffic at rush periods by providing more passenger cars or more doors on tube trains. The Operating Managers are concerned jointly with the Commercial Manager in forecasting, and in trying to influence the volume and incidence of traffic.

The Chief Civil Engineer deals with most construction works on the railway side, whereas all construction on the road side falls to the Architect. Some works, such as underground stations, are primarily civil engineering, and the Architect handles only such things as internal design of ticket halls. On the other hand, some schemes involve mainly surface building, but also some civil engineering work. In either case the officer concerned with the larger portion of the work agrees with the other to take overall responsibility for the design, and the latter works on the subordinate part by agreement with him. There are normally separate contracts as well as separate designs. The civil engineers, having provided the tracks and permanent way which run through a railway depot, would usually arrange the contract also for the drainage and foundations of the building—but in collaboration with the Architect. Designs, specifications and bills of quantities for civil engineering works are normally prepared by London Transport staff, except that consultants would be employed for any new tubes.

The Chief Mechanical Engineer (Railways) is assisted by four Mechanical Engineers—one for lifts and escalators, one for day-to-day maintenance of rolling stock, one for works and contracts and one for development and design work. The last mentioned—the Mechanical Engineer (Development)—is the one most concerned with capital work. He has a small staff. They do not produce all plans of new rolling stock in detail, but rather performance and other specifications, outline designs and directives. From these, contractors produce detailed designs, which are then discussed with the L.T.E. engineers. Moreover, the office of the Mechanical Engineer (Development) does not see the whole programme of construction through to its completion. When the designs and specifications are agreed supervision of manufacture and assembly is the responsibility of the Mechanical Engineer (Works and Contracts), who also has other responsibilities—provision of spare parts, maintenance and overhaul in the Executive's own workshops and depots. Indeed, at two stages below the Mechanical Engineer (Works and Contracts) there is still a combination of responsibilities for new development and current work. There is at this level one assistant concerned with progress and planning both of maintenance and overhaul and of new construction. There is also another assistant parallel with him responsible for the contract aspects of new rolling-stock construction. This absence of any one separate Department or Section exclusively concerned with new railway rolling-stock is probably due to the fact that, although there is a comparatively large total expenditure under this head, there are relatively few new designs being produced at any one time. At any rate the Executive prefer to rely largely on the resources of two or three competing contractors rather than to build up a considerable design staff of their own. London Transport do not seem to have had delays to their railway rolling-stock programme owing to lack of staff, whereas they have sometimes had such delays to their civil engineering and building works.

In addition to maintenance and overhauls the Chief Mechanical Engineer (Road Services) is responsible for design and development of new vehicles and garage equipment and improvements to existing vehicles and equipment. The Chief Supplies and Services Officer is responsible, among other things, for purchasing and stores control. For contracts for new capital works (as distinct from consumable stores and spare parts) he has quite a small staff, and he conducts the principal negotiations personally. He is responsible for the commercial side of contract arrangements and for the purchase of road and railway vehicles and other major equipment. But he is in no way concerned with either building or civil engineering contracts, except through his membership of a joint committee which reviews—after the event—all contracts over £30,000.

Capital schemes go up to the Executive with two reports— one by the initiating Department and another by the Chief Financial Officer—whereas in similar cases the Coal Board normally receive only one jointly agreed report. In London Transport it is considered important that there should be a completely independent financial report, because the Financial

Department is a completely independent department[4] in a position to give detached and impartial advice to the Executive. In most cases the Financial Department are consulted at the very earliest stages, but sometimes a scheme may be worked out up to a certain stage and then presented to the Financial Department for comment. There is within the Financial Department a 'Financial Investigation Officer', an important part of whose work is to make financial studies of the economics and profitability of capital schemes and other new proposals, and he can be called in by any other Department at any stage of such schemes.

The Research Department is relatively small (though in course of expansion) and concerned with scientific investigation of particular problems put to it (or aspects of larger problems) but not with development. It is also concerned with testing materials and technical control of certain works processes. It also has a Section for operational research, and a committee of Chief Engineering Officers guides it as regards priorities. There are small Economic and Statistical Sections (under the Assistant Secretary) which study population and general economic, business and social developments likely to affect traffic or general operations. They are not directly responsible for traffic forecasting—a matter for the Operating and Commercial Managers' Departments—but they produce material on which these and other Departments can work.

(d) *The General Planning and Control of Capital Development*

We saw that planning and control of new development under the Coal Board involved the preparation of schemes at Area Headquarters and their submission to and consideration by the Divisional and National Headquarters. Most of the schemes had very broadly similar objects, and there were large numbers of them which the Divisional and National Headquarters dealt with within the scope of long-term National Plans. Within

---

[4] This is London Transport Executive's reason for maintaining the practice they have. The author would rather not try to judge whether the Coal Board Finance Department is any less—or more—independent, or if it is, whether either Board's system is better suited than the other's to its own special purposes. The Coal Board Finance Department can, of course, also report independently—in case of disagreement—and there is one Member of the Coal Board itself responsible specifically for finance.

London Transport there are certainly long-term plans, but there are relatively few very large individual projects, and there is no question of subordinate local headquarters passing them up the line for consideration. Usually projects, large and small, are initiated in the Departments of one or other of the Chief Engineers in collaboration with the Operating Departments. They are submitted first to the Finance Department and/or otherwise considered at or below Chief Officer level and then put up to the Executive (and if they cost more than £100,000 to the British Transport Commission). We must bear in mind all along the relative smallness and compactness of the L.T.E.'s organisation. A capital project of any considerable size will be known to one or more of the Executive Members at a very early stage, often well before it has been worked on in any detail on paper. The really large and important schemes, such as the renewals of large fleets of road or rail vehicles, will almost certainly have been discussed from the outset at Executive Member level. One of the most important questions about capital development control in any organisation is who decides, and on what basis, between competing projects. Other large organisations may have separate Departments or inter-departmental committees to consider new capital schemes—and their relative priorities—before submission to the governing authority—or sometimes to make the final decisions. In London Transport there is no such body below the level of the Executive Members, and it is they personally, in conjunction with the Chief Officers, who decide on the size of the programme and the main projects and types of project which it should comprise. The programme is dealt with on a three-year basis and, like all programmes, there is more finality about its first year. A programme has in recent years been put forward and settled between October and December each year for the three subsequent years (beginning 1st January). About three-quarters of the proposed expenditure for each year will be allocated in the programme to specific named schemes and the remainder by broad groups of Departments. The programme is put forward by the Executive to the Commission, and, after any discussion between them, it is submitted along with the Commission's total programme to the Government. In practice, the programmes for the second and third years may, a year later, be varied either by the subsequent proposals of the Executive or by the Government.

Chief Officers can only authorise capital projects estimated to cost less than £1,000, and even the appropriate Executive Member only those estimated to cost less than £2,000. In effect, therefore, every significant individual item of capital expenditure has to go to the highest level for approval. The Executive deals with all projects over £2,000, either in full session or through a committee. In particular, the 'Executive Conference' of the full-time Members chaired by the Managing Director deals with individual approvals and also questions of priority between different schemes, reviews progress, both at the planning and at the execution stages, and supervises the drawing up of annual programmes. The Chief Financial Officer reports on projects over £25,000 individually. The Executive Conference is the pivotal body in considering all capital schemes. It reviews progress by receiving and discussing half-yearly reports on the out-turn of expenditure on all schemes costing over £100,000—taking in June and December schemes costing over £250,000 and in March and September schemes between £100,000 and £250,000. It usually discusses buildings schemes as soon as sketch plans are drawn, if not earlier, and engineering schemes are also taken at the formative stages. Final sketch plans are formally signed and approved by all the Executive Members and Chief Officers directly responsible for authorising the schemes. All this quite detailed consideration of capital expenditure at the highest levels is presumably made possible by the relatively small number of schemes. As we have seen, there are few occasions for putting up many sizeable new buildings, and the engineering programmes consist primarily of a very few large projects— usually large batches of identical vehicles.

Below Executive Member level nearly all capital expenditure is dealt with by some standing or *ad hoc* committee—the seniority of the members varying in the different committees. On the civil engineering side there is a New Works Planning Committee appointed by the Chief Civil Engineer but under the Chairmanship of his New Works Engineer. It includes an architect, a signals engineer and representatives of the Mechanical Engineer's and Operating Departments, but not the Finance Department. For buildings there are two committees, the Station and Railway Premises Committee and the Garage and Road Services Premises Committee. The first is chaired by the Operating Manager (Railways) and the second by the Chief Mechanical Engineer (Road Services). The secretary of both these committees is the Works Officer, who prepares all works submissions for the Executive Conference. For railway rolling stock the Chief Mechanical Engineer has a committee which consists of periodical meetings between himself and his Assistant Engineers, and there are other committees in his Department at rather lower level. His capital projects are, of course, much fewer in number, and some of them much costlier than most of those of the Civil Engineering Department. For a particularly large project the Executive will set up a special sub-committee. There is, for instance, a 'Trolleybus Conversion Committee' and the design of the new 'Routemaster' bus was supervised by a large working group comprising everyone concerned—mainly officers from the Road Services Mechanical Engineering and Operating Departments.

(e) *Provision of Road Vehicles*

Since the War the Executive has had three major problems of road vehicle design and manufacture:

(i) the final design and provision of the 'R.T.' buses (originally designed in 1939) to replace the general standard types 'S.T.' and 'S.T.L.' which by the end of the War were twelve to fifteen years old;

(ii) the decision to scrap the trams and trolleybuses; and

(iii) the design and provision of the new standard 'Routemaster' ('R.M.') bus.

There was a considerable degree of standardisation of London buses before 1939—indeed before 1914—but the R.T. buses which were delivered over the period 1947–54 were the first to be fully jig-built to a completely standard design, so that all parts (in particular engines, chassis and bodies) were interchangeable and the flow-line maintenance and overhaul system could be introduced. In earlier years it is said to have required some pressure to persuade the manufacturers to work to this standardised system.   London Transport paid the body-builders for the special jigs and tools required and took them over when the contracts were completed (to use for manufacturing spares).   The same procedure will be applied for the Routemasters.

Problems (ii) and (iii) above were really closely connected. The 'Routemaster' working group studied the essential requirements for a London bus quite afresh.   The resulting improvements, like those in rail vehicles, were introduced partly because of technical progress, partly for economic reasons (affected by changes in the statutory requirements as to public service vehicles) and in part simply to enable the services to cope with the increasing traffic problems.   The 'R.M.' bus is bigger, yet lighter, than the 'R.T.' It has power-assisted steering and automatic gear change.   These are not simply amenities for the driver.   They are intended to speed up the handling of traffic and the movement of buses in congested areas. Reduction of driver's fatigue should also, of course, improve safety.   The Routemaster bus is also designed to be rather more comfortable for the passengers than the 'R.T.' and to include heating. This too is not merely pleasant but economically important.   It may help to retain and attract traffic at a time when the service is engaged in really fierce competition for marginal traffic with private cars.

Separate manufacturing contracts are placed with different firms for the vehicle bodies and for the engines and chassis. Although they consulted manufacturers about particular points of design, the Road Services Mechanical Engineering Department produced drawings down to the last detail for the bodies, and specified in considerable detail the mechanical parts, before tenders were invited for prototypes. Four successive prototypes have been made by different manufacturers. Each has been run in service for many months, the first on and off since early 1956.   Comments have been obtained from members of the public and the bus crews, and the final design resulting has now been put into full production.   The entire double-decker road fleet will not be replaced by Routemaster buses all at once.   The first stage (roughly three years) is to replace trolleybuses.   It has not been finally decided whether the existing 'R.T.' buses will be replaced by Routemasters when they have reached the end of their economic life.

The decision to replace trolleybuses by oil buses, like the decision to replace the trams, was taken on traffic grounds after a detailed study had shown that there was little to choose between them financially. Trolleybuses, however, are less adaptable than oil buses. London Transport considered it reasonable, especially in view of the terms of the Act of Parliament under which it operates, to take into account larger considerations of public interest, such as traffic congestion and the availability of its service to the public in all conditions. (This approach might be thought to contrast with that of the Herbert Committee,[5] but their criticisms of the Electricity Boards' concern with 'matters of supposed national interest' seemed to refer primarily, if not exclusively, to cases where such considerations conflicted with those of cost. In the trolleybus case, in the London Transport Executive's view, no such conflict arose.)

(f) *The Provision of Railway Rolling Stock*

Orders for new railway rolling stock and for its major reconstruction are dealt with in very large blocks—the entire stock on the Central Line, for instance, by the ordering of some 350 new cars and the modernisation of 350 old ones[6]—the whole at a cost of about £9 million. Projects of this size require the approval of the British Transport Commission, to whom outline information about design is submitted, but all planning of programmes, specifications and placing of contracts is done by the Executive's own Departments direct with the manufacturers. London Transport designs are not standardised with those of British Railways, but the Executive's engineers keep in touch with technical developments in the Railway Regions, and vice versa—by various means, including personal contact, attendance at British Railways engineering meetings and the technical Press. The electric traction systems of London Transport and the Railway Regions differ considerably. The construction of London Transport rolling stock in British Railways carriage-building workshops has not

---

[5] *Report of the Committee of Enquiry into the Electricity Supply Industry*, 1956, Cmd. 9672, p. 97, para. 373. See p. 107 below.

[6] Some of the 350 old ones will be cars transferred from the Piccadilly Line.

G

hitherto been undertaken, largely because the latter have in the main been fully occupied with their own work.

Before placing bulk contracts for fleets of new rolling stock London Transport usually has prototypes made. The detailed design and manufacture of the prototypes, like that of the main bulk of the stock, is normally carried out by the contractors in close liaison with the Executive's own engineers. Recently, for one set of new rolling stock, a *design contract* was placed and the contractors were given a less detailed specification than normally, and hence more scope in the development of their own design. Although the construction of new prototypes is normally left to contractors, a prototype modification to an existing vehicle—or a 'mock-up', in very simple form (of the passenger accommodation only) may be produced in the Executive's own Works at Acton.

A single contract is not placed for complete vehicles. There is one contract for the vehicle body, another for the traction motors and another for control equipment. The manufacturers of the control equipment are usually made responsible for the installation work at the body-builder's works. There are also separate contracts for each of some seventeen items to be incorporated in the body as 'free issue items'. The manufacturers deliver these items to the works of the body-builders, who are responsible for fitting them into the body. The following is a specimen list:

> Air brake equipment
> Motor generator sets
> Air door equipment
> Car doors
> Auxiliary equipment
> Axle boxes and motor suspension bearing units
> Auxiliary contactors
> Loudaphones
> Chokes, capacitors, resistances and car heaters
> Auxiliary lighting equipment
> Auto-couplers and disconnecting units

The following items were to be supplied and fitted by London Transport staff into the body after delivery of the vehicle at the London Transport Depot:

Collector traction motors' shoegear
Fire extinguishers
Emergency tools and keys
Short-circuiting devices
Destination blinds
Batteries
Route diagrams

The degree of competition in tendering for the contracts for these different items apparently varies. In 1927, before the formation of the L.P.T.B., the Underground Group of Companies were concerned that the prices of rolling-stock bodies were not sufficiently competitive. So the Group formed a new body-building company, the Union Construction Company, and considered that this helped to reduce prices. The company ceased to function—at least for rolling-stock manufacture —before the formation of the L.P.T.B. in 1933. For some time in the post-War period there were only three body-building contractors whom the L.T.E. invited to tender, but recently they have added two other firms. They feel that they sometimes have a difficult choice between, on the one hand, enlarging the field of competition and the possibility of reducing prices and, on the other hand, confining their orders to firms who, they are confident, have the necessary resources and experience. The same applies to the contracts for the 'free issue items'. Some of these involve very specialised work in fields covered by patents. London Transport engineers apparently have in some cases to undertake a good deal of advance consultation, without commitment, with the principal manufacturers likely to be invited to tender, before the definite specification and order have been drawn up and approved. Such a procedure seems naturally to follow from the Executive's policy of keeping their own design staff small and not employing it on detailed planning. Whether this has tended to restrict the list of firms invited to tender it is hard to say, but there does seem to have been a definite policy (which has achieved certain results) in recent years of trying to get a larger number of tenders and keener competition. London Transport officers say that they have seldom, if ever, had to consider inviting tenders from abroad, and they would not normally do so unless they could not get satisfactory tenders from British firms.   The Executive, however, have placed no restriction as a matter of policy on buying abroad.   In contrast to the Civil Engineering and Architect's Departments, the Chief Mechanical Engineer (Railways) has experienced little, if any, delay in his capital programmes through lack of sufficient numbers of experienced design staff.   This appears to be the result partly of the considerable reliance that is placed on contractors for designs and partly of the Executive making special efforts during the post-War period to recruit, train and keep suitable young men. Railway engineering has strong traditions, and some men enter it through family connections.

A ten-year forward programme for the purchase and reconstruction of railway rolling stock has been prepared so as to try to avoid requirements for replacements coming in irregular peaks—as they did owing to the wartime deferment of replacements.   Although they are dealt with in large blocks, there is a good deal of complicated interlocking between the programmes of replacement and occasional reconstruction of the stock on different railway lines.   It is important to have the right numbers and types of cars so that they can be made up in train sets which can be divided at non-rush periods.   The manufacture of a fleet of cars in each bulk contract may be spread over three or four years.   The preliminary studies and planning and manufacture of prototypes have in the post-War years been spread over even longer periods.   It is thought best to run prototype cars for a year before making a decision on the final design—which should differ in only minor respects from the prototype.   A very considerable interval can therefore elapse between the first consideration of a proposal to renew a complete batch of rolling stock and its final delivery.   The design contract for prototypes for the new Central Line stock was placed in 1958.   The bulk orders were expected to be placed in 1960 and delivery spread over the period 1961–63. The delivery of over 230 new cars and conversion of nearly 150 for the District Line was spread over the years 1947–50.   When the provision of new rolling stock is tied up with a project for a new line or the expansion or electrification of an old line the periods can, of course, be very much longer.   Because projects of this magnitude (including the civil engineering work) take so very long to prepare, they can seldom get fully under way before being affected by some general national economic factors requiring deferment or financial restriction. For instance, the idea for new stock on the Piccadilly Line started in 1949 with the intention of getting into production in 1952. For financial reasons, however, there was a deferment for five years. Prototype designs were approved and the contract for manufacture placed in 1954. Delivery, originally promised for the spring of 1956, did not in fact start until mid-1957 and was only completed in the spring of 1958. In December 1957, in order to avoid a repetition of the current overlapping of replacement programmes, the Chief Mechanical Engineer, in collaboration with the other Chief Officers concerned, set up a committee to devise a ten-year forward plan for rolling-stock replacement. The Chairman is the Mechanical Engineer (Running), and the other members are an officer from the Railway Operating Department, the Financial Investigation Officer from the Finance Department and a representative of the Chief Supplies and Services Officer. The Committee have worked out a complex series of interlocking programmes of progressive renewal and regrouping of all the rolling stock.

Apart from the question of whether the body design will meet modern requirements of rapid loading and unloading, railway vehicles can be kept in service very much beyond their normal thirty years' life, so long as the technical performance (as to traction characteristics) is still acceptable, and provided the liability for expensive replacements is accepted. For instance, if the life of a car is extended by five years its wheels and axles may need to be completely replaced, yet such expensive new components will have run but a fraction of their life when the car itself is replaced, and it will be unlikely that wheels and axles of, say, thirty-five year old design could be re-used in cars of newer design. It is important to avoid sudden variations in the number of cars coming in for five-yearly 'heavy overhaul'. London Transport try to replace their vehicles at the times they would otherwise be due for heavy overhaul. Yet if the incidence of replacement is too greatly concentrated this will result in a sudden reduction in the overhaul requirement, without opportunity to save staff through the normal process of wastage. London Transport have found, particularly since the War, that discharge of staff because of redundancy is one of the things most certain to provoke labour trouble.   Their aim is, therefore, to avoid sudden variations in the number of vehicles coming for overhaul.   Among other reasons for trying to keep an even programme of replacements is that there is the prospect of better terms, because it naturally helps manufacturers.

Other factors in decisions to replace rolling stock are the opportunities for improvements in design, notably the substitution of light alloys for the entire bodies of railway cars.   Tests of these under control conditions showed that the saving in electricity is critically dependent upon the particular service being worked, and there are also subsidiary factors, such as the fact that aluminium alloy need not be painted.   For more than thirty years past the design of tube stock cars has been progressively improved.   Doorway openings have been increased in number and in width.   Traction motors have been reduced in size and the number per train increased.   Thus a motor bogie could be designed so as to allow a level floor throughout the car, and increase the space for passengers.   This change has also meant that the traction control and other auxiliary equipment has had to be designed so that it will fit in the 15 inches between the floor of the car and the gauge clearance level. These improvements are intended to reduce rush-hour crowding in central London.   The alternative—enlarging platforms below ground—might not be effective in all cases, and the cost would often be prohibitive.   So efforts have to be concentrated on getting the largest possible number of people on and off trains of limited length in the shortest possible time.

As this system of producing railway vehicles involves the activities of some dozen to twenty separate manufacturers in each case, there is clearly a problem of co-ordination and progress control.   The prime responsibility for this has been clearly laid on the car builder.   However, apart from maintaining timetables and progress control charts and discussing them internally and by correspondence, the L.T.E. Railway Mechanical Engineering Department has inspection staff who report on progress in manufacturers' works, check quality and ensure that the equipment is being produced in accordance with the agreed designs and specifications and by reliable methods.

London Transport staff consider that the close contact that these inspectors maintain with the manufacturers' staffs and the mutual confidence that can be built up provide a very effective means of getting warning at an early stage if progress at any point is falling behind the timetable. The car builders are responsible for the routine progressing of their requirements, including 'free issue' items, and are expected to call on London Transport for assistance only if their own efforts have failed.

(g) Provision of Buildings

There are hardly any buildings common to both road and rail services. Building schemes are initiated by one of the Engineering or Operating Departments, or by the two sides jointly. On the railway side, for example, the Electrical Engineering Department needs substations, the Civil Engineering Department, signal boxes (built to the requirements of the Operating Department) and the Mechanical Engineering Department occasionally new depots, or more often alteration or extension to old depots. There is no Department in London Transport responsible for co-ordinating all building requirements from the 'client's' point of view.[7] Probably there would not be enough work for any such special Department. The L.T.E. Architect, however, like many private architects, finds himself to some extent in the position of co-ordinating his clients' demands as well as meeting them. He is also responsible for controlling, co-ordinating and reporting on progress in planning, as well as progress in carrying out the work, and for liaison with the Estate and Rating Surveyors and with the Civil Engineers and the Mechanical Engineers (who have to install lighting, heating, lifts and other mechanical equipment). This applies to all schemes in which the Architect's work predominates. As we have seen, there are other types of scheme which are regarded primarily as civil engineering and where the Civil Engineers co-ordinate and the Architect does only a subsidiary part of the design. In relation to the size of London Transport's whole system there have not been very many new buildings in recent years. The bulk have been garages, and some of

---

[7] On the other hand, there are the Garage and Road Services Premises Committee, the Station and Railway Premises Committee and (at a higher level) the Executive Conference. See above pp. 84–85.

these and most of the others have formed subsidiary parts of larger schemes. It is natural, therefore, that we shall be disappointed if we look within London Transport for a special system for initiating and controlling all building schemes in isolation. There is nothing like the system which obtains within the Post Office [8] with its large building programmes and separate (administrative) Sites and Buildings Branch.

One can get an idea of the size and nature of L.T.E. building programmes from the following extract from the Architect's periodical report to the former 'Executive Works Committee' (now the Executive Conference) in 1958:

TABLE III

LONDON TRANSPORT BUILDINGS IN COURSE OF CONSTRUCTION
OR SHORTLY ABOUT TO START, 1958

		Amount Authorised £
Acton	Extension of Chief Mechanical Engineer's Offices	104,000
Leyton	Additional amendments to accommodation at Garage	127,000
Hatfield New Town	New Garage	160,000
Stevenage New Town	New Garage	156,000
Chiswick	New Central Laboratory (Stage I, £23,000, already completed)	300,000
Trolleybus conversion scheme	Total estimate for conversion of trolleybus depots for oil buses	1,596,000

Individual schemes forming part of the above:

Bexley	60,000
Carshalton	50,000
Clapton	87,000
Bow	91,000
Poplar	91,000

Nine other similar schemes expected to start 1959–61.

A somewhat different type of garage and local depot is provided when oil buses replace trolleybuses. The electrical wires, etc., are removed and fuel-storage facilities added, and the occasion has generally been taken to improve the whole garage accommodation and add mechanical cleaning equipment

[8] See R. J. S. Baker, 'Post Office Building Programmes', *Public Administration*, Summer 1958.

which it would not have been practicable to use with electrically driven vehicles. There are or will be new garages or garage extensions in most, but not all, of the New Towns in the London Transport area. Most other garage building since the War has either followed on tramway conversion or replaced old, overcrowded and dispersed garages. Other big schemes have been the new Aldenham depot and the extension at Chiswick (for the flow-line maintenance systems).

It is only under the head of garages and the smaller buildings, such as the substations and signal boxes along railway lines, that the Architect has had to provide a fairly long run of schemes of similar type. On the railway side there does not seem to have been a great deal of standardisation in planning, presumably because of the fairly limited number of buildings and the varying nature of the sites and volume of traffic. The electricity substations are fairly similar, and planning is fairly simple, but it has not been considered possible to use identical plans. Only the very small cabins for permanent-way workers have been completely standardised—as little concrete huts— and even these are not always acceptable in or near stations or other areas where appearance is regarded as important. On the garage side, however, there is pretty full standardisation in the sense of standardisation of requirements and dimensions— although not of plans—more standardisation indeed than for Coal Board buildings. For each portion of the garage (locker room, conductors' room, stores of various kinds, lavatories, offices, paint-shops and other subsidiary workshops and canteens) specific areas are laid down according to the number of buses or the number of staff. There are two standard sizes for 'parent' garages and five sizes for 'attached' garages. This system, of course, simplifies the settling of requirements and plans. The present standards are substantially as revised in 1955. Standardisation has been in force since before the War. London Transport has no standard cost yardsticks, but the Architect's and Financial Departments consider they have a broad idea of what a garage ought to cost in relation to its size.

The whole professional and specialist staff of the Architect's Department amounts to seventy-three, including quantity surveyors and site supervisors. At times of pressure and difficulty it is helped by the employment of outside firms of architects and quantity surveyors.   The Works and Building Section, which is not part of the Architect's Department, but is responsible to the Chief Civil Engineer, carries out by direct labour the bulk of maintenance of buildings and civil engineering works and also does small new works.   It has a permanent staff of about 1,200, mainly tradesmen.   It started because on railways certain work adjacent to running tracks must always be carried out by railway staff; but it is employed on other work too.   It is a great advantage—indeed often essential to the L.T.E.—to have an organisation under its own direct control to do work at short notice or phased in precisely with the timetable of engineering schemes.   For relatively small jobs there is no need to waste time on getting a number of competitive tenders and dealing with contractors.   Generally, competitive tendering should save money, but there may be times when much more money could be saved in other directions by having a small building job completed at the right time, even at the expense of streamlining preliminary work and cutting out formalities, and perhaps paying a little more for the building work.

The L.T.E., however, have considerable reserve about the apparent attractions of doing work in this way, and are most anxious to ensure that cutting out formalities does not mean cutting out necessary safeguards.   They do not believe that, except for the most trivial work, it is worth while, or indeed saves much time, to eliminate the making of at least a simple drawing.   This, however, will often be prepared by the Works and Buildings Section staff themselves rather than by the Architect's Department, unless the job is complicated or likely to cost more than a few hundred pounds.   Both for maintenance and small new works there is a system of cost and labour-time control associated with a bonus system.   London Transport say that otherwise it would be very easy for a large permanent staff of tradesmen, continually on call for small and urgent or allegedly urgent jobs, to be uneconomically employed. Nevertheless, their system does seem more flexible and adaptable than the alternative of complete dependence on outside contractors.   Their own Works Department may on occasion carry out jobs valued up to £5,000 or £6,000, and without competitive tendering up to the order of £500 or even £1,000. Above this sort of level it is usual for the Works Department to put in formal tenders to the Executive and for them to be treated with the same formality and opened at the same time as those of outside contractors. If the Works Department's tender is accepted its relations with the Architect in carrying out the job will be similar to those of a private contractor.

(h) *Railway Line Work*

Nowadays London Transport Area is largely closed to further outward development. Practically all the extensions of its railway lines took place before 1940, except the extensions of the Central Line to Epping and Ruislip (1946–49). No completely new lines have been constructed since, but the Epping–Ongar Line was electrified in November 1957. The only new line now contemplated in the next few years is the Victoria tube line. Other recent and current major civil engineering work includes track alterations at Wembley Park and Gloucester Road, work between Bow Road and Upminster on the District Line (in preparation for the transfer of the local lines from British Railways), a new station (in place of two old ones) at Notting Hill Gate and the widening and electrification scheme for the Amersham Line. Apart from the Victoria Line, all the schemes so far mentioned were planned—and indeed constructional work on some of them was started—before the War. They are all very different in form and purpose, and it is impossible now to speak of a *typical* railway extension or other civil engineering scheme in London Transport.

The Amersham scheme is in distinct parts and has been undertaken for various different reasons. At present the Metropolitan Line north-west from Baker Street is only electrified as far as Rickmansworth and on a branch to Watford. Certain Metropolitan Line trains are hauled by obsolete detachable electric locomotives from central London to Rickmansworth, and thence to Amersham and Aylesbury by steam locomotives. The rolling stock needs replacement. The population served by the line has been growing, and there are difficulties at peak periods; but the traffic beyond Amersham is not heavy. The L.T.E. therefore plans to:

(*a*)   increase the number of tracks from two to four between Harrow and the junction for the Watford Branch;

(*b*)   electrify the line from Rickmansworth to Amersham;

(*c*)   provide new unit rolling stock;

(*d*)   transfer the service beyond Amersham to British Railways.

This involves widening bridges and earthworks, extending stations, providing new electricity substations and extensive alterations to the signalling system, including new signal boxes. The project was planned, and indeed started, before the War, but held up until recently by financial restrictions. When it is all complete and the new rolling stock has been introduced it is calculated that the heavier traffic carried will make it financially attractive.

The timetable, both of planning and construction, has been worked out in advance in considerable detail and expressed in terms of bar graphs. (The rolling stock is dealt with quite separately.) Once the scheme was firmly authorised and detailed planning started, there had not (at the time of writing) been significant fallings back from the pre-arranged timetable —and the Executive's civil engineers were confident that they would continue to be able to adhere to it. They believed that the secret of doing so lay in the very fact of working out a detailed programme covering all sections of the planning work well in advance, and discussing and agreeing this with all Departments concerned. The present bar-graph programme allocates work between all the different sections of the Chief Civil Engineer's Department (including signalling) and also the Chief Electrical Engineer's and Architect's Departments. No outside consultants are employed, and no design work (apart from rolling stock) is done by contractors. There are frequent meetings, both to settle the programmes of design and construction and to watch progress in carrying them out. The New Works Planning Committee covers all major new works of London Transport in course of planning or construction on the civil engineering side, but the New Works Engineer also holds special and frequent meetings to settle in detail the programme for planning and construction of such major schemes as the Amersham Line. Below this level, for the Amersham or other really large schemes, a Resident Engineer and Liaison Officer is appointed. (He spends most of his time on the site and holds periodical progress meetings with all concerned, including contractors.) For the final planning and progress control of the Victoria Line, however, if and when it is finally authorised, some special enlarged planning organisation would appear to be needed.

(i) *Conclusions*

In the foregoing description of London Transport capital development arrangements certain contrasts with other public bodies, particularly the Coal Board, have been evident. London Transport has been run as a single public body for practically a generation. Even before then many of the activities it now runs were already under unified control, and like most transport organisations had a considerable public utility character. The changes after 1947, therefore, involved little or no internal upheaval. In planning their new developments since the War the Executive's staff have not been disturbed by an atmosphere of controversy like that surrounding the Coal Board. Indeed, in the earlier period of considerable expansion between 1933 and 1939, most of the staff were working under the same top management as before 1933. The controversies which preceded the passing of the 1933 Act were limited in scope and affected only certain portions of the services which eventually united under the L.P.T.B. The bulk had been unified before.

With these advantages, very considerable expansion and modernisation of capital equipment took place before the War, concurrently with the rapid expansion of Greater London. The L.T.E. took over from the L.P.T.B. an efficient, modern and integrated system. Much of the equipment was certainly near the end of its economic life and technical improvement has been possible since; but, apart from the trams, and to a lesser extent the trolleybuses, it was not fundamentally outdated equipment. Even the scrapping of trams and trolleybuses simply involved the more general introduction of buses of designs already basically settled. Similarly, the overwhelming bulk of the railway services had been electrified from the outset or for very many years, and the rolling stock, although much of it was old, was designed on lines which were advanced at the time of their introduction.

Further technical developments—both road and railway—although important, have been mainly secondary, at least in comparison with the fundamental and wholesale technical changes in the coal and electricity generating industries. They have, however, been very valuable: two-pedal control in buses, rubber suspension in rail vehicles, and light alloys in road and rail vehicles. There have also apparently been notable advances in railway signalling. Really large items of capital expenditure associated with technical advances have been, first, the new major overhaul depots for road vehicles based on centralised flow-line methods and, secondly, the extension of the Research Department and its laboratories. The Victoria Line, the largest single scheme of capital expenditure yet proposed, does not originate from any fundamental/technical change, nor does the Amersham scheme. Another characteristic of post-War conditions in London Transport has been the absence of any great rise of traffic or any heavy demand for extended services. There has indeed been contraction at some points, and the pressure for extended services has applied in the main only at limited times and places, such as the New Towns and the rush-hour periods in central London.

L.T.E., therefore, started after the War as a well-integrated organisation not having to face any fundamental upheavals. Some of its greatest problems were problems of loss of traffic rather than expansion, of pressures on day-to-day operating, of recruitment and of balancing running costs and revenue—rather than problems of capital. The bulk of the investment was in large blocks, but, apart from the electrification of tracks and the construction of the very large buildings, most of these large blocks of monetary expenditure did not involve proportionately large expenditure of design effort, because they comprised large numbers of vehicles, mostly of identical or similar design.

The result of all this is reflected in the Executive's organisation. They have not set up special Departments for planning or co-ordinating capital expenditure. They seem to have found it quite satisfactory to leave such work below Executive Member level mostly under the control of a number of separate Departments,[9] some of whose main responsibilities were in the field of day-to-day operating and maintenance. This apparently leaves a good deal of co-ordination to the Executive Members themselves. Such a system, however, may well be found inadequate to control such a huge operation as the construction of the Victoria Line, and it would no doubt have clogged up the organisation of such nation-wide bodies as the Coal Board or the Central Electricity Generating Board. London Transport, however, has been helped, not only by the *relatively* limited nature of its problems but also by the compactness of its geographical area, the established traditions of the organisation and the staff, and the long personal experience of the Executive Members. Other special characteristics have developed as a result of these same conditions.

The effect on relations with the contractors has been different on the railway and the road side. On the railway side a fair volume of new design work has been needed, but it has not been enough to justify the setting up of a really large planning staff within the London Transport's own organisation. Contractors, who manufacture also for British Railways and for export, have been able to help. London Transport engineers have initiated important ideas and principles of design and also specific changes, but have not attempted to take over the whole design work themselves. On the road side, however, where the total volume of design work was less, the Executive's own engineers have undertaken proportionately much more of it—indeed all the details of the bodies of large buses, and chassis, for which London Transport presumably has a rather special demand owing to their very large number of identical vehicles and the exceptionally severe congestion and pressure of traffic. How far these demands differ from those of other transport authorities it is hard for an outsider to judge, but London Transport seem quite assured it is worth while to do this designing themselves. Probably the most important reason is that it makes possible their unique system of standardised maintenance and overhaul. In order to make the Aldenham and Chiswick system work, it has been essential to have complete control of every detail of design and complete

---

[9] There is, however, co-ordinating machinery, such as the Station and Railway Premises Committee and the Garage and Road Services Committee.

interchangeability. Aldenham and Chiswick are impressive, but owing to the very special conditions of London Transport, it may be doubted if they could be copied by more than one or two other large transport fleet owners.

It is interesting to notice the relationship of the Financial Department to other Departments.   It is represented on some but not all of the co-ordinating committees.   It is consulted informally at fairly early stages in most, but not all, capital schemes.   Final proposals come to the Executive Members for decision—with separate detailed comments by the Chief Financial Officer.

It would be wrong to give any impression that London Transport's problems in recent years have been easy. But some (though not all) have been short-term and many have concerned day-to-day operating. L.T.E. is working within a number of major limitations, and there are certain features in its system which are probably unique.   It also has certain advantages of compactness and relative organisational stability. It is extremely interesting to any student of management to see how in recent years it has worked within these limitations and made use of these advantages.   But its experience should only be applied with great caution to the problems of other industries and public services—especially those which are rapidly changing and expanding.

CHAPTER IV

ELECTRICITY: LOCAL DISTRIBUTION

(a) *Electricity Supply—the Basic Pattern*

The production and distribution of electric currents form a single, virtually instantaneous process. As electricity cannot be stored[1] on any scale, production and use are simultaneous— and can be dictated by the consumer (once he is connected)— unless widespread breakdowns are to ensue. Table IV shows the total amount of electricity (in units) supplied to consumers in Great Britain (excluding North Scotland), and also the increase in the numbers of such consumers, since 1920:

TABLE IV [2]

Year	Number of consumers of all classes (millions)	Units sold (millions)
1920	1·0	3,660
1925	1·8	5,585
1930	3·8	8,930
1935	7·5	14,290
1940	10·4	23,775
1945	10·8	30,601
1950–51	13·1	46,580
1954–55	14·9	62,410
1958–59	16·5	84,088

We can see that before the last War the most striking growth was in the number of consumers, while since the War it has

[1] 'Heat storage' and 'pumped storage' (described below, pp. 211–212) are not really exceptions to this general statement. Pumped storage is a means of storing not electricity, but mechanical energy, to produce electricity. Heat storage, as its name implies, is the storage not of electricity but of heat produced by electricity, in water, concrete or other suitable material, at the place where it is needed. Both systems may in future prove of very considerable economic importance, but neither has done so yet.

[2] Central Electricity Authority, *Power and Prosperity* (1954), pp. 12, 13, and also *Annual Reports* of the C.E.A., South Scotland Board and Electricity Council. The figures may not be precisely comparable in every case, but broadly they cover England, Wales and South Scotland. The amount of electricity being produced and supplied at any given moment is measured in *watts*, the measure of 'rate of work done'—or more conveniently in *kilowatts* (kW—1,000 watts) or *megawatts* (1,000,000 watts). The total amount of electricity supplied to consumers over a period is measured in kW-hours or, for the purpose of charging, 'units'.

been in the amount of electricity sold.   The main problems on the distribution side of the industry are at least as much concerned with reinforcing the network to give more supplies to existing consumers as with connecting new consumers.

Nearly all electricity for public use in Great Britain is now generated and supplied as alternating current at a standard frequency of 50 cycles per second—and generated by rotary motion—the great bulk by steam (less than 4 per cent by water). The heat for the steam may come from coal, oil or nuclear energy.   Electricity is generated, distributed and used at varying pressures (measured in volts and kilovolts).   Standardisation of consumers' voltages (and hence of their appliances) throughout the country has now nearly been completed (240 domestic, etc., and 415 industrial).   Voltages affect the economics of transmission and distribution.   Subject to certain limiting factors, the higher the voltage, the greater the quantities of electricity that can be transmitted without disproportionate increase in the thickness or number of the lines, and hence the lower the cost of the network.   But high voltages are dangerous, and expensive equipment is needed to step up to them and down again.   So they are generally used only for bulk transmission over long distances.   Electricity is now normally generated at 11–16 kV, stepped up at transformer stations to the voltage of the grid (now usually 132 kV or 275 kV) for long-distance '*main transmission*' and down again at other stations through stages in the course of '*distribution*', usually 33kV, 11 kV or 6,600 volts and 415 volts (industrial) or 240 volts (domestic).   Associated with the transmission lines and transformer stations are switching centres and control centres. When electricity is passed through transformers or long transmission lines some of it is lost—just how much will depend on complex calculations of the voltages, distances and other factors (some local),[3] and such calculations may be crucial in siting the generating stations as well as planning the transmission routes.

The purpose of the main transmission and local distribution systems is not simply to connect each consumer by the shortest possible route to the nearest power station, but rather to enable

[3] Insulation of the transmission lines may be impaired and losses increased when they pass through areas where the atmosphere is polluted.

the total load to be carried throughout the changing conditions of each hour and each day by those power stations which can do so most economically. The 'load' is the total amount of electricity demanded and supplied at any one time—measured in kilowatts. There are, of course, peak loads to be expected at particular times of the day and of the year—not, it is important to note, at quite the same times everywhere—and sufficient generation, transmission and distribution equipment has to be provided to cope with these, plus reserve capacity for breakdown and exceptional demands owing to cold weather and so forth. (*Normal* planned maintenance and overhaul is done in the summer, when demand is well below the peak.) Thus, for much of the time a sizeable proportion of the equipment is producing no return to cover its capital charges. The transmission and control system, therefore, needs to be organised so that:

(*a*) By pooling reserve capacity for emergencies the total quantity of plant required can be kept to a minimum.

(*b*) The generating equipment which is least economic to run (normally the oldest) is brought into operation only for the shortest periods—that is at the highest peaks, and the 'base load' is carried by the most economic (normally the most modern) equipment.

(*c*) The generating stations can be sited most economically taking into account costs of fuel and its transport and of electrical transmission.

The Electricity Boards have had to guard against uneconomic or excessive provision of capital, on the one hand, and the risk of deterioration and ultimately failure of service, on the other. If consumers, by switching on too much equipment, place too great a load on a power station without alternative sources of supply the first thing that happens is that the frequency or voltage is reduced. If the overload becomes greater still, either a proportion of consumers have to be cut off or the whole supply of current comes temporarily to a standstill. National, regional and local control centres (and the heavy and elaborate switchgear they operate by remote control) exist to keep supply in line—minute by minute—with demand, to regulate the bringing of generating equipment into and out of operation and to switch power from one part of the country to another.   Whenever an increase of power is needed the control centre finds out which station can offer it at the lowest cost.

All this organisation exists to deal with loads[4] of very unequal incidence—a situation which seems universal in electricity supply, but which may be not incapable of some modification.   One major problem is to cater as economically as possible for this unbalanced pattern of demand.   Another is to influence the demand itself by encouraging the use of electricity at off-peak periods with such measures as suitably adjusted tariffs, and the stimulation of consumers' interest in equipment which can generate heat at off-peak periods and store it.

Before the War electricity generation and distribution was provided by local concerns (two-thirds Local Authorities, and one-third companies) subject to central control by the Government and the Electricity Commissioners; but main transmission and the pooling of generating capacity was recognised as a matter of national concern, and the Central Electricity Board (created in 1926) had:

(*a*) acted as wholesaler of electricity to buy from generating stations and sell to distributors;

(*b*) constructed and operated the grid and its control and switching centres for this purpose.

In 1944–47 the North of Scotland Hydro-Electric Board was given the task of generating electricity (mainly by water), distributing it within the Highlands and exporting the surplus south.   In 1947 local electricity distribution in England, Wales and South Scotland was concentrated in fourteen larger local units—Government-appointed Area Boards.   Generation was taken away from the local concerns and combined with the transmission functions of the former C.E.B. under a new British Electricity Authority (later Central Electricity Authority) which also had certain functions of control and co-ordina-

---

[4] The electricity authorities speak of the 'system load factor', which they define as: 'the ratio expressed as a percentage of (*a*) the number of units of electricity sent out to the supply system during a given period, to (*b*) the number which would have been sent out had the maximum demand on the system been maintained and supplied throughout the period'—in other words, a measure of the extent to which the full capacity of the system had been used.

tion of the Area Boards. Broadly the Area Boards distribute at and below 33 kV. The B.E.A./C.E.A. operated its power stations and the grid directly through fourteen Divisions— quite separate from the Area Boards. The Area Boards at first set up Sub-Areas and Districts—but some have since eliminated the first of these lower tiers of management. In 1954 the South of Scotland Electricity Board was set up to do all generation main transmission and distribution in its own District indepen- dently of the C.E.A. Its generation and main transmission are controlled centrally, but for distribution there are Areas (really equivalent to Sub-Areas in England and Wales) and Districts.

In 1955 the Government-appointed Herbert Committee reported on the whole electricity supply industry in England and Wales—broadly to the effect that it was efficient, but in danger of losing its efficiency and needed certain changes, notably decentralisation, which they advocated strongly in principle and in detail. Later we shall quote their views about power-station construction. Their only recommendations which concern us here are those of general philosophy:

> We attach great importance, therefore, to the industry being run on business lines. It should have one duty and one duty alone: to supply electricity to those who will meet the costs of it and to do so at the lowest possible expenditure of resources consistent with the maintenance of employment standards at the level of the best private firms. Any variation from this task should be undertaken only on precise instructions.[5]

They feared that the Boards 'may become too much concerned with interpreting what the national interest requires rather than with the proper commercial conduct of their business which is to generate and sell electricity as cheaply as possible'.[6] For similar reasons they were also critical of the C.E.A. because— in the interests of British industry and exports—it was reluctant to order equipment from abroad:

---

[5] *Report of the Committee of Enquiry into the Electricity Supply Industry*, Cmd. 9672, p. 137, para. 507. For a moderate criticism of this point of view and of the Report in general see A. H. Hanson, *Public Administration*, Vol. XXXIV, 1956, pp. 211– 214, 'Electricity Reviewed: The Herbert Report'.

[6] *Ibid.* pp. 95–97, paras. 364–371, especially 366.

Matters of supposed national interest, if they interfere with the economic operation of the industry, should be recognised as essentially political matters to be decided by the Minister subject to his responsibility to Parliament.[7]

Following in most but not all respects the Committee's other recommendations, the Electricity Act 1957 dissolved the C.E.A., handed over its generation and main transmission functions to a new Central Electricity Generating Board and some but not all its co-ordinating functions to a new Electricity Council[8]

TABLE V[9]

ELECTRICITY SUPPLY INDUSTRY
NEW CAPITAL EXPENDITURE ON FIXED ASSETS
IN THE YEAR 1958–59

£ million

	C.E.G.B.	English Area Boards	South Scotland	North Scotland	Total
Generation . .	142·4	—	20·4	11·6	174·4
Main transmission .	30·8	—	2·4	1·4	34·6
Local distribution and/ or miscellaneous .	0·8	83·0	7·6	2·4	93·8
TOTAL .	174·0	83·0	30·4	15·4	302·8

(composed largely of representatives of the C.E.G.B. and Area Boards).

The electricity supply industry's capital assets may be broadly divided between:

[7] *Ibid.* p. 97, para. 373.

[8] See the article by Mr. D. G. Dodds, the Council's Industrial Relations Adviser, in *Public Administration*, Vol. XXXVI, Spring 1957, p. 27.

The brevity of the references here and elsewhere in this book to the Electricity Council is not intended to carry any implication of doubt as to its importance. The reason is rather that most of the activities of the Council are concerned with matters of high policy, while this book is concerned primarily with management, administration and the internal organisation of concerns directly responsible for operating industries and public services.

[9] *Electricity Council Report and Accounts*, 1958–59, pp. 147–149.

North of Scotland Hydro-Electric Board Report and Accounts, 1958, p. 35.

South of Scotland Electricity Board Report and Accounts, 1958, p. 29.

The English figures are for the year ending 31st March 1959 and the Scottish figures for the year ending 31st December 1958.

(*a*) Generation

(*b*) Main Transmission

(*c*) Local Distribution and Miscellaneous

—the last two categories including transformers and switch-gear as well as lines and cables.

The balance of new capital expenditure is shown in Table V.

Clearly these are figures with which hardly any other organisation in the United Kingdom has anything to compare, whether for annual capital expenditure or total capital assets. For instance, the annual capital investment of the electricity supply industry is about three times that of the coal industry, and its total assets (about £1,936 million) almost twice as much.

(b) *Area Organisation*[10]

The Area Boards in England and Wales provide, extend and maintain the large networks between the Grid and the consumers, and also assess and collect payments, do internal contract work and sell electrical apparatus. Each Board consists of a full-time Chairman, a full-time Deputy Chairman and between six and eight part-time members. Every Board has broadly the same organisation of four Departments under the Chief Engineer, Chief Commercial Officer, Chief Accountant and a Secretary. The Chief Commercial Officer (in most but not all Areas an engineer) is responsible not only for proposing tariffs, for estimating demand and for promoting retail sales but also for contract work inside the consumers' premises. All other engineering work is the responsibility of the Chief Engineer. This includes responsibility for deciding what is required and planning and providing it. In his Department there will generally be separate sections for planning and design, construction, operation and maintenance—usually he also has an architect, sometimes responsible to him through a civil engineer and sometimes more directly. The organisation for building design and maintenance differs from one Area Board to another. There may be a large or small direct labour building

---

[10] The organisation in Scotland below Board Headquarters level is very similar to that described in this section, except that the Scottish 'Area' is similar to an English Sub-Area. At Headquarters there is a link between main transmission and distribution work.

organisation, not necessarily under the direct control of the architect. 'Non-operational' buildings may be controlled by the Secretary. There is always a Purchasing Officer, and he may have certain joint responsibilities with the Chief Engineer and Chief Commercial Officer and/or owe his main allegiance to the Chief Accountant or Secretary or to the Deputy Chairman or the Board as a whole.

The Chief Accountant's Department both assesses the amount of finance required and makes and receives payments and prepares accounts. The Area Boards, however, unlike the Generating Board and the South of Scotland Board, have no title of 'Chief Financial Officer'. The Chief Accountant is usually concerned with the make-up of total financial programmes and budgets and with checking the out-turn of expenditure, but he does not usually appear to be involved in financial estimation or criticism of individual capital projects. The Secretary's Department may (among other functions) obtain sites and wayleaves and statutory approvals for schemes from Government and Local Authorities. It includes salaried solicitors, estate surveyors and 'Wayleave Officers' (generally not professionally qualified).

The Areas vary markedly in size and character—between those selling 8,500 million and those selling 3,000 million units each year. No Areas are overwhelmingly rural, and only London is almost entirely urban. They were planned so as to be 'sufficiently large and contain a sufficient diversity of requirements to enable the load to be well spread out over the day . . . to avoid, as far as possible, rearrangements which would cut across the existing distribution networks and might involve an unnecessary outlay of capital'.[11]

At first the Area Boards generally had a three-tier local organisation—that is their own Headquarters, Sub-Areas and Districts. Most still do. The Sub-Areas—between four and nine in each Area—broadly reproduce the departmental organisation at the Area Headquarters—with a Manager, an Engineer, a Commercial Officer, an Accountant and a Secretary (the last two offices sometimes combined). The Districts —between eighteen and thirty-seven in each Area—have generally only two branches, under Engineers and Commercial

[11] White Paper, *Electricity Supply Areas*, Cmd. 7007, 1947.

Officers who are co-equal—with only sometimes District Managers controlling both. Sub-Areas have been abolished by the two (very different) London and the South-Western Areas, but only in combination with special measures to reduce the 'span of control', including reduction in the number of Districts.

In most Areas there appears to have been a trend of gradually increasing the powers of Sub-Area Managers. This has been done, in the field of capital expenditure, not necessarily by increasing the formal monetary powers, but by getting more of the planning work done at lower levels. This seems to have been a natural result of the progressive building up of planning staffs and their acquisition of experience.

The size and character, and hence the powers and functions, of the Districts vary considerably. For instance, measured by units consumed, the Bristol District is more than ten times as large as that of East Cornwall. The amount of effective independent management that can be done at the District H.Q. must depend on its size and character, on the practices of the Area and Sub-Area Headquarters, on personalities and so on. In some Areas, however, there are in effect (as indeed one Board Chairman described it) only two *management* levels—the Area and Sub-Area—and the District Engineers and District Commercial Engineers are regarded as heads of services rather than managers in the full sense. In some cases again there may be two levels of management in parts of the Area and three levels in others. Under the Yorkshire Board the Sub-Area Manager and his Headquarters are directly responsible for District functions in Bradford, Leeds, Sheffield, Hull, Huddersfield and Grimsby, although outside these towns they work through District Managers. The varying patterns of organisation may often owe something to the physical and technical form of the distribution network which the Area Board took over from its predecessors. On the whole there were a greater multiplicity of independent undertakings and of technical standards and distinct types of network in London than in the big industrial cities of the North, largely because the systems in London were the oldest. The replacement of the non-standard networks has involved probably more centralised planning at the Area Headquarters in London than elsewhere. In at least some large industrial cities there were large and well-developed municipal systems which could probably be more easily left to District or Sub-Area Headquarters to operate and extend. In smaller towns and country districts networks are on a smaller scale, and some may well remain so, while others are considered by the Boards to require integrating into larger units. The pattern seems to have been nowhere very uniform, however. There were some large companies with well-developed and efficient systems extending over very large areas partly urban and partly rural, and some of their systems could be maintained without any wholesale reorganisation.

(c) *Capital Equipment*

Well over half of all the assets of the Area Electricity Boards (by value) are line networks, overhead and underground, and about a third are the associated transformers and switchgear and the buildings that house them. Most of the other capital equipment is subsidiary to this—for instance depots for the stores and vehicles, mobile plant required for construction and maintenance and offices from which the work is controlled. The depots and offices also serve the 'commercial' side of the Boards' activities, contracting for work in consumers' premises and selling of apparatus—and there are service centres (showrooms) solely for this purpose.

The distribution network under Area Board control is broadly of three voltages—33 kV, 11 kV and 415/240 volts.[12] The conductor will be aluminium (with steel core for strengthening) or copper, according to the relative availability and cost of these metals at the time. The choice between different types and sizes of cable and between different voltages will rest broadly on economic calculations. We have referred to three voltages, but there are many types of cable, including considerable networks inherited from the former independent undertakings—some at other voltages, for instance 66 kV, 22 kV and 6·6 kV. Moreover, there is not simply one type of cable suitable for each voltage. There may be a choice of some half dozen different sizes of metal conductor—and the planning of a network will involve a careful choice of these

[12] Current is normally supplied to large industrial consumers at 415 or higher voltages and to small industrial, commercial and domestic consumers at 240 volts.

according to the load to be expected. Indeed, cable of a certain size may be put down with the intention of its working initially on a lower voltage and of the system being adapted

TABLE VI[13]

TOTAL FIXED ASSETS
OF ALL AREA BOARDS IN ENGLAND AND WALES
(Averages per Area in brackets)

	Total fixed assets (not depreciated) at 31st March 1959 £ million		Expenditure on fixed assets 1958–59 (£ million)	
Land and Buildings:				
Substations and other oper-ational properties .	. 43·2 (3·6)		2·9 (0·22)	
Offices and Service Centres	14·0 (1·2)		1·4 (0·12)	
Miscellaneous . . .	7·4 (0·6)		1·3 (0·11)	
Total Land and Buildings .	64·6 (5·4)	64·6 (5·4)	5·6 (0·46)	5·6 (0·46)
Plant and Machinery (mainly transformers and switchgear) . . .		263·7 (21·9)		26·7 (2·22)
Lines and Cables Existing at 1st April 1948 (all types) . . .279·0			—	
Constructed since 1st April 1948:				
Mains—underground	.195·9 (16·3)		24·0 (2·0)	
Mains—overhead .	. 82·3 (6·9)		9·3 (0·79)	
'Services'—(to individual consumers) .	. 99·0 (8·2)		10·7 (0·89)	
Total Lines and Cables .	.656·2 (54·7)	656·2 (54·7)	44·0 (3·68)	44·0 (3·68)
Meters		58·5 (4·9)		3·8 (0·32)
Vehicles and mobile plant .		9·2 (0·8)		1·5 (0·13)
Apparatus and wiring on hire		20·9 (1·7)		0·2 (0·22)
Remainder (tools, instruments, furniture, fittings, office equipment, public lighting) . . .		14·1 (1·2)		1·3 (0·11)
TOTAL undepreciated value		1,087·2 (90·6)	*Total*	83·1 (6·9)
Deduct depreciation and other capital provisions .		531·1 (44·3)		
TOTAL depreciated value .		556·1 (46·3)		

[13] Electricity Council, *Report and Accounts*, 1958–59, pp. 143–149, Statements A.25. and A.27. (Depreciation figures are not given for all the sub-heads.)

some years later to carry a higher voltage.   It is such considerations which produce the complex calculations often required in planning new networks and extensions and reinforcements.   As in most types of capital construction, there can be a choice between long-term and short-term economy.

Underground construction may vary from sixteen times as expensive as overhead to very little more, according to the voltage and the local conditions for construction.   In certain places it may be quite a controversial point which method is cheapest for the lower-voltage networks.   The main reason for the high cost of underground cabling is insulation.   The difference in cost increases greatly at the higher voltages, because so much more insulation is required.   Insulation of the whole conductor by a paper covering with outer metal armouring is only required when it is placed underground. With the higher voltages this paper covering will have to be thicker and the cable filled with oil or gas and special devices to maintain the oil pressure.   Higher voltage lines go overhead whenever possible and only underground either in places of special natural beauty or in towns.   In doubtful cases much may depend on negotiations with the Local Highway Authorities, landowners and other interests.   Sometimes the more costly method may be accepted to save time or goodwill.   In extremely congested urban areas there may not be room for cables even under a street, and sometimes costly deviations may be necessary.   The jointing of cables involves special skills and safety precautions—particularly on the higher voltages.   Generally both overhead and underground cables are constructed or laid by the Boards' own direct labour, but contractors may be employed for various reasons, for instance to deal with occasional peaks of work.   In some places there is not a sufficient continuous load of specialised higher-voltage work to justify the Board maintaining a permanent specialised labour force for this purpose.

The provision and laying of underground cables may cost between £4 and £6 a yard for 33 kV, and between £8 or £11 for 66 kV.   Overhead lines for these voltages may cost between £1 and £4 a yard.   Very roughly 11 kV lines underground may cost £1 to £3 a yard and the same overhead between 10s. and £2.   Lines at distribution voltages (415/240 kV) will cost somewhat less.   Costs of cable schemes may vary from two or three hundred pounds to tens of thousands according to the extent and nature of the area to be covered and the voltages involved.   There is really no typical size of cable scheme—whether it be an extension for new business, a reinforcement of existing cables, a replacement of sub-standard cables or a combination of any two or all three.

Oil-filled switching equipment is generally needed at 6·6 kV or 11 kV and the higher voltages, but not below.   It is generally specified and ordered specially for each scheme.   Its costs (without buildings or foundations) may be a few hundred pounds on the lower voltages and anything between, say, £3,500 and £35,000 for the higher voltages—depending, of course, on the number and nature of the switches.   Area Boards' transformer stations broadly fall into two groups:

(a) those required to bring the voltage down from 11 kV or 6·6 kV to the distribution voltages; and

(b) those stepping it down from the higher voltages (mainly 33 kV) to 11 kV or 6·6 kV.

TABLE VII [14]

NUMBER OF TRANSFORMING POINTS OF AREA BOARDS
ENGLAND AND WALES

(First figures are England and Wales totals; figures in brackets give average per Area Board)

Transforming points with secondary voltages	Taken out of commission 1958–59	Commissioned	In commission at 31st March 1959
(a) 650 volts or under	2,624	17,830	181,846
	(219)	(1,486)	(15,479)
(b) Over 650 volts .	81	223	3,777
	(7)	(12)	(315)
TOTAL . .	2,705	20,053	185,623
	(225)	(1,504)	(15,469)

Broadly, the transformers under (a) above are ordered in bulk and those under (b) individually.

The orders are based on detailed specifications of performance and main characteristics, which leave a good deal of discretion in design, particularly as regards overall size, to the

[14] Annual Reports of Area Electricity Boards for 1958–59.

manufacturers.   These specifications are standard throughout
Britain.   They are subject to continuous development and
review by the Conference of Chief Engineers of all Electricity
Boards (including both Scottish Boards and the C.E.G.B.) and
its Committees.   This, however, is the only organisation which
exists within the electricity supply industry on a national scale
for standardising electricity distribution equipment, and it has
no permanent secretariat.   It is apparently the general view
in the industry that although this type of standardisation works
well and is being applied to more types of equipment from time
to time, it should not be extended to the point where there
would be identical types of equipment for each purpose produced by all manufacturers for all Area Boards.   This, it is
suggested, would discourage the initiative and inventiveness of
manufacturers in producing new and competitive designs to
meet existing specifications in a more effective or economical
way.   There are also some types of equipment for which even
the performance specifications are not absolutely identical for
every Area.   Area Boards are prepared to accept the degree of
variation that all this involves, including the fact that transformers (throughout the range of sizes) are not always interchangeable with one another as regards the space occupied in
buildings.

The smaller transformers each cost usually a few hundred
pounds (anything in fact from under £100 to £2,000) and the
larger ones of the 33/11-kV type between, perhaps, £15,000
and £30,000.   In each case these figures are for the plant only.
The practice of accommodating transformers seems to vary a
good deal.   The smallest, on overhead routes, can be mounted
on the poles.   For others it is much cheaper to have no buildings, but only concrete foundations and a strong fence.   Nevertheless, buildings quite often are provided, sometimes because
of appearance and to meet the view of Local Authorities, sometimes to protect the equipment from damage and sometimes
because certain transformer equipment produces a continuous
humming noise which may be objectionable in residential areas.
Transformer and also switchgear equipment designed for use
out of doors is different from that used in buildings, and more
expensive.   The outdoor designs have to provide against damage and corrosion and may occupy rather more space.   Build-

ings for transformers and switchgear may vary in cost from a few hundred pounds to some thousands. Generally, but not always, Area Boards have standard plans and, where justified, standard bills of quantities for transformer stations of the smallest sizes, but others will usually be individually designed. In addition to many transformer and switching stations, each Area has one or more Control Centres from which all the switching stations are operated and which work in collaboration with the C.E.G.B. Grid Control Stations.

Until recent years the Area Boards did relatively little building for purposes other than transformer and switching stations and Control Centres. In the last year or two, however, there has been a fair amount of new building (as well as adaptation) for Area, Sub-Area and District offices and for depots for stores and vehicles, workshops and showrooms. For all these the Area Boards started, and to some extent still work, on the basis they inherited from their predecessors. This generally meant having showrooms and a good many District Offices, and some other offices, in the commercial centres of towns. The other accommodation (including Area Offices) was scattered about and split up into various fragments in whatever buildings happened to be available, including industrial buildings and adapted country houses, often in relatively remote places. A new policy of combining District Offices and depots, however, does seem to be emerging in some places. It is based on the view that it is best for the managerial organisation to be right on top of the practical work and that this is much more important than the District Manager's outside contacts, which can no doubt be fairly easily made by car. Where the District Office and depot are any significant distance from the central commercial or shopping area of a town, it is necessary to have a separate service centre. As combined District Offices and depots can easily cost between £50,000 and £200,000, they are only being built gradually—sometimes with the office portion following the rest after an interval of a year or two.

There are no mandatory standards for these 'non-operational buildings' in terms of cost or dimensions, but certain standards for staff and welfare accommodation and certain planning principles agreed within the electricity supply industry are recommended for guidance in the booklet *Standards of Provision for Welfare, Health and Safety in the Electricity Supply Industry* issued by the National Joint Advisory Council of the Electricity Industry, 1954. These are quite detailed for equipment and planning principles, but not for building dimensions. No cost standards are given.

Meters, although in consumers' premises, remain the property of the Area Boards. They are not precisely standardised, but subject to standard specifications covering performance and certain other points. It is open to manufacturers to compete in producing different designs aimed at improving efficiency or lowering cost.

(d) *Forms and Purposes of Capital Development*

Broadly, most of the Area Boards' capital development consists of extending or reinforcing their networks, primarily to cater for increased use of electricity by existing consumers and also to connect new consumers—only a very small proportion because existing equipment is worn out. Cables in the ground may last over fifty years, and many transformers and switching installations have to be replaced by others of different designs or greater capacity before the end of their economic lives (about twenty-five years). Poles need renewal, and the insulation o underground cables may occasionally suffer deterioration or accidents. Generally, however, the electricity distribution industry is so relatively young that it has not yet had to face any substantial plant renewal. Equipment may be superseded because it is of obsolete design; but more generally, to provide for greater loads, existing cables may be supplemented by others or the transformers may be changed so that the same cables can carry higher voltages—provided cables capable of doing so have been laid originally. Such practices are more usual than disconnecting cables completely or pulling them out of the ground (which may be done when non-standard working is being replaced—but not always even then). The Area Electricity Boards' capital development problems thus stand in complete contrast to those of the Coal Board, whose capital has to be constantly, and indeed massively, renewed merely to maintain current production.

The Area Boards' prime task is to keep pace everywhere and at every hour with consumer demand and to provide enough equipment to avoid breakdowns, accidents and failures in the quantity and quality of supply. Apart from some possible variations in the order of meeting rural demands and the influence that may be exercised on the load factor by selling different types of equipment, the Area Boards (unlike the Generating Board) have relatively little choice in the means they adopt to achieve this object. The choice of technical methods is usually severely limited, and they work within close geographical limits.

The Area Boards divide their capital development between:[15]

(a) reinforcement;
(b) standardisation;
(c) rural development;
(d) other new business.

Most Boards, however, find a good deal of difficulty in apportioning expenditure on particular schemes between these headings. Reinforcement means strengthening the network at any point or all along the line—from the bulk supply point to the consumers' premises—to carry heavier loads. This may take the form of all sorts of technical changes and rearrangements, from merely supplementing a few lines or cables and/or transformers by others of greater capacity, to complete reorganisations of whole networks and the bringing in of supplies over quite different routes, sometimes from new bulk supply points. The need for such reinforcement results partly from increased use of electricity by existing consumers and partly from increased *numbers* of consumers.

Imagine an urban area where a new housing estate and a new factory are being built. The new housing estate will involve the provision of a new network of cables for supplies mainly at 240 volts, but there will probably have to be one or more new substations, and hence some extension of the 11-kV network. The factory may want most of its supplies at 415 or higher voltages. It may have its own substation. All this new development will probably produce such an increased load on the whole system that a fair amount of strengthening of the 11-kV network will be needed, and perhaps a new 33/11-kV

[15] Particular accounts and statistics for different Areas and for different purposes may vary somewhat and go into more detail.

I

substation. It may possibly tip the scale in justifying a strengthening of the 33-kV network. If the factory and the housing estate were large and the 33-kV network already pretty heavily loaded a new bulk supply point might be justified. So far one might say that all this new development resulted from the 'new business' involved in connecting the new housing estate and the factory. But all the time one might expect the load produced by various other consumers in the neighbourhood—industrial and residential—also to be increasing and so adding to the justification for strengthening the network at 11 kV and above. A statistical and financial apportionment might be made, but if the existing networks and the new developments were at all complex it would not be very easy to say how much of the expenditure should be attributed to 'new business' and how much to 'reinforcement'. Similarly, the opportunity might be taken to complete some replacement of non-standard networks which might otherwise not have been regarded as so urgent. Again, a problem of apportionment would arise. London Electricity Board, who have had—and still have—the biggest problem of standardisation, say that they find it almost impossible to draw a useful distinction between expenditure attributable to this and to reinforcement.

It is a virtually inescapable duty of Area Boards to provide service to all urban consumers at all times of the day and year, at or as close as possible to the standard voltages and frequencies. (They have a statutory duty to keep to whatever voltage has been 'declared' for the locality concerned and a policy objective to bring all declared voltages to 240 throughout the country.) Their main choices in urban areas are in effect what risks of failure to take and how rapidly to standardise. Both may be influenced by the money available, but it is very hard to calculate the financial benefits of either. Standardisation is expensive, because it includes providing for the replacement or adaptation of consumers' appliances. The resulting convenience to consumers, Electricity Boards and manufacturers is hard to measure in money terms; but simplification of maintenance, design and storeholding must be of great economic value. On the other hand, almost every standardisation scheme will include some provision for reinforcement.

Reinforcement is largely a question of balancing risks and

methods of providing against those risks.   The principles on which all electrical distribution systems are laid out involve a great deal of duplication to ensure against breakdown and overloads, and as the load grows it is a question of how far these margins of safety can be relied upon.   In some cases consumers may already be suffering from some deduction in voltage at peak times, and it would be strange if such cases could all be treated with equal priority according to any statistical measurement of the degree of deterioration.   Variations in voltage may be more serious for some types of consumers than others.   The quality of the service over a number of years may be different in different parts of the country, so that some consumers may be more concerned about such failures than others.   The Area Board has its periodical records of load, but there cannot be a detailed record for every point in a system at every day, and indeed every hour, in the year.   If a reinforcement scheme is being considered in a place where there have been complaints of low voltages, recording voltmeters may be installed specially to make sample checks on a few consumers' premises.

Provision for new business in towns is completely inescapable, and thus has priority in any capital programme; but in the country the Board has more freedom of choice.   In theory it might proceed on a strict basis of priority for connections expected to show the best economic return.   But, of course, the question of how far people who have never had electricity will in fact use it is somewhat speculative.   The Electricity Council's Report for 1958–59 comments:[16]

> While a number of farm consumers make extensive use of the supply—some using over 60,000 units per annum—far too many on the other hand use electricity only for lighting and television, ignoring the benefits of putting it to work on the farm.   In one area, where metering arrangements enabled consumption to be analysed for 10,000 farms, it was found that 18 per cent. of consumers used less than five units per quarter for farming, as distinct from domestic requirements, 50 per cent. used less than 100 units per quarter, and 60 per cent. less than 200 units per quarter.

There has been much pressure in recent years for rural extension—in the interests of preventing depopulation and of encouraging farming—and Electricity Boards have clearly made

[16] *Electricity Council Report*, 1958–59, para. 77.

great efforts to meet it, although with varying results. In 1953, after a debate in Parliament, the Government encouraged them to speed up the process despite its increasing cost as it progressed, and authorised an extra £1 million a year for it. A special joint Committee of the C.E.A. and Area Boards prepared five-year and ten-year programmes. The latter aimed by 1963 to connect 85 per cent of all farms—which the Boards then regarded as the limit of what was practicable. The Herbert Committee, while not actually opposing rural extension, had:

> . . . certain misgivings about the industry's present policy, which seems to provide a blank cheque for uneconomic expenditure to be incurred by particular Boards under the guise of furthering their social obligations or the national interest.[17]

Under the policy referred to, the C.E.A. had agreed to contribute from the central funds:

> if any particular Board incurs expenditure in the promotion of rural electrification which cannot be recouped from the rural consumers concerned and without laying a burdensome charge on the general body of consumers in the Area.[18]

The South-Western Board had already, the Herbert Committee noted, received such a grant of £250,000. The grants have not continued since 1957. The Herbert Committee apparently wanted to see the cost of rural extension (at any rate in terms of long-term marginal costs) falling entirely on rural consumers and for the Area Boards to adjust their tariff and commercial policies accordingly—where necessary taking larger capital contributions and/or guarantees of future revenue.

The Electricity Council's Report for 1958–59 said that the ten-year programme was then ahead of schedule. Already five Area Boards had reached or passed the target of connecting 85 per cent of farms, and the only ones which had connected less than 78 per cent were the North-Eastern (76·7), Merseyside and North Wales (66·5), South-Western (64·3) and South Wales (55·1). On the whole, farms are the most difficult places to connect. The original target had been connection of 95 per cent of all 'rural premises' by 1963, and by March 1959

[17] Herbert Report, Cmd. 9672, p. 96, para. 366.
[18] Ibid., p. 96, para. 365.

about 91 per cent were covered.   Progress with rural electrification was bound to be uneven.   Despite the efforts to balance types of locality and electrical load when their boundaries
were drawn, it is clearly inevitable that Areas have different
problems.   Some took over less-efficient networks, and so have
had greater competing claims for standardisation and reinforcement.   Some are no doubt more fortunate in the type and
volume of the urban business which balances their rural business, and, of course, the nature and profitability of the rural
business itself must vary considerably.   The Area Boards are
very largely autonomous in tariff, financial and technical
policies, and the arrangements resulting from the Herbert
Report and the 1957 Act have clearly been intended to increase
their autonomy.

The amount of building done by Area Boards is small absolutely and relatively to their total capital development.   As the
Electricity Council's First Report says:

> In recent years, investment in new workshops, depots and
> offices has naturally taken second place to directly operational
> works because of the shortage of capital.   The resulting inade-
> quacy of such accommodation has become a serious obstacle to
> the concentration of administrative effort, and to operational
> economy.   Now that capital restraints are being eased, the
> Boards can plan urgently needed accommodation, which is
> necessary for more efficient and economical working.[19]

There does not seem to have been much standardisation of
buildings, but the smallest substations in urban areas enclosed
in brick buildings—largely standard—are an exception.

(e) *The Planning and Carrying out of Capital Schemes*

When it has to be decided from which offices a distribution
scheme is to be planned, authorised and supervised during construction, the decision will be based both on cost and on type—
in particular on voltages.   The Districts vary very much in
size and the extent to which they are staffed to plan and supervise development schemes.   Moreover, as their work increases
and they acquire more experience they can be given more discretion and authority.   There seems to have been a distinct
trend in this direction in recent years, with a consequent freeing

---

[19] *Electricity Council Report and Accounts* 1958–59, p. 50, para. 238.

of Sub-Areas to do other and larger-scale planning which would hitherto have been done at Area.   Clearly the situation differs not only between one Area and another but also in different parts of the same Areas, depending on many factors, including the experience of the staffs concerned and the nature and the scale of the planning needed.   (Within a single Area there may be some Districts twice the size of others.)   In London, and to a lesser extent elsewhere, there have been very large standardisation schemes which have involved the renewal or amplification of networks extending over large portions of the Area.   Such schemes have been planned at Area because, apart from any question of technical experience and competence, there was nowhere else where they could be dealt with as a whole.

All schemes involving new bulk supply points or otherwise needing discussion with the C.E.G.B. are always done by Area. (The planning of combined or complementary schemes with the C.E.G.B. and one or sometimes two other Areas must be complex enough without bringing in Sub-Areas.)   Each Area has a regular meeting with the Headquarters and the Regional or Divisional officers of the C.E.G.B., usually every two months, and all current schemes of mutual interest are reviewed.   The extent to which other planning (not involving the C.E.G.B.) is done at Area depends on the nature and size of the scheme and how far it extends or has repercussions beyond the boundaries of any one Sub-Area or District.   Most schemes mainly or wholly involving the 33-kV or 66-kV network will be planned at Area or Sub-Area, and schemes wholly or mainly on the 11-kV network at Sub-Area or District.   Districts should normally do all or most of the planning for the 415/240-volts mains—and, of course, also the 'services' (connections to particular consumers) at these voltages.

To describe where a scheme is initiated or where most of the detailed drawings are done would not necessarily tell the whole story.   The power of Districts to *authorise* schemes is generally limited to £1,000 or even £500 in any one case, and that of Sub-Areas to £5,000 or £3,000.   Distribution schemes vary greatly in cost, from a few hundred pounds up to tens of thousands, but generally the limits quoted mean that neither Sub-Areas nor Districts can finally approve the bulk of the schemes which they themselves plan. When schemes come up to Sub-Area or Area they are looked at wholly or mainly by engineers, and at least as much from a technical as from a financial point of view. How much technical review they actually get will depend partly on their size and complexity and partly on the experience and technical knowledge of the planning officers at the lower formation—and perhaps to some extent also on the views of those at the higher formation. The reviews may be quite considerable and far reaching, and Chief Engineers and indeed Board Chairmen and Deputy Chairmen may take a close interest in the larger schemes. It may not simply be a matter of technically amending or improving a scheme prepared at the lower level. If the scheme is closely integrated with a large network extending outside the District boundaries it is inevitable that the Sub-Area or Area will be closely involved in the planning. For instance, the Area or Sub-Area may be developing a comprehensive plan or policy for standardising or re-organising the networks of the whole or part of a town. The outstanding examples of this, but not the only ones, are in London. On the other hand, the District Headquarters in a large town, whether or not it is combined with that of a Sub-Area, may be quite large and with a well-qualified and experienced planning staff and be left to carry out a good many of its own schemes. Bristol District, for instance, has done a good deal of planning of its own in the 33-kV network.

It seems as difficult to quote typical time scales for distribution schemes as typical sizes and costs. A year or even more may sometimes pass between the time when it is decided to start planning a scheme and the time when work can actually begin on the site; but it may often be very much less, even only a matter of weeks. Time does not seem to vary in close proportion to cost. Of just what does 'planning' consist? The central process is no doubt that of a specialist engineer sitting down with large-scale maps and diagrams and technical and statistical data about the existing system, about the additional loads to be catered for, and the costs of different types of equipment—and then working out the most economical, efficient and speedy means of arriving at the desired result and getting it out in detailed drawings and specifications. The balancing of alternatives, which may arise in this kind of planning work, can, of course, be very complex, even when the matter is looked at from an ideal point of view before tackling the practical difficulties which we shall mention in a moment.   There will be a balancing of the costs of different types and quantities of cabling and of transformer and switching equipment, together with excavation costs and so on—possibly transmission losses in very large schemes.   There may be problems of carrying the loads by alternative routes in emergencies.   It is not apparently necessary nor even possible in most cases to set out all conceivable alternatives and make precise mathematical and financial comparisons between them.   Often all possible plans except one, or perhaps two, are ruled out on the basis of experienced engineering judgement.   Sometimes, however, there are complex calculations, and then it is common practice to use a 'network analyser'—an electrical model working at very low voltages which can simulate the effect of various alternative schemes.

We must not, however, leave the impression that a period of months or even a year or more can be entirely occupied by planning engineers continuously poring over drawing-boards and figures and electrical models.   One knows from the analogy of architectural planning, which is perhaps a little easier for the layman to appreciate, that it is not in work on the drawing-board and with the slide rule that all, or perhaps most, of the weeks go by.   It is in arguments with other people, concerned with the building and its site, usually non-technical people—sometimes completely outside the organisation concerned—and indeed in waiting for such people to come to meetings and answer letters.   The same sort of thing can happen in electricity distribution planning.   Of course, schemes also have to wait until planning engineers have finished other work on the drawing-board or with the slide rule, but again longer periods may go by waiting for them to be released, not from purely technical work, but from these outside arguments.   Indeed, one scheme may well depend a good deal upon another, and the technical planning of the first perhaps cannot start until an agreement in principle on the second has been achieved.

In building work of almost every kind many of these delaying factors arise from differences between people other than architects about the way a building is to be constructed—its future occupants, the engineers who have to put equipment into it, those who are going to provide the money, the Local Planning Authorities, neighbouring property owners and so on. Electrical distribution systems afford much less scope for argument by non-technical people about how the job is to be done. Generally, as we shall see, neither the Accounts nor other Departments of an Area Electricity Board (save perhaps the Commercial Department) comment on the planning of particular schemes. Outside people are not much interested except on the all-important point of whether the lines go overhead—and also possibly on how far cables can be laid under crowded streets—that is streets crowded either with road traffic or with other underground cables, pipes or ducts. Of course, if the scheme includes substations there may naturally be many people with views on their siting and appearance. If there are objections to granting wayleaves for overhead lines or underground cables or to allotting land for substation sites, a great deal of engineering time may be spent in investigating whether there are practicable alternatives before the people who originally objected are pressed to give way. One may sum up by saying that while it may take a year or even more to finalise the planning of a large or difficult scheme, most of this will be spent on matters that arise directly or indirectly from wayleave and land difficulties, and possibly only a few weeks continuously—perhaps even only two or three weeks—on the detailed technical calculations and drawing.

All this does not mean that there is normally much delay to immediately urgent schemes owing to wayleave or similar difficulties. A planning office may well have up to a year's work in hand which its staff could not in any case cope with all at once. Again, this does not necessarily mean that the office is understaffed. The schemes concerned will probably meet essential needs if they are started within a year. They will have accumulated simply because the planning office is tending to look well ahead, to work to long-term programmes and to plan its network as a whole. The existing network probably contains considerable margins for safety which will not be needed provided unforeseen developments do not occur. When, however, industrial or house building goes ahead quicker than expected or if sufficient notice of such building has not been obtained, then a scheme may have to be taken quickly out of the queue and given exceptional treatment.   The whole process of orderly planning depends on good liaison all round—notably with Local Authorities—both in estimating demand and obtaining wayleaves.   Wayleave negotiation is primarily a matter for wayleave officers (from Sub-Area or District), but some of it, and indeed some negotiations for buying land, seems to be done and at least started by engineers.   On the other hand, professional estate surveyors from Area Headquarters usually carry through and complete *purchase* negotiations, at least for the larger sites.

Rural development does not depend solely, and in some places perhaps not even mainly, on economic and technical considerations; but also on obstacles to putting up lines on poles.   The lines themselves and their insulators are somewhat bigger and more obtrusive than those used for the telephone service, and it is often desirable to mount small transformers half-way up the poles.   No one claims these things are beautiful, and there may be much opposition to them in some places—depending no doubt not only on the intrinsic beauty of the districts but also on how well known they are and how many people (and what people) are interested in preserving their appearance.   For instance, as might be expected, the North-Western Board has very special problems in the Lake District. Apart from questions of appearance, there may often be difficulties of fitting in with the interests and convenience of farmers and landowners.   To get a reasonably economic layout of lines in any country district it may often be necessary or desirable to leave the public roads and go across fields.   This may not be at all welcome to the farmers concerned, and however helpful they are, a great deal of negotiation may be involved.   All the time, however, there will be pressure for extension of electricity supply to particular places.   There may also, as we have seen, be uncertainty about the extent to which the services will in fact be used when they have been provided.   In country districts therefore the Area Boards are faced with difficult problems of planning and priority—quite different from the more technical and economic problems in towns.   Technical and immediate economic considerations have to be balanced against judgements about priorities and potential use, and, above all about the time needed to settle wayleave negotiations.

Rural electrical development in South Scotland was dealt with by special published plans, the essence of which was a series of intensive programmes in one locality after another. These provided for the connection of every potential consumer who wanted the supply, so that everyone could know to the nearest month when they could expect service. The Plans consisted basically of tables (accompanied by outline maps) showing the detailed programmes consisting of individual named schemes, and the numbers of farms and of other premises to be connected were given against each, with the miles of line, cost and dates of start and finish of work. Costs of schemes varied from a few hundred pounds to just over £100,000 and the time from a couple of months to nearly a year and a half—the times seemed roughly proportional to costs. The Plans were qualified by the statement that the schemes would be carried out:

> in the order and at the times shown in the programmes provided there is a satisfactory response from the occupiers of the properties ... that wayleaves are readily obtainable and subject to the availability of the necessary capital and labour.

Tariffs were to be arranged with special terms for these rural extensions—including individually settled capital contributions based on the size of the property and a guarantee of revenue for five years. The maximum contribution was for a farm over 200 acres—£200 and a guarantee of £40 a year revenue—and it was explained that the average cost to the Board of connecting a farm was £800. The great value of publishing such a Plan was, of course, to make clear to potential rural consumers just what they could expect, and also the favourable financial terms they were getting. Broadly the work of extension has kept pace with the programme and was expected to be finished to time.

Most Area Boards have some arrangements for getting at least minor building work done by their own direct labour, but these arrangements vary very much. Relatively few (and simple) buildings are needed on the operational side. Much equipment needs only foundations and fencing. Alterations and extensions to equipment, however, may involve various small kinds of building and civil engineering work, even if only in manholes.   Generally, therefore, Sub-Areas and Districts have at least a few bricklayers and other building workers in their permanent employ.   The London Board has a direct labour Works Department employing over 400 building-trade workmen and about 140 engineering-trades workmen.   It is concentrated on four depots, each with a Superintendent, an Assistant and four Foremen.   This Department does much minor work and maintenance and also builds all the smaller transformer stations.   More buildings are required for these in towns than in the country, and in London the builders' work is often of a peculiar kind—adaptations of cellars and parts of other buildings and other underground work which has to be fitted in with a timetable of engineering work, and possibly other public services.   London Electricity Board does not claim that this organisation necessarily gets its building work done cheaper or even quicker than contractors could—its justi- fication is rather that there are so many complications that it would be hard to get contractors to undertake such work at all.

Area Boards generally employ their own salaried architects and civil engineers.   Sometimes the civil engineers are respons- ible to an architect and sometimes the architects to a civil engineer—sometimes both independently to the Chief Engineer or his deputy.   The Boards' own architects and civil engineers generally do most of the building design and supervision work unless there is temporarily an exceptionally heavy load.

(f) *Long-term and Annual Programming*

Detailed systems of control of capital development differ between one Area and another, but a certain broad pattern seems common to all.   There is always a background of long- term estimating, the pattern of which is now set for the whole country by the Electricity Council, with six-year plans (until recently five-year plans).   Each January the Council asks each Board for bulk estimates of expenditure on fixed assets, varia- tions in working capital requirements and how they should be financed—each estimate to be given for each of the succeed- ing seven financial years.   For the current and succeeding financial years, it is broken down by classes of expenditure—supplies to different types of new consumers, reinforcement, standardisation, new buildings, vehicles, etc.

Before it can arrive at the bulk totals, of course, each Area Board has to do a good deal of forward planning in more detail, at least for larger schemes. On the whole, Area Boards now seem to plan capital construction in terms of five-year programmes, at any rate for their larger schemes, and they usually expect their Sub-Areas, although not usually their Districts, to do likewise. They naturally find their planning and estimating more accurate for the first two years of any five-year programme than for later periods. After that the broad trend over a period of years may come out quite close to their predictions, but there may be considerable variation as to the particular year in which development becomes necessary, and more as to when it actually gets done. It is interesting that in terms of either time or money the large bulk supply point schemes are always difficult to estimate for more than a year or two ahead. The degree of detail in which Areas expect their Sub-Areas and Districts to plan still varies. We have seen that the planning not only of bulk supply point schemes, but also of many other large schemes, may take a year or more from the time they are first thought of to the time when work starts on site and money begins to be spent. Some fairly detailed planning two or three years ahead is, therefore, essential, but nevertheless considerable fluctuations of demand—particularly major industrial demand—may well make everything but the next year's programme somewhat tentative. Delays and uncertainties in supplies of major equipment could have the same effect, but this was not a serious factor at the time of writing—though it had been a few years before.

Firm programmes and final capital investment allocations by the Government through the Electricity Council to Areas, and by them to Sub-Areas and Districts, are on an annual basis. The Sub-Area programmes are built up partly by Sub-Areas and Districts putting forward their proposals to Area Headquarters and partly by Area Headquarters themselves laying down certain main features of the programme—particularly as regards rural development, standardisation and major reinforcements. Planning on these lines is understandably more centralised in the London Area than elsewhere. The immediate reason is that there are no Sub-Areas, but basically it is because the London system is more concentrated and its standardisation and reinforcement has involved major re-planning schemes affecting the Area as a whole or large parts of it.   This, of course, was one of the factors taken into account when the Sub-Areas were abolished.

There will naturally be a two-way traffic between Area, Sub-Areas and Districts in the formulation of plans. Area Chief Engineers, for instance, will tell their Sub-Area Engineers and others concerned whether they consider it most important to get on with replacing non-standard networks or with providing for growth.   In the end there will have to be an allocation in terms of money from the Area to the Sub-Areas and from the Sub-Areas to the Districts.   How difficult a process this will be will depend on whether, in each particular year, the limitations on new capital development have been principally monetary restrictions or restrictions on staff and physical resources.   The Electricity Council's Report for 1958–59 says that ever since nationalisation there have been restrictions on capital expenditure, that these have fallen most heavily on the Area Boards, but that recently they have been eased.   In any event, whether the money available is relatively plentiful or scarce there has to be some allocation at each level in view of the competition between different types of scheme and between many schemes of the same type throughout the Area.   Area Boards do not seem to have had any special formula for making the allocations.   The figures have to be finally settled as a matter of experienced judgement.   This will normally be done personally by the Chairman, Deputy Chairman or Area Chief Engineer (or by the Board itself) so far as division between the Sub-Areas (and the Districts in London) is concerned, and by the Sub-Area Engineer for the District programmes in the provinces.   The allocation process will usually be preceded by separate individual discussions with each of the Sub-Area and District Engineers.   As with all such monetary allocations dependent on a variety of factors rather than any simple formula, the people concerned would probably find it hard to set down in a few words just why each decision had been made. Broadly, however, one of the main factors is usually whether the

Sub-Area or District is *able* to spend all the money it proposes in the year concerned—whether in fact it has the resources (of all kinds) to get the job done and whether the wayleave and planning problems involved are capable of being solved in time. Of course, this does not mean that the relative rate of progress of the different Sub-Areas and Districts will be determined only by the amount of their existing resources. If it is known that some have a relatively greater burden than others efforts will be made to increase their resources by the allocation of staff and if necessary by the diversion of plant and stores—if these are scarce. But such measures would probably be taken at an earlier stage. By the time the annual programme came to be settled—in fact just before the year opened—it would probably have to be assumed that the existing distribution of resources could not then be altered very much.

(g) *Financial Control of Individual Schemes*

Authorisation of an annual programme with named schemes included in it does not constitute financial authorisation of these schemes themselves. They will have to be submitted, before or after the submission of the annual programme, individually to the authority competent to approve them. The levels of delegated powers vary from one Area to another (and sometimes within an Area), but any distribution scheme of any size at all will have to go at least to a Chief Officer at Area Headquarters and really large schemes will go to the *full* Board.

Some Area Boards allow District Managers to authorise up to £1,000 on any one engineering scheme—some £500—the South-Western Board (which has no Sub-Areas) £5,000. The Yorkshire Board leaves it to the discretion of its Sub-Area Managers to propose the delegation to District Managers of authority to approve schemes up to £1,000, subject to prior confirmation of such delegation arrangements in each case by the Board Chairman or Deputy Chairman. Sub-Area Managers themselves have authority up to such limits as £3,000, £5,000 or £10,000 on any one capital scheme. Sometimes Chief Engineers may authorise up to £7,000, sometimes they have no powers greater than Sub-Area Managers. Any proposals above these amounts—which must mean the great bulk of schemes of any size—go at least to the Chairman or Deputy

Chairman, and above certain limits to the Management Committee (Chairman, Deputy Chairman and Chief Officers) or to the Board or a Committee thereof.   The limit of the personal authority of the Chairman or Deputy Chairman may be fixed at £10,000 or £15,000 or £25,000, and that of a Board Committee at £40,000.   In some Areas every authorisation by every subordinate authority—from District Managers to Board Committees—or by some of them—must be reported after the event all the way up the line to the full Board.   Normally 'non-operational' schemes are subject to much lower limits (generally £500), so that buildings for offices, depots and service centres need full Board authority.

The channels through which capital schemes are submitted at Area Headquarters are particularly interesting.   In general, it seems Area Electricity Boards' Accounting Departments play a much smaller part in examining such schemes before authorisation than do the Finance Departments of the Coal Board, London Transport or the C.E.G.B.   In the London and Southern Electricity Areas, at any rate, individual (operational) capital expenditure proposals—as distinct from annual programmes and reports on the out-turn of expenditure—are not examined separately by the Area Chief Accountants or their staffs at any stage before authorisation.   The London Area has two Board Committees which examine, among other things, proposals for capital expenditure—the Finance Committee and the Technical Committee—but the Finance Committee, with which the Chief Accountant is associated, normally only authorises items which have been placed within the Chief Accountant's special sphere—mainly office machinery and furniture.   All other capital expenditure proposals—that is the great bulk, including all operational projects—go direct from the Chief Engineer to the Technical Committee, with which the Chief Accountant is not associated.   Indeed, the Chief Accountant is not brought in at all till after authorisation.   In some Areas, however, the Chief Accountant, and/or the Secretary, will see capital projects before authorisation.   As in the Southern Area, the Commercial Department may also examine schemes for connection of new consumers to see whether a sufficient return on capital can be expected, but in most Areas most of the examination will be done by the Chief Engineer and his staff.   Usually even when the scheme is to go to other Departments it will be submitted by the Sub-Area or District in the first instance to the Area Headquarters Engineering Department, which will be responsible for its submission to the Board.   In Areas where they are consulted the part played by the Chief Accountant and his staff in examining capital projects and in submitting them to the Board or the Chairman will no doubt vary both between Areas and also according to the nature of particular schemes.   It appears, however, to be a fairly general view among most—but not all—Area Boards and their staffs that Accounting Departments can contribute very little to the assessment of technical schemes.   The Accounting Departments' functions are usually, it seems, considered to be those of assessing the total amount of money that is likely to be required and likely to be available for successive annual programmes and of watching the actual out-turn of expenditure on particular schemes, and on total programmes and sub-heads, so as to check prospective or actual overspending.

All this does not necessarily mean that capital expenditure projects fail to get thorough financial examination.   Even if Accounting Branches do not see them, or make little comment on them, they will generally have a fairly thorough examination in the 'Budgeting Section' of the Engineering Department, where the cost will be compared with that of other schemes and with the total amount of money available.   The engineering Budgeting Sections may well be performing very similar functions to those performed elsewhere by Finance Departments. The same may sometimes be said of the Commercial Departments.   Moreover, in organisations such as the Coal Board, where the Finance Departments do more, there may be more factors affecting each case and which can be expressed in financial terms—not only material costs and labour costs, but proceeds from the sale of products of different types and qualities.   In an electricity distribution scheme there may be a choice of methods of achieving the same result and as to the margin of safety against risks of failure of supplies.   There will also be questions about lives of plant and value of old plant. But most of these factors are technical, and the engineers concerned would no doubt claim that they could make all the

K

financial and economic calculations required.   Despite all this,
however, it does seem to be a somewhat open question whether,
where it is not already given, an independent 'second opinion'
from a Finance Department would be valuable.   If the answer
is 'No' it may raise interesting implications about the activities
of accounting and finance departments in the organisations where they do spend a good deal of time examining
capital expenditure proposals—sometimes of quite a technical
nature.

The detailed procedure for the submission and review of
schemes also differs somewhat between Areas.   That of the
Yorkshire Electricity Board, for example, has been fairly
recently revised and amplified and appears to be particularly
thorough.[20]   They have, like other Areas, standard forms for
the submission of capital proposals, designed to ensure that
certain points are always brought out.   Expenditure must be
broken down under certain standard headings—building and
civil engineering, transformers, switchgear, underground cable
and overhead lines (under the separate voltages in each case)
with certain percentages for transport and other overhead
costs.[21]   In addition to the net cost for which authorisation has
to be sought, other items are added in to make up the gross
cost—land, 'services' (connections to consumers), meters and
'materials at nil value' (the present-day cost of plant, etc., taken
out of commission from a previous scheme and available and
suitable for a new scheme).   The total gross cost determines
the level at which the expenditure is authorised.   The proposed starting date has to be given, construction time and
(when it is to cost over £10,000) the number identifying the
scheme in the capital expenditure budget.   In any case its
classification in the budget has to be shown and the total
amount apportioned (as far as necessary and possible) between
new business, reinforcement, bulk supply points and standardisation.   Where appropriate the number of new consumers to
be connected has to be shown, together with gross revenue,

[20] This does not imply that the systems of various other Boards, which it has not
been possible to examine in the time available, are necessarily any less thorough.
It is understood indeed that others are on similar lines, and some may be of longer
standing.

[21] Which the electricity supply industry calls 'on-costs'—presumably to avoid
confusion with the other meaning of the word 'overhead'.

estimated annual return on the capital and how far revenue has been guaranteed by consumers.

Other Area Boards have similar forms. The North-Western Board's form, for instance, is virtually the same, but there are also further spaces for additional information in support of particular types of proposal. For large industrial or commercial schemes described as 'maximum demand tariff supplies' this includes the period of the agreement, the type of premises, the minimum payment, the voltage (delivered, metered and utilised) and particulars of any private generating plant to work in conjunction with the Board's supplies, including the extent to which the Board is to provide standby capacity. For 'new business' schemes classed as 'domestic, farming and small commercial' the statement includes the revenue to be covered by guarantee, the number of different types of premises taking the supply and their main appliances (cookers, water heaters and washboilers) and the wiring to be provided for these. Similarly for street-lighting schemes, the number, type and size of the lamps is to be quoted, the total load in kW and the number of hours of burning to be expected.

The Yorkshire Board requires each Sub-Area to submit annually one of the standard forms in respect of all proposed expenditure bulked together for the whole year for 'low-voltage services' (that is individual connections to domestic and small commercial and industrial users), and also for meters. If the total expected to be spent in the year under these heads goes up during the year a supplementary application has to be made rather like that required when the expected cost of an individual scheme goes up. (The proportion of expenditure on low-voltage services and meters has also to be shown on the form relating to each larger individual scheme.)

The Yorkshire Board's instructions not only lay down delegated authorities in terms of maximum sums which may be authorised but also state precise conditions for these delegations. Chief Officers before authorising any scheme within their powers must consult, and obtain the agreement of, any other Chief Officers who may have responsibilities in connection with any aspect of the scheme. Sub-Area Managers before exercising their powers must obtain the approval of the appropriate Chief Officers at Area Headquarters in respect of:

(a) schemes involving any alterations to bulk supply points, points of supply from other Area Boards or where consultation with the Generating Board is required;

(b) schemes directly affecting the 66-kV and 33-kV systems;

(c) schemes for taking existing property for non-operational purposes if they involve new building work or major alterations (or *any* alterations in the case of service centres);

(d) any scheme which may greatly affect another scheme costing over £3,000—whether yet authorised or not.

Several Area Boards have at varying times developed estimating systems based on standard engineering cost data. That of the Southern Board, for instance, is of very long standing. We will quote the Yorkshire Board's system—started within the past two years. The data covers every size of transformer (classified according to capacity in kilovolt/amperes—kVA), switchgear of each voltage and cables of each voltage classified by material and diameter of conductor. A standard cost is given for each of these—and further information is calculated from time to time either to supplement these figures or to enable them to be adjusted for variations in metal prices. There are also standard costs for transformer buildings, for overhead routes and for the labour of construction and excavation—in yards for each main type of cable (varying according for roadway or open ground)—and also for other standard items of plant and work, including meters and their installation. There are also percentages to be added for transport and other 'oncosts'. With these standard figures it should be possible for Sub-Area or District planning staff to construct a complete estimate of the cost of any scheme they have planned. They normally rely on these figures alone in preparing first estimates for formal authorisation. The main object of the data, however, is not merely to speed up and simplify estimating but also to provide standards with which actual costs can be compared. Revised estimates made just before the scheme is due to start may provide the first opportunity for such comparisons. Detailed comparisons can be made when further reports are received during the course of the work and after its completion. A further advantage of the standard data will presumably be to make it easier to work out broad cost comparisons of alternatives on a reliable basis before schemes are finalised.

The Board's instructions particularly state that it is 'advantageous'—so as to avoid abortive work on plans, specifications, etc.—to seek approval in principle in the early stages of preparing any scheme likely to cost more than £3,000. This approval is to be sought by letter without the detailed printed form or plans and specifications, but with 'information sufficient to enable proper consideration to be given to the proposal'. It is particularly to be noted that the instructions, at any rate of the Yorkshire Board, and no doubt of others, provide for approvals in principle for schemes over £3,000 to be sought in advance from whatever authority has to approve the scheme finally. We have seen the value of similar formal instructions by the Coal Board. Probably other organisations have some practice of advance consultation with high authority when large schemes are being planned, but if the arrangements are merely informal they may not be put into effect in just those cases where they would be most valuable. Moreover, where advance consultation does take place, it may not, unless there is an explicit instruction to this effect, be taken to a high enough level. In such cases when the fully detailed scheme comes up there is always a danger that the final approving authorities may be faced with the choice of 'rubber stamping' something which they feel may be unsound or seriously delaying an urgent scheme. This may not always be such a serious consideration if the higher authority is mainly concerned to decide whether a project should go ahead or not and does not have a choice of alternative methods. But in electricity distribution, just as in the coal industry, the most important questions to be decided in authorising schemes may concern the choice of methods. *Some* scheme may often be inescapable to meet a particular need, but quite technical questions of method may be at the root of the whole question of the economics and financial soundness of what is proposed. In the electricity supply industry questions of technical method cannot necessarily be settled at lower or middle levels in the organisation. They may constitute major questions of policy. Many of the Chairmen and Deputy Chairmen of Area Boards are electrical engineers and have long and detailed experience of electricity distribution work.   It is, therefore, natural that they can criticise fundamentally and improve the technical aspects of schemes which come up to them.

There are detailed provisions about amendment and review of estimates already authorised.   The Yorkshire Board seem particularly concerned to guard against increases in cost owing to variations in the scheme itself or for other reasons.   Their instructions state:

> If it is proposed to make any material variation to an authorised scheme the complete scheme in its modified form will become the subject of new authorisation which will cancel the previous authorisation.

If at any stage, either before or after work starts, it seems likely that the total cost of any scheme will exceed the amount authorised by more than 15 per cent a revised estimate has to be prepared and a supplementary authorisation applied for. This 15 per cent is calculated in relation to the total cost of the scheme:

> Overspending on part will be permitted up to a maximum of 20 per cent on any one item

and subject to there being:

> no material modification of the scheme.

The Board's instructions add:

> In applying for supplementary authorisation the estimated cost of the whole scheme will be reviewed and detailed reasons given for the variations.

Estimated costs of all schemes are to be reviewed before work starts on site and where they 'are likely to show significant variations from the authorised amounts' a new revised estimate must be made on a form with similar headings to the original submission.   Normally at this stage actual prices quoted for plant, stores or constructional work can be substituted for the standard costs used for the first estimate.   The foregoing provisions about the conditions under which powers are delegated seem to be somewhat more detailed in the Yorkshire Area than in some others.

Area Boards have standing procedures for review of the out-turn of expenditure and of the final costs of completed schemes. In the Yorkshire Area, and somewhat similarly in other Areas, there is a standard form for reporting each month the expenditure during that month, and the total expenditure to date, on each authorised scheme—in both cases under the three headings of materials, labour and contract payments. For reporting on the final cost of schemes after completion there is another form with headings corresponding to those of the form submitted in seeking the original authority. Reports are required for all schemes except those costing less than £500 and where the net difference between authorised and actual expenditure is less than £50. The Chief Accountant submits the reports to the Board for approval. Reasons must be given:

(a) Where the final cost of the *whole scheme* is more than 10 per cent above or below the original amount authorised (or more than £50 above or below where the original amount authorised was under £500).

(b) Where the expenditure on *any particular cost heading* within the scheme differs from the original amount authorised by more than 20 per cent either way (or by more than £100 where the total amount authorised was under £500).

There generally seems to be a standing drill for the submission to Area Boards of periodical reports of progress with capital expenditure. Normally reports of out-turn of expenditure, and deviations (up or down) from targets in a budget, are reported for each month (or four-weekly period) and also for each half year—in every case broken down under the main standard headings of the annual programme. There may be slight variations in the classifications and breakdown between one Area and another, but broadly they are common to all. Such periodical reports are normally given in total figures under each head for the whole Sub-Area. Sub-Areas receive periodical reports, sometimes weekly, on the progress of all schemes over a certain amount (normally the limit of the District Manager's authority). Other important instruments of control are the monthly reports of completed or cancelled schemes and of schemes authorised by Sub-Areas under their own powers. Reports of completed and cancelled schemes, for instance, are made by Sub-Areas in the North-Western Area in duplicate once a month to the Area Chief Engineer, for all operational schemes over £1,000 each (and for all other schemes over £500). One copy of each is passed to the Chief Accountant, and all the reports are then summarised for the Board Chairman. This enables comparison to be made of the actual expenditure with that estimated and also a review of the reasons why schemes previously proposed have been dropped.

(h) *Stores and Purchasing*

All Areas have Purchasing Officers, although their lines of responsibility and relationships with other officers and Departments vary slightly. In most large organisations purchasing and contracts work involves co-operation between a purchasing department, a technical department and an accounting department. In Electricity Areas the commercial departments are also concerned. Area Headquarters controls the purchasing and ordering of the bulk of stores, including all the largest transformers and switchgear and the higher-voltage cables. For other transformers, switchgear and cables Areas normally settle contracts and overall purchasing arrangements and then empower Sub-Areas (or sometimes Districts) to order supplies direct from the manufacturers within the terms of these contracts and within the limits of their own budgets and programmes. Sometimes Sub-Areas or Districts prepare the order forms and send them to the Purchasing Department at Area Headquarters, where they are checked, certain details added and the orders despatched.

As far as possible, stores are delivered to the places where they are used—otherwise to Sub-Area or District stores, where stocks are kept down to a few weeks supply. Except for a few special items, there are no central Area stores. Sub-Areas do not normally keep stocks for reissue to District stores, and the extent to which Sub-Areas have stores of their own will depend on the amount and type of constructional work which they do direct. All the Electricity Boards[22] use common specifications

---

[22] The C.E.G.B., the twelve Area Boards in England and Wales and the two Scottish Boards are represented at the Conference of Chief Engineers which agrees the standard specifications, but the importance of standardisation is mainly on the distribution side, and the major generating equipment is not standardised, but is constantly developing. See p. 116 above.

for most major types of equipment, but not identical designs. Each Area Board makes its own arrangements with the manufacturers. There are not, and apparently never have been, any bulk supply agreements between manufacturers and the electricity supply industry as a whole. Arrangements with manufacturers have altered from time to time in recent years. Indeed, the situation as regards prices and the degree of competition in the cable and heavy electrical manufacturing industries as a whole seemed to be somewhat fluid at the time of writing. Generally, the Area Boards seem to get a fair degree of competition in price for most items of equipment, but they may not always place all their orders with the lowest tenderers. There are a fair number of firms in the fields concerned—for instance, some dozen making larger transformers, some fifty making small transformers and about a dozen making meters. Nevertheless, there is some 'allocation' of orders, either by the firms among themselves or more recently by the Area Boards in placing their orders. For any particular type of equipment the firms fall into two groups. There are the few very large ones with considerable manufacturing and research capacity, and development and design facilities, who could be expected to maintain a level of supply and to contribute most to the improvement of designs. On the other hand, there might be smaller firms who have less of these resources, but whose present prices might be lower. They probably would not have sufficient capacity for all the orders that had to be placed, and Area Boards seem generally to try to spread their orders somewhat between the two groups of firms.

At the time of writing the delivery period for the larger transformers and switchgear was something of the order of nine to twelve months. Cable generally took nearly the same time. This, of course, was one reason for the major schemes having to be planned well in advance. This situation had fluctuated since the War, and at some periods delivery of plant was a major delaying factor in carrying out new schemes. Partly because large stocks of small stores had not (at least in recent years) been held, and partly because the larger equipment could on the whole be delivered direct to a site or stored in the open, the Area Boards (unlike the Coal Board) had not faced any very large problem of building stores accommodation.

One cannot leave this subject of plant and stores purchasing without raising the question whether some more unified arrangements for the whole electricity supply industry would be worthwhile. We have seen[22] how much importance the Coal Board have attached to arrangements on a national scale for purchasing, stocking and distributing stores of all kinds, and how, despite the varieties of mining methods, they are moving towards further standardisation of equipment. In the electricity supply industry there seems to be a smaller range of main types of equipment and, as we have seen, the specifications (at least of performance) are broadly common to the whole country. Generally, moreover, variations are between manufacturers' designs and not between different Area Boards' requirements. Nevertheless, the Area Boards' purchasing arrangements are conducted independently, and it is understood that they do not, and would not, disclose to one another the details of the prices they pay. It seems impossible to say whether any organisation for purchasing on the national scale would be worthwhile without much more knowledge than the present author possesses of the manufacturing industries concerned, of the economics of the prices which the Area Boards are paying and of the efficiency of the delivery arrangements. Bulk purchasing would no doubt raise questions of organisation within the industry. These might well be controversial, but perhaps they should not without more enquiry be accepted as insoluble. If, however, the final answer was that the advantages of national bulk purchasing and stores control would not counter-balance its disadvantages in the electricity supply industry, that would surely raise the question of whether national bulk purchasing and stores control in the coal industry have been worthwhile. The two industries are, of course, very different, and it may well be that each now has the best system for its own needs. But until fuller answers are given than can be attempted in this book the questions still seem worth asking.

[22] See pp. 26–27 above.

CHAPTER V

POWER STATIONS AND THE GRID (I)

(a) *Coal- and Oil-fired Power Stations*

A generator (or 'alternator') may be very crudely described as a huge complex of wire coils (the 'rotor') revolving on a central shaft inside a casing containing another mass of coils (the 'stator'). To produce alternating current of the standard frequency requires precisely fixed speeds of rotation, which cannot be increased to produce any more electricity. To put it very broadly and crudely, an increase in the capacity of the generator—its 'load' in kilowatts—is obtained only by extending and elaborating the system of coils in the stator and the rotor, and hence increasing their weight and the mechanical power required to drive them. The alternator and turbine are directly coupled together to form a single piece of machinery, the 'turbo-alternator', which, with its whole combined apparatus, is called a 'generating set'. Modern sets each have their own separate and distinct boilers when they are fired by coal or oil; nuclear reactors each feed two or more sets through common boilers. The largest type of single turbo-alternator (200 or 300 MW) may cost over a million pounds.

Generating sets are getting more and more powerful—although not of much greater overall physical bulk. Units of 375 and 550 MW are now being planned (the latter a sort of double-barrelled design with two alternators and two turbines but one steam-circulation system). Within limits, the greater capacity a generating set has, the cheaper and more efficient it is—both in capital and running costs. Table VIII brings out the striking effects (achieved and expected) of improved design in recent years.

Some of the limitations on the size of sets in the immediate post-war years were those of manufacture. In 1947–50 sizes were kept standardised at 30 and 60 MW by Government Regulation to achieve more rapid production. There are many technical and practical problems in increasing the capacity of generators. No single piece of equipment weighing over 150 tons can be carried on British public roads.   This is important in any comparisons with the United States, where—at least until recently—higher thermal efficiencies were achieved.   To enable the larger alternators to be built a method had to be

TABLE VIII [1]

Size of set in MWs	Thermal [2] efficiency	Capital cost £ per kW sent out (broadly adjusted to 1959 price levels)
30	26	80–85
60	29	65–70
100	32	60–65
120	34	55–60
200	36	50–55
275	36	40–42
550	36·5	40

devised of cooling the windings by hydrogen for the rotor and water for the stator.[3]

Besides heat, a steam turbine requires good supplies of water for steam raising and cooling.   For steam raising alone the largest type of coal-fired station now being planned (with three or four turbo-alternators, each of 360 or 375 MW) would require between 600,000 and 900,000 gallons of water a day (of sufficient chemical purity).   Much more water is needed to cool and condense the steam after passing through the turbine— so as to create enough vacuum to draw more steam through. After use for cooling the water has, of course, absorbed so much heat that it cannot be used again without being itself put through a somewhat elaborate process in a cooling tower (up to 350 feet high).   A basic requirement in planning a power station is, therefore, either to site it immediately beside a very large river or estuary (or by the coast) where water can be

[1] These figures supplied to me by the C.E.G.B. are more up to date than those quoted in the *Report of the Committee of Enquiry into the Electricity Supply Industry* (the Herbert Report), 1956, Cmd. 9672, p. 28.   The differences are slight, and both sets of figures clearly point to the same conclusions.

[2] Thermal efficiency is the ratio (as a percentage) of the heat value of the electricity sent out from the power station to the heat value of the fuel consumed in generation.

[3] For fuller accounts of the reductions in generating costs see an article in *The Times* of 9th February 1960, by F. H. S. Brown (then Member for Engineering, C.E.G.B.) and 'Costs of Conventional Power', by J. L. Gray (Turbine Plant Engineer, C.E.G.B.) in *The New Scientist*, 28th January 1960.

continuously drawn and discharged or else to build huge cooling towers—or both. The cooling water needs screening apparatus to remove extraneous solid matter and chlorination plant to prevent micro-organisms growing.

The boilers are the most expensive single pieces of equipment in a non-nuclear station, costing well over £2 million each—vast metal structures some 150–200 feet high through which run a labyrinth of water pipes. Into these are injected jets of flame, which may be produced by oil or powdered coal. The boilers work on broadly the same principles with either. Some have been built for oil, but capable of conversion to coal—and some designed for coal have been converted to oil. The latter process, however, may involve some technical difficulties and loss of thermal efficiency. If a station is to burn coal it must have a large coal hopper and pulverising mills in front of each boiler (or space for them on conversion to coal). Oil is normally delivered to power stations by water-borne tankers and stored in very large tanks. It needs a system of pipes and pumps and also a heating plant—it arrives in too thick and treacly a state to be sprayed direct into the furnaces. Coal needs much more elaborate handling plant, including a substantial wharf and cranes if it is water-borne, whereas a simpler floating discharge point would suffice for water-borne oil supply. Rail-borne coal needs substantial sidings and a marshalling yard and connections with the main lines. The coal storage and conveyors may together absorb as much space as the rest of the station. Provision is also needed for temporary storage and disposal of ash.

The control systems for the station plant and its interconnection with the national grid are extremely complex. A large station (coal, oil or nuclear) may employ 200 to 300 men or more with proportionate canteen and office space. The workshop may be more than half the size of the turbine room. On-the-spot repairs and overhauls of station plant are obviously important in a service whose economics depend so much on keeping the highest possible proportion of plant running in the peak periods.

The chimneys may be up to 500 feet high, and it is important to have plant—usually electro-static—for cleansing the smoke. The whole site may be over 100 acres. Buildings may rise to a height over 200 feet and extend over 700 feet in length. They give a tremendous impression of height and mass. The Electricity Boards have had to face the rather opposite criticisms:

(a) That they provide extravagant cathedral-like structures unnecessary for a utilitarian engineering purpose.
(b) That they are blind to considerations of architectural aesthetics and amenity.

In fact, they have in recent years substantially reduced the station building costs in proportion to capacity, partly by eliminating brickwork or replacing it by lighter forms of cladding, but more by reducing the size of the plant relative to its output and grouping it more economically.

Yet in recent years the absolute sizes and costs of power stations have been increasing. So it is difficult to give typical costs, but the following are the estimates under the principal heads of one of the very largest non-nuclear stations now under construction. They cover four sets (two 200-MW and two 300-MW) and associated equipment for a total installed capacity of 1,000 MW. Further equipment may be added later to bring the capacity up to about 1,300 MW, but all the foundations and certain civil engineering and other work will be provided for this ultimate capacity from the outset:

TABLE IX

	£ million
Land purchase, etc.	0·15
Civil engineering contracts	8·95
Mechanical engineering contracts	28·22
Electrical engineering contracts	4·13
'Engineering' (salaries and/or fees of design staff, etc.)	1·15
	43·20

(b) *Nuclear Power Stations*

Basically a nuclear power station is a variant on a modern coal- or oil-fired station—with a new kind of heat source. The total bulk of both types of station and the site areas they occupy are comparable. Nuclear stations now being built will cost between £45 million and £65 million each, excluding the initial fuel charge (about £15 million for each station with two reactors and also counting as capital). The total capacities of the C.E.G.B.'s first four nuclear stations will be as follows:

Bradwell	300 MW
Berkeley	275 MW
Hinkley Point	500 MW
Trawsfynydd	500 MW

So among stations now being planned and built the nuclear ones will be of a good deal smaller capacity than the others, and the capital cost per kilowatt of the first two or three will be some two and a half to three times as great. Future nuclear stations may be of larger kilowatt capacity and larger total cost.

The principles of generation of electricity by steam and the types of plant used are basically similar in a nuclear and in a coal- or oil-fired station. The main special features of nuclear stations are:

(a) Nuclear reactors supplying hot gases to separate boilers replace coal- or oil-fired boilers.

(b) Reactor fuel storage and handling plant takes only a fraction of the space of coal-handling plants or oil supply and storage.

(c) It is Government policy that 'the first stations even though they will be of inherently safe design will not be built in heavily built-up areas'.[4]

In nuclear stations steam is used at lower pressures and temperatures, and that is why the turbo-alternators are each of *smaller* output than those in a large non-nuclear station; but up to 50 per cent more cooling water is used (in proportion to the capacity).

Briefly and very crudely a nuclear reactor is an enormous steel and concrete structure inside which heat is produced and drawn off by a gas or liquid cooling agent. The nuclear stations now being built in Britain are cooled by gas, which circulates round the reactor and then through heat exchangers (boilers), where it produces steam. The reactor becomes

[4] White Paper, *A Programme of Nuclear Power*, 1955, Cmd. 9389, para. 37, p. 9.

'critical' and nuclear fission takes place when a certain number of uranium rods are in position inside the reactor.   The process is finely controlled by the extent to which other moving rods of neutron-absorbing material (at present boron steel) are lowered into and out of the graphite core or 'moderator'. Nuclear fission not only produces heat but also turns at least part of the uranium into plutonium—which might be used in other types of reactor or for military or scientific purposes.

The boilers are different from those in a 'conventional' station.   They are cylindrical pressure vessels about 90 feet by 20 feet—constructed off site, if they can be transported there by water.   (They are far too big for road or rail.)   The basic component of the reactors is the spherical pressure vessel into which the graphite moderator is packed in blocks and into which the uranium and steel control rods can be moved by complex remotely controlled machinery.   The pressure vessel is made on site of welded steel and is over 60 feet in diameter, enclosed all round in a concrete 'biological' shield over 8 feet thick.   The total weight of the two reactors with their foundations, shields, control machinery and fuel is about 75,000 tons.   The control of the whole station—nuclear equipment, boilers, turbo-generators, switch-gear and transformers— is all concentrated in one control room, whose electronic and other equipment is probably of greater extent and complexity than anything similar in the world.   The boilers, reactors and their buildings thus represent unique problems of mechanical and civil engineering construction.   The pressure sections of the reactor vessel have all to be manually welded to Lloyd's Class A standard, which calls for 100 per cent radiographic examination of all weld material.

The economics of the use of nuclear heat for electricity generation depend on:

(*a*)   the cost of building the station;
(*b*)   its thermal efficiency;
(*c*)   the cost of the initial and subsequent charges of uranium fuel;
(*d*)   the quantity of heat that can be expected from the fuel before it is 'burnt up';
(*e*)   the price obtainable for 'burnt-up' fuel (plutonium);

(*f*) the time the reactor will last before developing defects which may make it inefficient or dangerous.

The C.E.A. and C.E.G.B. have so far looked to the Atomic Energy Authority for advice, and as a source of uranium and a market for plutonium.

Problems of reactor design are far too abstruse for the layman to discuss, but we must note certain effects which these problems produce on the organisation and economics of the power-station programme generally:

(*a*) The capital cost per kilowatt of nuclear stations, excluding the initial fuel charge, is at present estimated at about two and a half times that of coal- or oil-fired stations, and the costs of generation (including capital charges) at about 40 per cent more.

(*b*) *But* no one can say at all exactly whether these estimates are correct—and how costs might be reduced—until at least one full-size station[5] has been working a number of years. The estimates might well be wrong—either way —by as much as 40 per cent.

(*c*) A great deal of the uncertainty concerns time. The life of the whole station, although now estimated at twenty years, could conceivably be as little as ten. The life of the initial fuel charge is equally uncertain.

(*d*) Much uncertainty also concerns the metals which may be used for the containers for the uranium fuel rods and the lining of the whole reactor vessel. There is uncertainty about how far the better-known metals or alloys would absorb neutrons and so affect the time within which the fuel would need renewal, and also about whether they might be made brittle by radiation. There is also uncertainty about the technology and general behaviour of the less-common metals, which are, however, expected to be unlikely or less likely to absorb neutrons. It is also hard to predict all aspects of the behaviour of graphite under radiation.

(*e*) These and/or many other types of uncertainty surround the problems of design of other types of reactor which

---

[5] Calder Hall is not a full-size station, and Bradwell and Berkeley were not due to start working till 1961, and they actually started in 1962.

L

may have other types of coolant or moderator—possibly a liquid for both—even though there are indications that such types—or a more advanced type of the present gas-cooled reactor—would be substantially cheaper than the present types.

(f) It is equally difficult to predict the price either of the fuel in the form in which it is put into the reactor or in that in which it is taken out. All this depends on world supplies of these and other types of fissile material and the possible uses to which they might be put, and leads one into speculations extending beyond any narrowly commercial or economic field.

(g) Prices tendered for the construction of nuclear power stations may depend—far more than those for other plant—on the contractors' prospects of getting similar orders abroad—prospects which seemed to have worsened somewhat at the time of writing.

(h) Due to the limited practical experience, design of all parts of a nuclear station (which may involve radiation risks) tends to be based on a more theoretical calculation than is normal for other types of safety risks. Some features which may later turn out to be over-insurance and over-elaboration, in at least some parts of the design, would seem inevitable in the first few stations.

The Fifth Report of the Select Committee on the Estimates on the U.K. Atomic Energy Authority[6] contained a most fascinating and lucid discussion of the factors affecting the present and prospective comparative costs of electricity generated by coal-fired stations and different kinds of nuclear station. Although the White Paper *A Programme of Nuclear Power* in 1955[7] had predicted that the costs of nuclear- and coal-generated electricity would be comparable, the Select Committee said nuclear-generated electricity was now expected to cost $0 \cdot 7d$. per unit 'or perhaps a little higher' against $0 \cdot 51-0 \cdot 52d$. per unit for coal-generated electricity—or some 40 per cent higher. The Report commented that these comparisons assumed particularly favourable siting and general condi-

[6] House of Commons, 316, July 1959, paras. 117–123, pp. xlvi–xlix.
[7] Cmd. 9389, p. 5, para. 19 ($0 \cdot 6d$. per unit)

tions for coal-fired stations and that 15–20 per cent might be a fairer estimate of the disparity.   It said the changed prediction resulted partly from a reduction in 1956 in the 'plutonium credit' allowed by the A.E.A. to the C.E.G.B., but otherwise mainly from reduction in the estimated costs of coal-fired generation.

The Select Committee, after citing the expert evidence, suggested that Advanced Gas Cooled Reactor stations might come into service 'at the beginning of 1964 or even earlier'[8] and produce electricity at 0·5d. to 0·54d. per unit and Fast Reactors in the early 1970s, at 0·3d. and 0·4d. per unit but use plutonium—thus providing an economic use for the 'burnt-out' fuel of all the other reactors.   It would, however, take five years for such reactors to 'burn out' or rather 'irradiate' the fuel.   Hence if Fast Reactors were to be working in the 1970s so as to produce plenty of really cheap electricity it was necessary not only to give high priority to the related research and development programmes of the A.E.A. and the C.E.G.B. but also to have enough other reactors working well in advance in time to produce sufficient plutonium fuel—even though these other reactors might not themselves be economic.

We cannot pursue this vast subject here.   But one obvious conclusion emerges.   We are clearly outside the field where anyone can be guided simply by the kind of economic and financial criteria that a competent accountant would apply to a proposal to build a factory next year.   Decisions must be taken on inadequate scientific, engineering, commercial and financial information.   *This includes information about the availability and costs of coal and oil for more than a decade ahead.*   Considerations of national—and international—policy are—despite all that the Herbert Committee said—bound to enter very largely into the picture.   It is not only because of the military aspects of nuclear energy that the the nuclear-power programme takes us into a field where laws and principles derived from quite different forms of economic activity may be of little relevance.

[8] See also Sir Christopher Hinton's article on 'Nuclear Power' in *The Three Banks Review*, No. 52, December 1961. J.A. Jukes (U.K. Atomic Energy Authority) in *Financial Times Supplement: World Energy*, 24 September 1947, p. 47, put the Advanced Gas Cooled Reactors some years hence: ' The technology will be tested in the next year or two in the prototype . . . a full-sized station could then be ordered.'

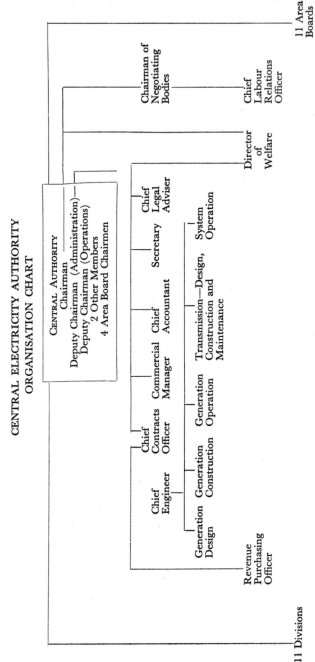

CENTRAL ELECTRICITY AUTHORITY
ORGANISATION CHART

11 Area Boards

Chairman of Negotiating Bodies

Chief Labour Relations Officer

Director of Welfare

CENTRAL AUTHORITY
Chairman
Deputy Chairman (Administration)
Deputy Chairman (Operations)
2 Other Members
4 Area Board Chairmen

Chief Legal Adviser

Secretary

Chief Accountant

Commercial Manager

Chief Contracts Officer

Chief Engineer

System Operation

Transmission—Design, Construction and Maintenance

Generation Operation

Generation Construction

Generation Design

Revenue Purchasing Officer

11 Divisions

This Chart is derived from the Herbert Report 1955, pp. 154–155 and 165. There were various changes in Departments, Branches and titles of Chief Officers before and since.

CENTRAL ELECTRICITY GENERATING BOARD
ORGANISATION CHART

Chairman:

Sir Christopher Hinton K.B.E., F.R.S., D.SC., D.ENG., M.I.C.E., M.I.MECH.E., M.I.CHEM.E.

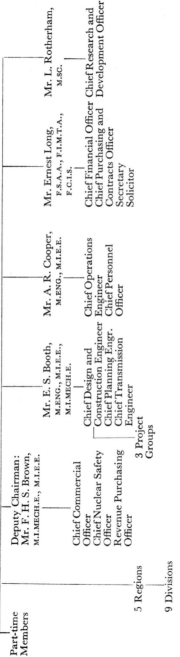

Part-time Members

Deputy Chairman:
Mr. F. H. S. Brown,
M.I.MECH.E., M.I.E.E.

Chief Commercial Officer
Chief Nuclear Safety Officer
Revenue Purchasing Officer

3 Project Groups

Mr. E. S. Booth,
M.ENG., M.I.E.E.,
M.I.MECH.E.

Chief Design and Construction Engineer
Chief Planning Engr.
Chief Transmission Engineer

Mr. A. R. Cooper,
M.ENG., M.I.E.E.

Chief Operations Engineer
Chief Personnel Officer

Mr. Ernest Long,
F.S.A.A., F.I.M.T.A.,
F.C.I.S.

Chief Financial Officer
Chief Purchasing and Contracts Officer
Secretary
Solicitor

Mr. L. Rotherham,
M.SC.

Chief Research and Development Officer

5 Regions

9 Divisions

Note: Under the Board there is a Central Executive Committee comprising the Full-time Board Members and the Regional Directors.

(c) *Overall Organisation for Generation Development in England and Wales*

The general internal organisation of the C.E.A. and of the C.E.G.B. are shown on the charts on pp. 154 and 155.   We are interested in those parts concerned with capital projects—both power stations and the main transmission network.   Under the B.E.A./C.E.A. they were somewhat complex.   There were for some time three engineering Sub-Departments for Generation, Transmission and Research.   The Generation Sub-Department had three Branches—Operation, Design and Construction—the last two being mainly responsible for capital works.   The Design Branch covered not only design and standardisation of plant but investigation of possible power-station sites, negotiations with other interests such as Planning Authorities and River Boards, negotiations (jointly with the Secretary's Department) for statutory and other consents and approvals and preparation of the Authority's evidence at Public Enquiries.   The Generation Construction Branch dealt with specifications and contracts, co-ordination of plant erection and inspection of plant at works during manufacture. The Generation Operation Branch did an analysis of performance of plant and negotiations with the Coal Board about future coal supply, the last function in association with the Design Branch because of its effect on station planning.   Later on the Construction Branch was hived off to form a new Sub-Department, and later still the Design Branch was combined with it.

The Transmission Sub-Department very largely carried on the functions of the former Central Electricity Board, and was indeed mainly composed of C.E.B. staff.   It had three branches:

   (i) Design
  (ii) Construction and Maintenance
 (iii) System operation

(iii) went beyond day-to-day operation and included both long- and short-term planning of the whole system, including general advice as to the siting of power stations.   The day-to-day operating function (including operational planning as far as the second winter ahead, usually referred to as short-term planning) was later taken away from the Transmission Sub-Department and combined with the Generation Operation Branch of the Generation Sub-Department to form a new Generation and System Operations Sub-Department. The long-term planning section of the original System Operation Branch was left as the System Planning Branch of the Transmission Sub-Department.

Throughout these permutations, however, there were always quite a number of sets of people involved in the planning of power-station construction. The Herbert Committee criticised the arrangements (as it found them) as leading to overlapping and delay.[9] It was, however, and still is, considered essential that questions of major plant design and of the programming of generating stations should be dealt with centrally, and also that there should be a local organisation responsible for such matters as supervision of construction on site. Between these two sets of functions there was a considerable area of responsibility in the field of power-station construction within which the C.E.A. were not apparently able to draw ideal lines of demarcation. Nevertheless, they built a large number of increasingly efficient power stations—fifty-five major stations in all—and closed eighty-six old ones, and more than doubled their circuit miles of main transmission links.[10]

The Herbert Committee considered where the planning and construction of new power stations could best be controlled. (Main transmission and other capital construction they did not discuss.) They said they had been much concerned at the duplication of work as between the C.E.A. Headquarters and its Divisions and also with the problem of the size of constructional staffs where the work load fluctuated according to developments in the power-station programme. They started from the assumption that:

the stations to be built over the next 15 years can be divided into two broad categories for which we will adopt the descriptions 'conventional' and 'advanced'.

[9] The last stage of the changes described above, however, only took place after the Herbert Committee had reported and the C.E.A. were further reconsidering their organisation not long before they were dissolved.

[10] Central Electricity, *Report and Accounts*, 1957–58, pp. 5–10, includes these and other statistics for the ten years 1947–57.

They explained:

> By 'conventional' stations we mean stations involving no particularly novel technical or constructional features and of a size in no way exceptional having regard to the current practice for the time being.

With these they contrasted the 'advanced stations':

> which are either of very large size or in some other respect incorporate novel, experimental or other features outside the common practice for the time being.

They then recommended that—subject to Headquarters approval of the sites, the capacity 'and the proposed amenities' —the entire responsibility for design and construction of 'conventional' stations should rest with the Divisions:

> The responsibility for the design and probably for the construction of the 'advanced' stations should . . . belong to Headquarters.[11]

The C.E.A. at the time of the Herbert Committee's Report had twelve Generation Divisions. As the Committee were concerned about evening out the load of planning work, they presumably expected there would be, for a number of years, at least two or three 'conventional' stations in course of planning and construction in each Division. However, in another part of their Report[12] they drew attention to the great advances in the design of generating sets and reproduced a table showing how in future years the generation construction programme would come to comprise a smaller number of bigger sets. The Committee in that part of their Report appear to be taking 30-MW and 60-MW sets as 'conventional' and sets of 100 MW and above as 'advanced'. But their table shows only eighteen sets (not stations) of 60 MW and below to be commissioned in 1958, twelve in 1959 and fourteen in 1960—that is sets which would presumably have been ordered in 1953, 1954 and 1955

[11] *Report of the Committee of Enquiry into the Electricity Supply Industry*, Cmd. 9672, 1956, pp. 71–72, paras. 267–268. This is confusing, because the C.E.G.B. uses the term 'conventional' for all non-nuclear stations. The Herbert Committee's distinction was derived from that in the C.E.A.'s standard instructions (dated January 1951, but still operative when the Committee took evidence) between 'routine stations with standard ratings and type of plant' and 'advanced design stations'. In 1951 standard ratings were 30 and 60 MW.

[12] Pp. 28–29, paras. 102–103.

respectively.   It is hard to see on this basis how an even load of planning work could have been envisaged for twelve Generating Divisions even as far back as 1955.   Admittedly 100-MW and 120-MW sets might in due course be so developed as to come into the 'conventional' category, but according to the same table there were only eight of these sets due to be commissioned in 1960.   Since the Herbert Committee reported, sets and stations of even larger capacity have been planned—200, 275, 325 and 550 MW for an individual set and 1,300 MW for a complete station.   This has involved:

(a) Rapid advances in various features of design requiring specialisation by a few highly skilled design engineers on the Board's staff in collaboration with a few highly developed manufacturing firms.

(b) Much smaller numbers of stations (and of sets) to be commissioned annually in future years.

The following table shows that *after 1961–62 there will be far fewer stations commissioned.   And it is the stations to be commissioned in those later years that are being planned now*—1959:

TABLE X

NUMBERS OF NEW GENERATING STATIONS
UNDER CONSTRUCTION EACH YEAR

Year	No. of Stations where construction starts on site during the year	No. of Stations having their first set commissioned during the year	No. of Stations having their last set commissioned during the year
1955	4	7	9
1956	5	3	13
1957	11	4	13
1958	2	2	8
1959	3	7	7
1960	2	4	7
1961		7	6
1962		3	8
1963		2	4
1964		2	3

(The figures up to and including 1958 are actual.   Those from 1959 onwards estimated or programmed.   The figures include nuclear stations.)

In the light of these figures it seems clear that there could not possibly be a balanced run of work for each of twelve separate Divisional planning staffs as envisaged by the Herbert Committee.

The Herbert Committee were at least partially aware that there would be some problem of uneven loading of Divisional planning staffs if their recommendations were accepted, and they added:

> It may be that from time to time the concentration of stations required to be built in one particular Division might result in the Construction Department being overloaded. In that case the Divisional Controller should be able to call upon the services, so far as he needs them, of Construction Departments of less heavily loaded Divisions. It appears to us, however, that the use of consultants should add a further element of flexibility.[13]

The Committee added that they had considered, but set aside for possible 'further review', the suggestion that constructional staffs should be concentrated in three or four regional centres. Where Headquarters took responsibility for 'construction' as well as 'designing' advanced stations:

> The work would be carried out by mobile teams organised for the purpose . . . if at any time one or another of these teams was not engaged on the construction of an 'advanced' station it could be seconded to an overworked Division and there help in the construction of a 'conventional' station under the directions of the Divisional Controller.[14]

The Committee recognised that all this would 'pose difficult organisational problems', but added:

> We do not feel competent to go at this stage beyond the proposals we have set out and cannot pretend to have said the last word.[15]

Certainly they do not seem to have considered the human as well as the organisational problems of treating a considerable number of highly qualified engineering staff as 'mobile' and repeatedly moving them and many other staff up and down the country to work under different chiefs. (Some of these problems already existed in respect of the very important site engineers and their staffs, but the Committee's suggestion would have created such problems on a much greater scale—combined with problems of changing or even divided control.)

[13] Pp. 71–72, para. 267.   [14] P. 72, para. 268.   [15] P. 72, para. 269.

There was also the point, which the Committee do not mention, that the more infrequent an event the planning of a new station became, the smaller would be the part which such work would take up out of a Divisional Controller's personal responsibilities. Each Controller would, therefore, presumably feel justified in giving a smaller part of his time and thought to it, while still being required to intervene and give decisions at important stages of the planning and constructional work.

In discussing the Herbert Report and the new legislation in the House of Commons on 17th December 1956[16] the then Minister of Power referred specially to power-station construction:

> To build a conventional power station in this country takes about seven years. Calder Hall . . . took three-and-a-half years. . . . There were of course special circumstances. . . . Nevertheless the disparity is . . . too great. If we are to speed up the nuclear power programme . . . this time must be abridged.
>
> There is in the light of the Herbert Report only one way of doing that and that is to break down this over-concentration of functions—to make each one of them more manageable and to entrust it to a body which can give undivided attention to it.

So the C.E.G.B. was to be set up with its separate functions. He added:

> I hope, however, that the Board . . . will pay particular heed to one suggestion by the Herbert Committee . . . that conventional stations not incorporating special features should be delegated to the Divisional Controllers so that the Generating Board for its part can be free to concentrate on the more advanced stations; and at this stage of time, the most advanced are of course the nuclear stations.[17]

The C.E.G.B., however, also had before them, when they took over a year after the Parliamentary debate referred to, not only the Herbert Committee's proposals but also later programmes of generation construction, which showed that, especially since the Herbert Committee reported, designs of both nuclear and other stations were continually advancing—their size increasing and their total number decreasing. They decided neither to

---

[16] Hansard, 17th December 1956, col. 941.   [17] Hansard, col. 942.

de-centralise to the Divisions nor to continue or intensify centralisation at Headquarters, but to set up a fundamentally different system.   This probably contains many lessons for other organisations, although there will be few, if any, who will have a load of planning work based on a capital development programme of comparable dimensions.   Moreover, although it comprises revolutionary changes and improvements, it may not, owing to the rapidity of technical change, represent the last word.   It may indeed already have produced some problems of organisation which are not yet solved.

The C.E.G.B. seem to have started by recognising a situation which could be summed up as follows:

(*a*) On the generating side the planning and control of new capital development was too vast a responsibility to be combined with that of day-to-day operations.   The two functions required quite separate organs of management.

(*b*) Detailed planning and construction of generating stations, on the one hand, and of transmission links and their associated transformers and substations, on the other, were each large enough spheres of responsibility on their own, and should not be combined in one Department.

(*c*) The smaller number of separate generation projects to be expected in the future would necessitate the concentration of planning and control work into a number of units considerably smaller than the number of the Divisions.

But

(*d*) Complete concentration of all design, planning and control of construction at Headquarters would involve too large and unwieldy an organisation there.

But

(*e*) Much work in connection with planning and design of the major items of equipment and practically all the work of planning the generation and main transmission system for the country as a whole ought to be concentrated in a few highly specialised staff at Headquarters.

The C.E.G.B., therefore, set up the following organisation:

(*a*) *A new Engineering Planning Department* at Headquarters to plan and programme the extensions of the generating and main transmission system for the country as a whole, including decisions as to the size, character and location of individual generating stations and of the more important new main transmission links. (The essentials of this 'system planning' and station programming work are the same as those of the B.E.A./C.E.A., and indeed very similar to those of the C.E.B. before the War.)

(*b*) *A new Engineering Design and Construction Department:*

    (i) to be responsible for design and construction policy generally;

    (ii) to deal almost entirely with the design of the major items of equipment, turbo-generators, boilers and nuclear reactors; and

    (iii) to advise and be concerned with many general factors affecting the development, design and production of other plant and structures.

(*c*) *Three 'Project Groups'* at Finchley in North London, at Birmingham and at Manchester, to deal (subject to Headquarters control on certain aspects) with most other questions involved in the design and construction of new generating stations (and substantial extensions to them),[18] and supervision and progress control of work on sites.

(*d*) *A separate Transmission Engineering Department* at Headquarters—in effect the same as the former Transmission Sub-Department—but confined in future to major functions—that is its functions are broadly similar to those exercised for generating stations by the Design and Construction Department. It will have executive responsibility only for larger national schemes and leave other work of planning and supervising construction of transmission works to the Transmission Departments under the control of the Regions.

[18] Regions and Divisions will still deal with extensions and renewals of subsidiary plant at existing stations costing less than about £250,000, but this is a small sum of money to spend in a generating station.

The Headquarter Departments mentioned work in collaboration with others which are being built up on a considerably
wider scale than those of the C.E.A.—notably the Secretary's
Department, concerned with sites and statutory approvals of
outside authorities, and the Research and Development
Department.   The Atomic Energy Authority act as the Board's
consultants for much of the research and development work on
nuclear stations.   Apart from this and the special arrangements with the 'consortia' of contractors, the basic organisation
for planning and constructing all types of new power stations—
nuclear and non-nuclear—is the same.   No distinction, as
suggested by the Herbert Committee, between the arrangements and planning for designing 'conventional' and 'advanced'
non-nuclear stations seems practicable.

(d) *'System Planning' and Forward Programming*

The C.E.G.B. Engineering Planning Department starts with
the various estimates of demand and translates them, first, into
a plan for the whole system of generation and main transmission
and thence into programmes for particular power stations and
main transmission links.   Responsibility for detailed planning
and construction of stations and links then passes to other
Departments.   The Planning Department is divided into three
Sections for 'Development Policy', 'System Planning' and
'Station Planning and Development'.   We can start with
System Planning.   The 'system' (built up originally by the
C.E.B. before the War) is all the C.E.G.B. generating stations,
transformer and switching stations, and transmission lines, and
its complete interconnection enables all electricity generation
in England and Wales to be planned as a whole.   The System
Planning Engineer, therefore, assembles estimates of plant
requirements for this whole system a number of years ahead.
The Station Planning and Development Engineer makes proposals for particular stations and their siting.   Then from all
these estimates and proposals complete programmes are built
up.   From the very beginning both these Planning Engineers
and their Sections have to consult together very closely, and the
final making up of the programmes is largely a joint operation.

The starting-point of system planning is the Electricity

Council's 'adopted estimates', but in using them the C.E.G.B. makes allowance for the degree of risk it must take for departures from average conditions. An allowance—about 5 per cent—is added for weather of maximum severity. The C.E.A. made considerable studies of the relationship of electricity demand to weather conditions. The whole exercise is largely a mathematical one of risks and averages, and policy decisions are concerned with what percentage risks that can be accepted —risks of having to vary frequency or voltage beyond certain tolerable margins or risks of consumers being actually cut off.

To translate all this into plant needs, a review is required covering:

(a) generating plant at present fully efficient and economic and the percentage allowance for breakdowns or failures;
(b) the economics and practicability of keeping old and less-efficient plant in service;
(c) expected progress in bringing into full service plant already planned and authorised;
(d) Supplies from sources outside C.E.G.B.'s direct control (e.g. Scotland, Atomic Energy Authority and the proposed cable link with France).

The assessment of future serviceability of old plant is primarily the responsibility of the C.E.G.B. Regions (under the general guidance of the Operations Department at Headquarters). It covers not only efficiency but also reliability. Plant over twenty-five years old in each year concerned is classified as 'time-expired', and a special estimate of its capacity is made. The percentage of all plant which can be assumed to be available for service at the times of maximum demand is, of course, a crucial one for the whole exercise. In their 1958–59 Report[19] the C.E.G.B. say that the percentage is being increased by 'careful planning of overhaul and maintenance work, together with improvements in plant design and operating techniques, and that in planning their programme of plant to be commissioned in 1964 they are assuming 90 per cent will be available.

The assessments of plant capacity on the basis described

[19] Para. 17, p. 5, and para. 49, p. 12.

above are reviewed annually by the Planning Department and the new programmes discussed with Regions at the beginning of the annual planning process.   Thereafter 'Final', 'Provisional' and 'Tentative' generating-plant programmes in terms of total capacity are drawn up for the fifth, sixth and seventh year ahead respectively.   The above calculations and their conclusions are embodied in a paper submitted by the Board Member for Engineering first to the Central Executive Committee, then to the Board.

When these authorities have settled the planning requirements the next task is to translate them into proposals for particular stations and transmission links.   The starting-point for this is the whole of the data of demand estimates broken down to particular supply points.   As electricity can be transmitted from any part of the country to any other, the field is in theory completely open for decisions about location of generating plant.   Any major modern power station, however, needs:

(a) Adequate water for cooling and steam-raising (without the former very large cooling towers are needed).
(b) Very strong foundations.
(c) A large site, which may be some hundred acres, and the agreement of the interests concerned to use it.
(d) Access to adequate and continuing fuel supplies.
(e) Transmission links to the places where the supply is required.

Requirements (a) and (b) are especially exacting for nuclear stations.   Although a modern power station, either nuclear or 'conventional', may employ permanently some two or three hundred staff or more, staff recruitment and housing do not seem, so far, to have been major factors.   They have, however, to be considered, and may well be more serious as stations are developed in remoter places.

Basic to any detailed assessments of particular sites two major national considerations have had to be taken into account in recent years:

(a) The balancing of electricity transmission costs against coal transport costs.

(*b*) The Government decision that nuclear power stations should for the time being be sited away from populous areas.

We have spoken of the 132-kV Grid as giving flexibility to the whole generation and supply system and enabling it to be planned on a national basis. This Grid certainly at first enabled spare generating capacity to be pooled, but after the War its capacity was not sufficient to allow transmission from one end of the country to another whenever required. However, in 1953–55 the first stage of the 275-kV Supergrid relieved this situation, although its prime purpose was not such occasional transfers for pooling purposes but permanent bulk transfers from places where electricity is generated to places where it is used. A most important part of this network was that which linked with London and South-East England the very large new stations on the River Trent and the East Midland coalfields. This plan was deliberately chosen as an alternative to building stations in South-East England and transporting the coal from the Midlands by rail. Taken overall, it was reckoned that to provide these extra 275-kV transmission links at a cost of £9 million would produce an annual saving by 1950 of about £1 million a year. These calculations took into account capital charges and all other financial considerations so far as the electricity authorities were concerned.[20]

It would be interesting, however, to know how the calculation would have appeared if it were worked out on a national basis, taking into account also the financial effect on British Railways. A decision to transport less coal by rail might not represent entirely a real saving in the provision of railway facilities, but rather—at least in part—a saving in money payments from the electricity authorities to the B.T.C. The B.T.C. have large capital assets in their permanent way, whose capacity may or may not be saturated, and in their wagons and locomotives, which might or might not be sold or put to other economic uses than coal-carrying for electricity generating.

[20] Such savings can be achieved only if the transmission lines are reasonably fully loaded; long-distance transmission of peak loads cannot be justified in this way. Sir Christopher Hinton, 'Power Production and Transmission in the Countryside', paper read before the Royal Society of Arts, 25th November 1959.

M

To raise these points is not, of course, to argue—on the basis of quite inadequate information—that the decision in favour of electrical transmission and against coal transport was wrong. All the indications indeed are that it was right and that the electricity authorities considered the matter as widely and deeply as they were able to do. It is interesting, however, to ask how this question might have been considered if the electricity authorities and British Railways had been regarded for this purpose as parts of a single publicly owned undertaking. It may be argued, as the Herbert Committee indeed argued, that the sole duty of the electricity authorities is to make their own concerns pay and not to help any other organisations, public or private, out of their difficulties. Can such policy, however, be reconciled with the interests of the public as a whole, who stand to gain or lose just as much from the activities of British Railways as from those of the electricity authorities? Would a privately owned company allow one of its subsidiaries to make a substantial loss if it could avoid or reduce this loss by reducing the profits on another of its subsidiaries to a smaller extent? (It is only fair to add that when the calculations were made British Railways were not legally as free as they are now to negotiate special terms for long-term contracts for particular transport users.)

Such major questions of the economics of bulk transmission of electricity and fuel represent only a part of the many problems to be considered in translating proposals for total increases in generating capacity into projects for particular power stations. The effective decision in favour of bulk transmission of electricity rather than further massive transport of coal was taken by the former C.E.A. when it decided to plan and complete the construction of the Supergrid of 275 kV. When links in the Supergrid are already there (or being provided) there must be a general bias in favour of siting conventional power stations in or near the coalfields rather than in any other areas of growing demand. There is, however, considerable scope for choice of sites. The C.E.G.B. have calculated that transmission of electricity is only cheaper than the equivalent rail haulage of coal at distances of over 50–60 miles. Some coal may come by road or water. It is also apparently seldom possible to find a site for a power station immediately at the surface of a coal mine which will supply all its fuel required throughout its life.[21]

To consider these intricate questions of fuel-transport economics, as well as larger questions of mutual concern, good standing liaison arrangements seem to have been established between the C.E.G.B. and the N.C.B., on the one hand, and between the C.E.G.B. and the B.T.C., on the other—both by permanent formal machinery and by informal *ad hoc* contacts as required.   There are regular meetings between the Chief Planning Engineer, C.E.G.B., and the Director-General of Marketing, N.C.B., and their staffs also often meet separately to discuss particular problems.   Somewhat similar liaison arrangements exist with British Railways.   As we have seen, the Coal Board's long-term planning looks ten, fifteen or twenty years ahead, and the C.E.G.B. need to know about this, because their stations are planned for a life of about twenty years.   This period is bound to be somewhat speculative and provisional, because no one can say how soon nuclear or other developments in power-station engineering will have rendered the present designs relatively uneconomic.   Clearly, however, some broad assurance about fuel supplies for about ten years ahead is needed before a station is built.

Questions of water and coal supply, along with that of nuclear safety, now compel the siting of both nuclear and non-nuclear power stations to be considered on a nation-wide basis rather than in any sense locally or even regionally.   The Chairman of the C.E.G.B., Sir Christopher Hinton, has described some of the basic considerations.[22]   Even without nuclear power the C.E.G.B. would have been forced to put some of their future stations on sites not very different from those now

[21] Though this was done at Grimethorpe in Yorkshire, where the Coal Board built a pithead power station.   On the wider issue the President of the Operational Research Society recently said that British Railways, C.E.G.B. and N.C.B., although they all had professional operational research groups, 'go on planning, buying, selling and shipping as though they were playing games against nature. What is best for them individually is not necessarily best for the nation and indeed by acting together their own interests would be better served.   One does not have to be an operational research enthusiast to see the great gains, running into millions of pounds, that could arise from joint planning and combined operational research carried out at a supra authority level.'   B. H. P. Rivett in *Operational Research Quarterly*, Vol. 13, No. 2, June 1962, pp. 142–143.

[22] 'Power Production and Transmission in the Countryside', paper read to the Royal Society of Arts, 25th November 1959.

proposed for nuclear stations. Taking into account site space, transport and water supplies, the best and least controversial sites had already been used, and it was exceptional to find a suitable urban site at all. Even if it had not been decided to build on the Trent, most of the Thames estuary would be ruled out because the deep-water frontages were largely taken up by port installations. The Board would in any case have had to go beyond the estuary to more isolated stretches of coast, like that at Bradwell, even for coal- or oil-fired stations. Moreover, there were limits to the amount of water that could be taken out of the Trent, and also to the extent to which warm water could be put back into the Thames. Questions of water supplies, water discharge and water-loading facilities are much more difficult than coal supply, because on this subject the C.E.G.B. is not dealing with a single nationwide public authority which is itself carrying out long-term planning. Local Planning Authorities (Counties or County Boroughs), river and drainage boards, port authorities and water-supply undertakings (some private and some Local Authority) all have to be consulted, as to the quantity of water available, its chemical composition, arrangements for its discharge and the general effect on rivers and ports.

Availability of land, town and country planning and general amenity considerations have also to be considered. We shall describe later the processes involved in getting agreement about particular sites. At the stage we are describing now, however —the working out of the broad programme eight years ahead— the first task will be to consider the arguments for and against certain parts of the country in general. At this, as at later stages, the C.E.G.B. Planning Department consult with a number of public authorities who may be able to advise or who may be affected—the Ministries of Housing and Local Government, Agriculture and Transport, other Government Departments, the National Parks Commission (who have an interest in amenity questions extending beyond the boundaries of the Parks themselves), the Nature Conservancy and so on. The C.E.G.B. Planning Department also study the various published County Development Plans.

Of course, it is much easier to get agreement from all concerned (even within the C.E.G.B.) to building new stations

adjacent to existing stations than to stations in new places.[23]
On the other hand, a concentration of generating plant in one
particular area may create special difficulties under the heads
we have already mentioned—transport of fuel, water and even
disposal of ash.   All these main questions of how far the provision of new generating capacity will fit in with existing
stations involves consultation with the C.E.G.B.'s Regions and
Divisions.   The siting of new plant in existing stations or
near by will often avoid construction of new main transmission
facilities or—if they have to be provided—it may reduce their
extent and cost.

The programming timetable which has recently been
followed has involved the approval of the programme of total
new generating capacity by the C.E.G.B.'s Central Executive
Committee at the end of August, and by the full Board at the
beginning of September.   Discussion about the detailed programme of stations then proceeds between the Board's Headquarters Planning Department and the Regions and Divisions
and other Headquarter Departments concerned, and this cul-
minates in a big meeting in January, under the Chairmanship
of the Board Member for Engineering.   This results in a full
paper with programmes of individual stations which is submitted to the Central Executive Committee at the end of
February and the full Board in March.   There is indeed
a programme of planning and consultation starting with the
Area Boards' estimates in March of one year and concluding
with the 'Final', 'Provisional' and 'Tentative' programmes of
stations approved in March the following year—that is seven
years before the plan shown in the provisional programme is to
be brought into service.   This timetable was under review
at the time of writing.

The crux of the proposals in the paper submitted to the
Board is contained in a table, with the particular stations and
their capacity in megawatts and the order in which they are to
be brought into service.   The effect of this programme is then
given in a calculation showing, for the past and current years

---

[23] It is, of course, generally more economic to complete a half-finished station
by adding the remaining generating sets than to provide the same additional
capacity in a completely new station, but the reference in the text is to putting one
new station beside an existing completed one.

and each of the six subsequent years: (*a*) the capacity available against expected demand; (*b*) the margins allowed to cover abnormal conditions; (*c*) the extent to which reliance will have to be placed on plant over twenty-five years old and plant over thirty years old.   There are also estimates of the cost of particular stations and their fuel consumption—including initial fuel charges for nuclear stations.   The programme distinguishes between nuclear and other stations and also between new stations and the addition of further generating sets in existing stations.   It has been usual in recent years to plan a large station with three, four, five or six sets[24] and to bring the first one into commission at the earliest possible date (even before the completion of the steelwork for the housing of the last one). The other sets followed at yearly intervals.   (In future it will be at about six-monthly intervals.)   The bringing of the plant of a coal- or oil-fired station into commission, therefore, may be spread over two, three or more years.   For a nuclear station it is the reactors (each with two or three generating sets dependent on it) which will normally be phased successively.   The programme in some cases names particular sites, and the supporting paper may indicate whether they are already in the Board's possession or substantially agreed.   The tentative programme at least is likely to contain one or more stations whose location has only been determined very generally.

The supporting paper will indicate how far the programme is conditioned by any general directions of Government policy. The nuclear-power programme, for instance, is obviously a matter of national concern.   There will also be brief references to any major considerations emerging from discussions with the National Coal Board, the Atomic Energy Authority and so on.   The statement shows capital costs per kilowatt of installed capacity.   For the first full year's working of the stations in the final programme only there is a comparison of the 'fixed annual costs and charges' (capital management, etc.) with the annual fuel saving.   (The latter is derived from comparison with average costs of existing stations.)   The useful life of any new generating project to be brought into commis-

---

[24] But as sets get larger there may be only three or four of them in each station—so that in any case the total capacity of a complete station is unlikely to exceed 1,000–1,500 MW.

sion some five or six years from now may well extend to the end of the present century, and the Generating Board have not so far made a full economic appraisal of the working of such a station throughout its economic life.   Such an appraisal could only be made in comparison with the operating costs of other stations, including nuclear stations of rapidly changing design.

In recent years the planning and construction of large coal- or oil-fired stations has generally taken the following times:

TABLE XI

	Approximate number of years
(a) Preliminary consideration (mainly in the Planning Department)	1
(b) Detailed design and placing of contracts (2–3) .	
(c) Start of construction to bringing of first generating set into commission (3–4)	About 5
(d) To bringing of last set into commission and final completion	2
TOTAL	8

[Stages (b) and (c) may overlap.]

The timetable for a nuclear station will be broadly similar, but there are rather more chances of delays—particularly about the site.   Although some stations may not take quite as long as this and all kinds of efforts are being made to shorten the timetable, construction on site of the stations in the final programme clearly ought to start within a few months of the final approval of this final programme, and the preliminary consideration of any station ought to start as soon as it is in the provisional programme.   Even this assumes hardly any unforeseen delays—although some unforeseen delays at some points among a group of projects of this magnitude all over the country, with the work spread over a number of years, would seem almost inevitable. We shall describe later the kind of things that can happen in site negotiations.   A labour dispute or failure of supplies affecting almost any one of the forty or so main contractors or many more sub-contractors involved in each station could also well put a project back for months—certainly if it involved a major job, such as the steelwork.   Even if the C.E.G.B. are able to shorten the total length of the timetable in normal cases, their system of planning at least seven to eight years ahead would seem to be fully justified.   Indeed, any even longer-term planning that may be practicable would surely seem to be well worth while.   The Coal Board's major programming seems to go farther ahead than eight years, although the costs of their largest individual projects are only about a quarter of those of the largest projects of the Generating Board, and seem to be rather less dependent on contractors and the agreement of outside authorities and interests.

It goes without saying that the C.E.G.B. is bound to become effectively committed to very large sums of capital expenditure for further periods ahead than those for which anyone, including Governments, is normally prepared to give unqualified financial assurances.   All these considerations apply (although in a somewhat lesser degree) to main transmission.   Moreover, in most cases in the event of an unexpected shortage of capital resources the deferment of construction of main transmission links might well render the new generating stations largely ineffective—and vice versa.   Again, although the constructional problems may be less, an agreement about the *siting* of main transmission links may be as difficult to achieve as that about the siting of power stations.

(e) *Sites*

Siting problems are a major factor in delaying the capital development programmes of many—probably most—public bodies.   The C.E.G.B., like the C.E.A. before it, has great difficulty in reconciling its needs with those of 'amenity', but relatively few difficulties with land *purchase*.   Under the Electricity Acts, 1947, 1954 and 1957, all Electricity Boards[25] can buy land compulsorily subject to the consent of the Minister of Power and subject to the statutory safeguards[26] (broadly—that fair notice must be given to all concerned and a public enquiry held if any interested party desires it).   No doubt the mere existence of these purchase powers has been of some help; but

[25] That is originally the B.E.A./C.E.A., the North of Scotland Board and the Area Boards. Under the 1954 and 1957 Acts the South of Scotland Board and the C.E.G.B. also have such powers.

[26] Acquisition of Land (Authorisation Procedure) Act, 1946.

since 1948 they have only been actually used in some twenty-five cases (sometimes only to resolve doubts about ownership).

Most purchases for C.E.G.B. power stations are negotiated by estate surveyors in the Headquarters Secretary's Department. Preliminary searches, however, may be made by the Planning Department's engineers. Any approaches to land-owners for permission to survey or bore are normally made by the Wayleave Officers in the Divisions, but when compulsory powers[27] to enter land are to be used the Headquarters estate surveyors come in.

The Board works within a rather exceptional legal framework which has some influence on the way in which the discussions and controversies are conducted. The essence of the difficulties, however, lies not in the legal requirements, but in the very nature of power stations and the extent of competing claims for land use or land preservation in this crowded island. This should make us a little cautious about accepting the comparisons with the speed of power-station construction in the U.S.A. mentioned by the Herbert Committee.[28] The Electricity Act 1957 (S.37) specially requires that all Electricity Boards:

> in formulating or considering any proposals relative to the functions of any of the Boards, shall each take into account any effect which the proposals would have on the natural beauty of the countryside or on such flora, fauna, features, buildings or objects

The C.E.G.B. cannot put up a power station without consent of the Minister of Power under Section 2 of the Electric Lighting Act, 1909 (as since amended)—'Section 2 Consent'. The building (or extension) of a power station, like that of any other building, also requires 'planning permission'; but the Minister of Power may direct that his 'Section 2 Consent' may be 'deemed' to be planning permission. The C.E.G.B. send a copy of their application for 'Section 2 Consent' to the Local Planning Authority, who in due course reply with their

[27] Under Section 35 of the Electricity Act, 1957, which gives rights of entry for these purposes to all Electricity Boards—without reference to a Minister, but subject to 28 days' notice: to 'enter upon and survey any land . . . for the purpose of ascertaining whether the land will be suitable for use for the purposes of any functions of the Board'.

[28] Herbert Report, paras. 90–92, pp. 27–28.

comments and the results of their consultations with other bodies, and all these the C.E.G.B. then send on to the Minister of Power. If the Planning Authority object, or agree only subject to conditions which the C.E.G.B. do not accept, the Minister must hold a public enquiry, and he usually decides to do so if there are substantial objections from anyone else.

This public enquiry is normally conducted jointly by two Inspectors from the Ministries of Power and of Housing and Local Government. Both Ministers consider both Inspectors' reports, and if they agree the Minister of Power grants both 'Section 2 Consent' and 'Deemed Planning Permission'. He may include conditions such as measures to avoid discharge of sulphur and about consultation with his Ministry on engineering design and with the Local Authority about architectural design. If compulsory purchase of the land is also proposed it is generally arranged to deal with any objections to this at the same public enquiry.

Controversy has been most serious and prolonged in the case of the nuclear power stations—partly because of fears about radio-activity and partly because of the stricter limitations on the choice of sites. The difficulties that can occur and the time that can be consumed are illustrated by the early history of the Trawsfynydd nuclear power station site in the Snowdonia National Park.

Between May 1956 and August 1957	C.E.G.B. officers search various areas in North Wales for one or more nuclear stations and meet officers of the Caernarvon and Merioneth County Councils and the National Parks Commission.
August 1957	C.E.G.B. formally notify the two County Councils, the National Parks Commission, the Royal Fine Arts Commission, the Nature Conservancy, local M.P.s and landowners, of their proposal to establish a station on land they already own at Trawsfynydd; apply for 'Section 2 Consent' and issue a notice to the Press. Objections made by the National Parks Commission, the Youth Hostels Association for England and Wales, the Ramblers' Association and the North Wales (Hydroelectricity) Protection Committee.

12th, 13th and 14th February 1958	Public Enquiry by Inspectors at which the proposal is *supported* by: The Merioneth County Council The Snowdonian National Park Advisory Committee The Duedraeth Rural District Council The Ffestiniog Urban District Council Two Parish Councils Mr. T. W. Jones, M.P. for Merioneth, on behalf of the Welsh Labour Group of M.P.s The North Wales Region of The Transport and General Workers' Union The National Farmers' Union and the Welsh Farmers Union also support the proposals subject to certain stipulations
17th April 1958	The two Inspectors report jointly on facts, but with separate and differing conclusions. Ministry of Power Inspector recommends approval of the scheme. Ministry of Housing Inspector feels there is a fundamental conflict between the requirements of the National Park and of electric power, and that this is a matter of high policy on which he cannot make any recommendation. The burden of many of his remarks, however, is distinctly unfavourable to the proposal.
15th May 1958	Ministry of Power write to C.E.G.B. that the latter's evidence 'does not seem to have convinced the representatives of the National Parks Commission and certain other bodies', in particular on the point of alternative sites. C.E.G.B. are therefore invited to submit a further memorandum to the Minister; Ministry send a copy of their letter to all the parties who had given evidence and ask C.E.G.B. to send copies of their reply to the same parties for any further comments.
2nd June 1958	C.E.G.B. reply, saying, among other things, that officers of the National Parks Commission had been consulted at an early stage about alternative sites and had expressed a preference for Trawsfynydd.
6th June 1958	North Wales (Hydro-Electricity) Protection Committee send further comments.

16th June 1958	Council for Preservation of Rural Wales send further comments.
27th June 1958	National Parks Commission write contesting C.E.G.B. claims and saying that the discussions with their officers referred to were intended to be confidential and non-committal.
August 1958	Minister of Power grants 'Section 2 Consent' and 'Deemed Planning Permission'.

For the Dungeness (Kent) nuclear station site the application to the Minister was made in June 1958 and approved in July 1959.

Taking a fair average of cases of both nuclear and non-nuclear power stations in recent years, it seems that *at least two years* must normally elapse between the time when the C.E.G.B.'s estate surveyors are first consulted by their Engineering Planning Department about the choice of sites within a particular area and the time when access is obtained.   This is indeed the time effectively allowed within the whole eight-year programming timetable referred to above on the assumptions:

(*a*) that the first year is occupied in deciding what stations are required and within what broad divisions of the whole country; and

(*b*) that it takes five years to get all the generating sets into commission after construction on the site starts (this time, as we shall see, may be shortened *if nothing at all goes wrong*).

Two years, however, is not always sufficient for the whole process of site selection and acquisition.   A good deal of time must have been spent by the Engineering Planning Department in considering possible localities within very wide areas of choice before any proposal for a specific site can be agreed with the Board's estate surveyors and definite negotiations started with owners and public authorities.   Moreover, even counting from this point, two years may often be too short.   As far as possible, negotiations with landowners and applications for the Minister's and other authorities' consent will go in parallel. But an owner might not be willing to negotiate at all until planning permission had been obtained.   Moreover, difficulties seem bound to increase as the programme of nuclear stations gets under way. The Trawsfynydd proceedings tended to develop into debates on general issues of national policy, and the arguments were conducted mainly between organisations (both public and private) which were national in their scope.[29] If there had been much *local* opposition, the whole process might well have taken much longer.

It is interesting to note the way in which these questions have been treated in authoritative reports during the past two decades. In 1942 the Cooper Committee on *Hydro-electric Development in Scotland*[30] said that they had been impressed by the delays and the resulting 'substantial weight of wholly un-remunerative expenditure' in promoting Parliamentary Bills for hydro-electric schemes. They therefore proposed:

> that these leisurely and expensive methods should be superseded by more business-like and modern machinery . . . under the proposals which we advance it will be impossible to perpetuate the system under which any person whose property or interests may in any way be affected by the execution of a large public utility scheme is entitled not only to claim compensation . . . —for to that he is entitled—but also to oppose the entire scheme on its merits. Once Parliament has determined as a matter of high policy that a series of schemes should be carried into execution for the benefit of the Highlands and the national advantage, and once the technical programme has been mapped out to the satis-faction of the appropriate authorities,[31] it appears to us that vested interests, whether of property owners . . . or of the various unofficial organisations which have been in the habit of interven-ing in such proceedings, should no longer be permitted to oppose the policy thus determined upon, or to delay or add to the expense of its execution.

They, therefore, contemplated a:

> public general Act which . . . will in outline authorise once and for all the scheme of development.

and, thereafter,

> that lands and wayleaves should be acquired, failing agreement, by simple requisition.

[29] The term 'national' is used in this context as applying to England and Wales as a whole and not to Wales only.

[30] December 1942, Cmd. 6406, paras. 71–72.

[31] At the time the Committee reported these would be the Electricity Com-missioners.

These comments, which read a little strangely today, were, of course, made during the War. However, the Committee's Chairman, the late Lord Cooper, was then a distinguished Judge and shortly afterwards Lord President of the Court of Session and Lord Justice General of Scotland and, at least at a later date, a trenchant critic of what he felt to be the bureaucratic tendencies of modern Government.[32]   Sir Hugh Beaver's Committee on the construction of power stations said in 1953:[33]

> It is impossible to defer to all vested interests if rapid and effective decisions are to be made and if costs are to be minimised. Consequently procedures for consultation and approval between the many statutory and interested bodies should be rationalised.

The Herbert Committee[34] spoke of the possibility of 'facilitating the grant of the necessary approvals and consents'.

However, other trends of public opinion and recommendations made to the Government in recent years have been in a somewhat contrary direction.   The whole tenor of the Report of Sir Oliver Franks' Committee on Administrative Tribunals and Enquiries, which was accepted almost in its entirety by the Government—and indeed by Parliament as a whole—was in the direction of giving more sympathetic and careful consideration to objections to public authorities' proposals and greater scope to each objector to develop his case.   The Franks Committee indeed said:

> We do not claim that the effect of our recommendations taken together will be to reduce the time taken by the entire process. We are indeed doubtful whether any recommendations within the scope of our enquiry could produce any substantial saving of time.[35]

Despite this, the following final recommendations by the Beaver Committee would probably command more general acceptance than their first comments, which we have quoted (or those of the Cooper Committee):

> The aim should be to evolve a system of collaboration between Departments whereby agreement on future power station sites

[32] See Lord Cooper's lecture printed in *Public Administration*, Vol. XXXII, 1954, pp. 165–171.
[33] Paras. 10 and 11, pp. 3 and 4.
[34] p. 26, para. 93.
[35] Cmd. 218, August 1957, para. 353, p. 76.

should be reached long before they are actually going to be used. This recommendation would call for a detailed appreciation by the [Central Electricity] Authority of their site requirements and locations over a period of years.   Such an estimate need not be tied dogmatically to a meticulous forecast of future electricity demand year by year.[36]

In fact, the C.E.G.B. might well extend their programmes even farther ahead, say up to ten years, and apply for the necessary consents considerably earlier.   This need commit neither them nor the Government to the approval of a capital investment programme for any particular year.   (London Transport got Parliamentary approval for the compulsory purchase of land and underground rights for the Victoria Line at a time when the Government had made it quite clear they were in no way committed to its actual construction.)   In fact, at the time of writing indications were that advance programming was being taken farther ahead by the C.E.G.B.—up to ten or fifteen years. Long-term programmes had been attempted by the C.E.A., but it seems that the trend now will be to start considering *particular sites* farther in advance.   This would certainly seem to be most necessary.

Much of what has been said about sites for power stations applies broadly to sites and wayleaves for main transmission, and this is one of the reasons why a system of long-term trans-mission route planning seems clearly to be required.

There is some special interest in the way in which the South of Scotland Electricity Board deals with site and wayleave questions—in particular, the way in which the processes are streamlined.   There are no professional estate surveyors on the staff.   The organisation for acquiring sites and wayleaves con-sists simply of the legal side of the Secretary's Department and the Wayleave Officers.   The former also take an important executive part in the planning and controlling of the whole process of site acquisition from the earliest stages.   The Deputy Secretary (a solicitor) is Chairman of the sub-com-mittee which plans the power-station site programme several years ahead.   Similar forward planning is done jointly, by engineers and solicitors, for the main Grid system.   The solicitors take an active part in progressing site acquisitions

[36] Para. 11, p. 4, and summary of recommendations, 1, p. 16.

along the settled Grid routes, and also in considering diversions where serious local opposition is met.   They are directly engaged in the negotiations for important sites or in difficult wayleave cases from the outset.

These arrangements, which involve largely eliminating the professional estate surveyor, certainly seem to save time, both by avoiding reference of papers and discussion between two professional advisers and also by ensuring that the legal aspects of any case are considered from the outset before commitment. This system is especially suitable for Scotland, but it should surely have advantages elsewhere.

CHAPTER VI

POWER STATIONS AND THE GRID (II)

(a) *Preliminary Planning of Individual Power Stations*

The stage of 'preliminary consideration'[1] of power-station projects is primarily a matter for the Station Planning and Development Engineer's side of the Planning Department. He takes a project from the point when it is first included in a 'tentative' programme to the point when sufficient details can be worked out to hand it over (through the Chief Design and Construction Engineer) to one of the Project Groups for detailed planning and supervision of construction. No very clear-cut line of distinction between the three broad stages can be drawn. The Station Planning and Development Engineer and his staff are closely consulted and deeply involved in the planning and the working out of the main programmes, even though these are primarily the responsibility of the System Planning Engineer. As we have seen, if everything is to be completed in time, much work in connection with the site has to be done at a very early stage—usually a good while before the Final Programme is finally approved by the Board. At the other end, the Design and Construction Department Headquarters Branches and the Project Groups are consulted some considerable time before the job is finally handed over to them. The Project Groups make the first cost estimates. The Station Planning and Development Engineer, however, produces the 'Station Development Particulars' (SDPs) as the data on which the Project Group will work. SDPs comprise up to fifty or more sheets of foolscap plans and diagrams arranged under twenty or more heads, with possibly a dozen appendices. In broad outline the SDPs are similar to those of the B.E.A./C.E.A. (when they used to be sent from the Chief Engineer's Department at Headquarters to the Divisions), but in recent years they seem to have become a good deal fuller. The reasons are no doubt partly the increasing complexity and novel features in the design of power stations, and partly recent efforts to get major

---

[1] See p. 173, and pp. 164–174 generally.

planning questions more precisely settled in the earlier stages to save delays later.

The SDPs begin with 'Site Particulars' stating whether the land is already in the Board's ownership and/or occupation and what further negotiations have to be carried out and by whom. Before turning a case over to a Project Group the Planning Department will normally take it at least to the point where the site purchase is assured, but there may often be some negotiations (e.g. about outstanding leases) to be completed (usually, by the Estates Branch of the Secretary's Department, but on occasion jointly by the Planning Department and the Project Group). At these stages questions of flooding and river works will be dealt with and the Project Group will be advised of the results of tests and borings and warned if any special drainage or piling measures may be needed, or negotiations with River or Drainage Boards. Detailed results of borings will be shown in drawings, with a statement of what further boring is needed. Other points, such as mining rights, may need negotiation by the Project Group or by the Secretary's Department (Estates Branch).

Next there will be a brief but precise statement of the station's capacity in megawatts, the number of generating sets, the load factors, and the turbine and boiler characteristics (steam temperatures and pressures). Sometimes these technical factors have to be related to other factors. A note in one SDP reads:

> The implications of making provision in the layout . . . for one or more of the major units in the station being super-critical[2] . . . should be examined, and any difficulties which can be foreseen in making such provision should be reported to the Chief Planning Engineer. Particular attention should be given in this respect to changes in the main building outlines and their aesthetic effects and the effect on layout of any additional ground space which it is considered expedient to allow for the super-critical units.

A section on 'Planning and Amenity Considerations' states whether the land is 'designated' for a power station in the County Development Plan and whether separate building

---

[2] That is having certain steam conditions of specially advanced design and efficiency.

architects and landscape architects will be engaged. The Planning Department will normally have arranged for the appointment of civil engineers and architects and a landscape architect if required, but the Project Group will have to arrange early consultation between the latter and the County Planning Officer.

SDPs contain a good many meticulous notes on amenity questions, for instance:

> . . . —— was a private park until a few years ago. The most attractive features which remain of the original parkland are the copses of trees . . . care should be taken in evolving the station layout to avoid unnecessary destruction of trees.

SDPs also describe briefly the main transmission connections, existing or proposed.

There will be a considerable section on various aspects of fuel supply, normally with minutes of full discussions with British Railways and the Coal Board, estimated annual and daily consumption and the mean daily delivery of coal and its sources of supply (with detailed chemical composition). The fuel—coal or oil—will not only affect the design of the boiler and the type of storage and handling equipment but also the transport and access and ash-disposal facilities, which may affect the whole layout of the site and the efficiency and cost of its working. Rail facilities and/or wharves or jetties will be specified. The type of wagons to be used, the size of the trains and turn-round arrangements will be of very great importance, both for the efficient working of the station and to British Railways. The Planning Department are unlikely to have finalised all these matters with the railway, river, road or other authorities, but the SDPs should make it clear how far matters have been taken and what remains to be done. Both cooling and boiler water will always be major factors, and will have affected the choice of site and the calculation of the cost of the whole project in various ways, including the need for cooling towers. It may sometimes be necessary to negotiate about cooling-water supplies, and their eventual discharge, with River Boards and Port Authorities, who will also be concerned with water transport facilities. Heated water returned to a river or estuary may affect pollution, and there will have to be calculations of tides and so forth.   Negotiations about water transport—unloading and berth facilities—will involve bringing in the firm of shipping managers who advise and make water-transport arrangements for the Board.   It seems that the Headquarters Planning Department usually take all these negotiations up to the stage of reasonable assurance that there is no major obstacle to developing a station of the size and type proposed on the particular site.   There will then usually be a good deal of further detail to be worked out by the Project Group and the Secretary's Department.   Sometimes indeed substantial questions cannot be cleared before the case leaves the Planning Department, and they will have to be negotiated by the Project Group.   Water questions (particularly pollution) often impinge on Town Planning considerations, and indeed conditions about water, drainage and effluent may be embodied in the Minister's 'Section 2 Consent' and 'Deemed Planning Permission'. Although boiler-feed water will not be required in anything like such volume as cooling water, it can be a problem.   In one case a local water company could not undertake to supply water of the volume and purity required until it had settled major plans for expanding its own well borings and other facilities, and correspondence and negotiations went on for eighteen months before the C.E.G.B. received the assurances in principle which it needed before going on with the planning of the station.   (This shows the difficulties of a national public utility concern dependent on a local public utility concern for one of its major projects, which may not be of any special local benefit.)   The SDP may have to include a detailed chemical and bacteriological analysis of the boiler-feed water and some analysis of the proposed cooling water.   All this may affect the design of the circulating-water plant and determine what chemical and bacteriological purification plant and/or physical screening plant will be needed.

The number and height of chimneys required for smoke-cleansing plant will have to be noted, and under the Clean Air Act and the Alkali Act the (Government) Chief Alkali Inspector has to be informed.   Conditions about smoke and height of chimneys may also concern Local Authorities and be embodied in the Minister's Section 2 Consent.   The Air Ministry and the Ministry of Aviation also need to be consulted about chimneys. The Planning Department, after obtaining a detailed local meteorological survey, will have had at least preliminary negotiations about chimneys and probably ascertained in outline the main requirements, leaving it to the Project Group to work out and agree precisely how they shall be met.

Most of these questions covered in the SDPs involve also considerations of cost—direct constructional costs, running costs or any compensation and other payments to outside interests. The settling of these questions is, of course, also a vital factor in getting the planning and construction carried out to time, and many of the factors may also affect the working efficiency of the station. One of the main tasks of the Planning Department is to balance all these interlocking or conflicting considerations. It will seldom, if ever, be possible at the planning stage to express this balance wholly in financial terms. Moreover, there would seem to be a real problem of where the Planning Department should leave off and the Project Group take over. Further detailed investigation may produce a balance rather different from that struck at an earlier stage. Yet if the Planning Department kept the case too long, or if the Project Group itself made too many investigations before reaching final decisions, the whole programme would be delayed. We must remember that all along the timing of generating-plant construction is itself significant in financial terms. The effect of delay in bringing a new station into commission may not in future be wholly or mainly to jeopardise the full provision of supplies to consumers: it may be rather that much less efficient and less economic plant is kept longer in commission. If major delay occurs after construction has started, of course, there will be a longer period during which interest charges have to be paid without any equivalent revenue return or saving.

(b) *Functions and Policies of the C.E.G.B. Design and Construction Department*

In the Design and Construction Department the Power Plant Design Branch is concerned largely, and the Nuclear Plant Design Branch entirely, with equipment whose specification is primarily a matter for Headquarters. Most of this—boilers, turbo-alternators, and reactors and their ancillary

CENTRAL ELECTRICITY GENERATING BOARD
DESIGN AND CONSTRUCTION DEPARTMENT

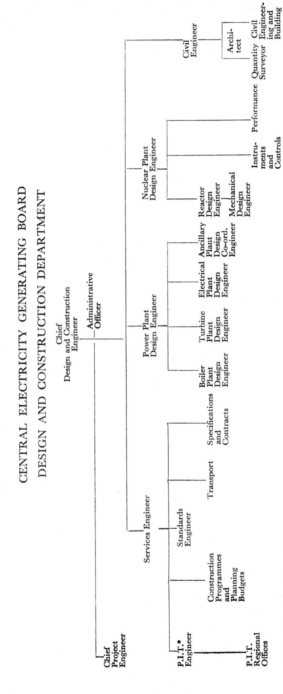

* Production Inspection and Test.

plant—is very large and liable to great advances in design. We have seen how the number of power stations programmed is steadily decreasing as the capacity of each increases. In future only some half-dozen stations of both kinds may be commissioned each year. Moreover, very few manufacturers are in the field—perhaps five for turbo-alternators, seven, eight or at the most nine for boilers; and for complete nuclear power stations (each comprised in a single contract) competition is only confined to the three 'consortia' of large electrical, mechanical and civil engineering firms. Hence the main work of drawing up specifications, considering manufacturers' designs and consulting with manufacturers about future developments is concentrated with a few highly specialised C.E.G.B. staff. *Working drawings* are not prepared by the C.E.G.B., and the precise form and dimensions of plant produced by different manufacturers to meet the same specifications may differ considerably. But for the main types of plant the C.E.G.B. produces *specifications* in considerable detail. One for a boiler or a turbo-alternator may run to some 100 pages of foolscap. More important perhaps than the final specifications is the continuous consultation between the C.E.G.B. and manufacturers' design engineers. Ideas about future development are exchanged, and the Board will try to encourage more efficient designs. C.E.G.B. engineers regard this field as one in which both sides can help one another, both in the development of the generation system at home and also in exports. They say this is a more realistic approach to the development of such a technically advanced industry than a purely commercial relationship between supplier and customer with totally separate interests and functions.

Other C.E.G.B. Departments, notably Purchasing and Contracts, are concerned with this relationship with manufacturers and the working out of specifications. The Research and Operations Departments also need to be consulted from time to time. The Atomic Energy Authority are largely responsible for nuclear research and development, and indeed for much design work, and act as the Board's consultants. For both nuclear and non-nuclear plant the Project Groups carry much responsibility. For nuclear reactors, boilers and turbo-alternators, as we have seen, Headquarters Branches of the

Design and Construction Department write specifications and assess tenders, but consult with the Project Groups.   Subject to certain Headquarters directions, the Project Groups are then authorised to place the contracts and/or supervise the work. However specifications for the other plant are primarily the responsibility of the Project Groups.   The Project Groups, however, must consult with Headquarters Branches of the Design and Construction Department, and a good deal of development work and consultation with manufacturers is carried out by the latter.   In particular, and in addition to the general control and supervision exercised by the Purchasing and Contracts Department, these Branches have the chance to comment on tenders for the following types of plant:

(a)	Condensing plant.	(g)	High-pressure pipework.
(b)	Feed heating plant.	(h)	Water-treatment and
(c)	Feed Pumps.		evaporation plant.
(d)	Cooling water pumps.	(i)	Generator and Grid
(e)	Coal handling plant.		transformers.
(f)	Ash- and dust-handling	(j)	Transmission switchgear.
	plant.	(k)	Cooling towers.

Moreover, tender lists for all contracts over £10,000 have to be agreed with the Headquarters Purchasing and Contracts Department.

In these fields of design and specification the lines of division of responsibility between Headquarters Branches and the Project Groups may not yet be finally settled.   As long as important new developments are taking place, there are probably bound to be many aspects of the work in which both parties are involved.

The other Branches ('Services' and 'Civil') of the Design and Construction Departments have some different functions from the first and from each other.   On the civil side there are many more contractors, while most of the design work is done by consultants.   The pre-War electricity concerns normally employed consultants for all design and supervision of construction of power stations.   Generally for each station there would be main consultants for the different items of plant and generally also for the civil engineering work as a whole (possibly with other specialists for such things as river works).   At first the B.E.A./C.E.A. continued on these lines, but as it built up its own specialist staff, it began to undertake more design work direct.   Sometimes it would do most of the electrical and mechanical work internally, but employ consultants for civil work, or it might employ different consultants for all sides of the work, but use its own staff for overall design and co-ordination.   In other cases it would still employ main consultants to arrange everything.   The practice varied according to the circumstances of each scheme and on the availability of qualified and experienced staff within the firms of consultants and within the C.E.A.   There are still some variations, but the present policy of the C.E.G.B. is to employ consultants for civil but not for electrical and mechanical work in non-nuclear stations.   There are, however, and apparently will continue to be, one or two stations where civil work is designed and supervised by the Board's own staff.   The arguments for and against these varying practices seem to be fairly evenly balanced.   The experience which they gain from working for the Board may be of value to the civil consultants in getting similar work overseas, and the C.E.G.B. can no doubt benefit much from the experience they gain with other clients.   Yet in keeping a certain amount of work for its own staff, the Board retains at its own disposal a reserve of independent experience and a source of independent advice.

Most of the architectural work is done by private firms of architects working either directly for the Board or for civil engineering consultants.   In power station construction generally the C.E.G.B. and its predecessors seem to have regarded the architect's function as ancillary and subordinate to that of the civil engineers.   A power station is primarily a grouping of electrical and mechanical plant supported as necessary by concrete and steelwork—not a building into which machinery is fitted.   Indeed, the tendency has been successively to reduce the amount of 'traditional' *building* work, particularly brickwork, which covers and surrounds the engineering plant and structures, putting switchgear, transformers, and in three cases even main boilers, in the open.   Where covering is undoubtedly required, brickwork has recently tended to be replaced by asbestos, aluminium or other sheet materials.   Yet emphasis on the aesthetic importance of the design has increased —ever since some years before the War when the size of stations increased, but more particularly since the War, along with the general public concern about 'amenities', and since stations—particularly, but not only, nuclear stations—have had to be sited in remote and sometimes beautiful places. All this seems to have brought architects back into a position of rather greater importance, but they still seem mainly concerned with adapting or modifying the external forms of already settled basic designs. They would now probably claim to be trying not to conceal or disguise a power station, but to adapt its essential and characteristic features into a pleasing form.

All this affects the architectural set-up within the Board's organisation. They have few salaried architects—only three in the Headquarters Branches of the Design and Construction Department, none of them designing individual schemes. Their function is research, development work, cost studies and general advice. Sir William Holford (part-time Board Member) takes a special interest in the design, siting and landscaping of power stations and other structures, and is Chairman of the Board's advisory panel of distinguished architects. The senior of the three salaried architects acts as Secretary to this Panel and works immediately under Sir William's directions, assisted by the other two. For each power station it is now usual to appoint a firm of architects to assist the civil engineers (whether consultants or C.E.G.B.'s staff) with the design of the main structure and in particular to design the administrative block and other ancillary buildings. A consultant landscape architect is also usually appointed separately to advise on land formation (the levelling of ground and the making of embankments) and the planting of trees and shrubs in relation to the buildings. (The layout and grouping of these buildings will already have been decided upon.) Both the main consultants' architect and the landscape architect consult with the Local Planning Authority, the Royal Fine Art Commission and other bodies interested in amenities and advise the Board on how the requirements or requests of these authorities may best be met.

There are relatively few civil engineers and quantity surveyors in the Civil Engineering Branch. Their main functions are:

(a) Development work, study of the economic aspects of designs and methods of construction, of types of materials, cost studies and preparation of standard specifications.

(b) Technical responsibility for the general conditions of civil engineering and building contracts and oversight and advice in respect of important individual contracts.

(c) Collaboration in negotiations for extensions of civil engineering contracts and with the assessment and negotiation of variations to civil engineering works on nuclear stations.

The Services Branch, among other functions, runs the 'Progress, Inspection and Test' (P.I.T.) service which operates both from Headquarters and its own eight Regional offices (quite distinct from the main C.E.G.B. Regions) and which is responsible for liaison with manufacturers within their own works. P.I.T. Inspectors maintain very close contact with the whole process of manufacture of plant from its earliest stages, report monthly or more often on progress, and check quality and conformity with specifications. (Progress control and programming of plant manufacture seemed to be very much a developing field at the time of writing.) The monthly reports are based on visits to works, and in recent years have been prepared more and more closely in collaboration with manufacturers—to whom copies are sent. The process is so much a joint one between the C.E.G.B. and its contractors that in some cases the P.I.T. Officers sit in on the manufacturers' own progress meetings. It is no doubt to the ultimate advantage both of the manufacturers and the Board to have realistic programmes laid out well in advance and firmly adhered to. However, with quite exceptionally large and new types of plant involving many sub-contractors, such firm programmes are extremely difficult to achieve. Although liaison with plant manufacturers at their works seems to be mainly carried out through the P.I.T. service, the Project Groups have an overall responsibility for the progress of each project. This was a field in which at the time of writing the division of functions did not seem to be finally settled. The Services Branch appeared to have a number of functions which were in the course of developing or likely to develop much more extensively,

CENTRAL ELECTRICITY GENERATING BOARD

ORGANISATION OF A PROJECT GROUP

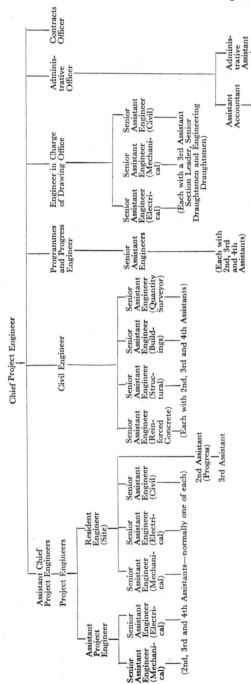

Note 1. The precise number of posts may be higher or lower than those shown according to the incidence of work in each Project Group.
Note 2. All engineers shown in the chart down to and including 4th Assistants are normally professionally qualified.

both in progress and cost control systems and in standardisation.

As new stations are so few and technical progress so rapid, the prospects of standardisation might seem fairly limited. In fact, however, there is thought to be considerable scope for standardisation in the designs of components which are not themselves materially affected by changes in the main plant— also in the field of general stores.

The Service Branch also deals with transport, which constitutes one of the main limits on the size of turbo-alternators and of transformers. The maximum weight of any loaded vehicle on British public roads, even with special permission and on special routes, is generally 200 tons (including about 50 tons for the vehicle). The design of a major plant may very largely depend on what special arrangements can be made for transport by road, rail and/or sea. For the Trawsfynydd power station, for instance, special docking facilities will have to be provided at Portmadoc and a special road part of the way to the site. For Bradwell the boilers were floated down from Teeside by sea.

(c) *The Project Groups and their Work*

The prime responsibility for the detailed design and construction of a power station rests with the Project Group, and it is to the Chief Project Engineer that the 'letter of authority to proceed', Station Development Particulars and 'Master Programme' are sent by the Chief Design and Construction Engineer as soon as the Board's approval has been given to the Final Programme. The Master Programme shows the overall dates for planning and construction and the commissioning of successive turbo-alternator sets.

The three Project Groups' respective areas have geographical boundaries, but these are not intended to be as definite or permanent as Regional and Divisional boundaries, and they do not follow the same lines. Their object is simply to provide for roughly equal loads of work for all three Groups, and if an exceptionally heavy load developed within the boundaries of one Group some schemes would be transferred to another Group. The Groups were set up in January 1958 and were fully functioning before the end of the year. (The Southern and Northern Groups housed themselves within about six months in large two-storey prefabricated buildings.)   Although there is a certain functional liaison between the Project Group civil engineers, administrative officers and contracts officers and their opposite numbers at Headquarters, the Project Group is a quite separate command comparable in status to a Region, and all staff take their orders from the Chief Project Engineer.

The Project Engineers—seven at the time of writing in the Southern Group—form the basis of the organisation.   A Project Engineer is in theory in charge of just one project, but he might have three or even four in the interim stage reached at the time of writing—when the jobs taken over from the Divisions still remained to be completed and before the total number of stations in course of planning had been reduced to the level expected in future.   Each Project Engineer has a staff of qualified mechanical and electrical engineers, and in some cases an Assistant Project Engineer—all at the Project Group Headquarters.   The Project Engineers also control the very important Resident Site Engineers, who are permanently on site throughout the construction period.   There is usually no separate group of civil engineers for each project, because, as we saw, consultants are normally employed.   Instead there is a fairly small staff of civil engineers serving the Group as a whole.   They, with the Administrative Officer's section (which includes finance and accounting), the contracts staff, the drawing office and the programmes section, provide service as required for each of the Project Engineers—and for the Chief Project Engineer in co-ordinating work for the whole Group. The Programmes Officer has very important functions in this respect.   He receives the 'Master Programme' as soon as the project is formally handed over to the Group and is responsible for compiling at the start the more detailed 'Contracts Planning Chart' and other programmes showing just when the various stages of planning and construction ought to start and finish.

There is a Resident Site Engineer for each station under construction, and his staff, status and salary vary somewhat according to the size of station.   Projects are in fact graded into three classes for this purpose.   Every Resident Engineer, however, has a mechanical, a civil and an electrical engineer under him, and each of these three will have one, two or three assistants. The junior assistants on the larger sites are occupied whole-time with inspection.   The size of the civil engineering team will depend on the extent to which consultants are employed. Where they are employed for any considerable section of the work or all of it they will themselves provide a resident engineer, who will be responsible directly to the C.E.G.B. Resident Engineer.   In addition to the various specialists there is normally a C.E.G.B. Progress Engineer on site, who may have an assistant and who will be occupied whole-time with questions of co-ordination and progress control—maintenance and checking of control charts and so forth—over the whole field of work —civil, mechanical and electrical.

This organisation of Resident Engineers is crucial to the C.E.G.B.'s whole system for the control of power station construction.   It has been developed and expanded considerably from the system which formed part of the Divisional organisation under the C.E.A.   The Resident Engineers and their staffs require a very high degree of practical and theoretical engineering knowledge and also force and drive.   They must have an understanding of the technical difficulties that can arise during any stage of the construction and assembly of very expensive and very advanced types of plant and structures— including nuclear plant—and also an ability to smooth out difficulties between the many groups of people whose co-operation is needed to complete an extremely complex programme. Some of the forty main contractors will be working mainly or wholly on site, and others will do most of the work in their own factories, but nearly all will be involved to some extent in delivery and construction on site.   So each of their timetables has to be co-ordinated with those of the others.   The Resident Engineer and his staff (fifteen or more in all, including the clerks and typists) have semi-permanent offices on the site throughout the four to five years construction period.   Good modern prefabricated buildings rather than huts are therefore normally provided, or sometimes a brick building which can be used later as part of the station.

Control is exercised by meetings, by individual contacts with contractors and by constant supervision around the site itself. There are normally three series of regular progress meetings:

(a) Between the Resident Site Engineer and each contractor's representatives separately—weekly or fortnightly.

(b) A general meeting with all contractors' representatives together—monthly.

(c) A meeting of C.E.G.B. staff—Project Group and Site Engineers—at the Project Group Headquarters—monthly.

In addition there are, of course, frequent—almost daily—meetings and small discussions with individual contractor's representatives or groups of them. The monthly site meetings ((b) above) are usually chaired by the Resident Site Engineer, but the Project Engineer will attend and 'sit in', possibly accompanied by the Programmes Engineer or other engineers from the Project Group Headquarters. Some Project Engineers, however, prefer to preside at these meetings themselves. They include all contractors on site at the time (or shortly about to start there). Most contractors send head office staff as well as their permanent site representatives.

These site meetings are primarily for co-ordination of time-tables and checking of progress, but many matters of common interest, particularly safety measures, are discussed. So many different contractors' jobs—such as foundations, steel framework, boilers, pipework and water and oil pumps—are physically interconnected and interdependent that constant co-ordination is required. Construction and testing have to be intricately phased in together. Meetings may be largely occupied with settling dates of tests and interconnections of different jobs, enquiring when essential subsidiary equipment will be delivered or when one contractor can make room for another. The following are random extracts from actual minutes of such meetings:

> Mr. —— [the pipework contractors' representative] said he was concerned about the delivery of the boiler stop valves and strainers in time for the hydraulic test. He was under the impression that a modification had to be carried out to the strainers and he had only been made aware of this two days previously. To date he had had no time to contact . . . [other contractors] for details. Following delivery to site of these items eight welds had to be done, which constituted approximately

three weeks' work. He said he favoured having these welds gamma-rayed prior to the hydraulic test. Mr. —— [C.E.G.B.] promised to investigate the delivery situation regarding the stop valves and strainers. . . .

Mr. —— [representing contractors for instruments etc.] stated that the steam flow indicator pipework had not been designed in accordance with the recommendations of his company and in his opinion it required modification. It was agreed to discuss this matter outside the meeting . . . welding of the steam main was complete and results of the X-rays were awaited. As soon as these were received the whole main would be released for lagging. Welding of the flow meter pipework was still outstanding. . . .

All these regular meetings with contractors and various special meetings are formally recorded in minutes which fix responsibility for action on all outstanding points on named individuals —either contractors' or C.E.G.B. staff.

If unexpected developments occur, particularly as regards civil engineering work on or under the ground, Site Engineers may have to decide as to what revised conditions the Board can accept, and such decisions could save—or cost—the Board very considerable sums of money or periods of time. Site Engineers also have to decide whether to accept and certify as satisfactory the amount and quality of equipment delivered and constructional and other work completed on site. These certificates in the case of civil and constructional engineering work form the basis of payments to contractors and the whole system of control of progress and out-turn of capital expenditure.

At nuclear station sites the work of co-ordination is very similar, but there are different methods. The 'consortia' maintained their own progress control systems and their own Resident Site Engineers and very large staffs. On one site they had seventy-nine in all, including about thirty civil and about twenty mechanical engineers. Apparently their object was to give a large number of engineers training and experience so that the consortium would be well equipped for other nuclear-power-station projects at home or overseas. Despite this, the C.E.G.B. is at every nuclear site providing its own Resident Site Engineers, with the status at least equal to those at the non-nuclear sites, but with fewer staff—for three reasons:

o

(a) certification of quantity and quality of work done;
(b) additional check on progress;
(c) to give experience and training to C.E.G.B. staff.

This last point would be of exceptional importance if the Board ever decided to have nuclear stations designed and constructed under arrangements similar to those employed for the non-nuclear stations.

The design of the nuclear reactors themselves and their associated equipment and the supply and loading up of the fuel and the moderator material directly involve the Atomic Energy Authority, partly as advisers and consultants to the C.E.G.B. and partly as advisers, consultants and sub-contractors to the consortia.   The A.E.A. do not maintain staff permanently on C.E.G.B. construction sites, but their officers make frequent visits, normally at least weekly during the whole period of construction.

The Station Superintendent and his staff who will ultimately run the station (whether nuclear or non-nuclear) usually arrive on site about twelve months before the first generating set is due to come into commission, and thereafter they attend all progress meetings.   They are in no sense responsible to the Resident Site Engineer or the Project Group, but to the Chief Generation Engineer (at Division).   For each project a Commissioning Panel is set up about six months before the first item of plant is due to be commissioned.   This comprises the Station Superintendent and other representatives of the Division and the Project Engineer, Resident Site Engineer and other Project Group officers, and is responsible for programming and planning the actual commissioning of plant —taking into account safety of men and plant, making sure that the various staff and services will be available when needed and generally that the work is carried out stage by stage under proper control.

It is most unlikely that there are in this country any other individual capital construction projects—except very occasionally in the oil, chemical, steel and railway industries—in any way comparable in size and complexity with power stations and coal mines.   The Coal Board also have site engineers for very large colliery schemes, and in particular for the surface work thereof; but their organisation seems not quite so elaborate as that of the C.E.G.B., as a large section of the work can be entrusted to the Colliery Manager. It is, therefore, probable that the C.E.G.B.'s site organisation is almost unique. In view of the enormous importance of time and cost control in these projects, it would seem to represent money extremely well spent. Indeed, the tendency of recent years seems to have been to strengthen the site organisation, and possibly the limit to which this process could usefully be taken has not yet been reached. The largest and most successful civil engineering contractors are understood to attribute much of their superiority over their smaller competitors to the employment of really high-grade site supervision staff. With the very much larger investments of capital at stake in power stations than in most civil engineering works the C.E.G.B. must obviously want to spare nothing within reason which can improve the efficiency of their site control work.

(d) *Construction on Site*

The Herbert Committee[3] in 1955 gave the normal time between start of site works of power stations and commissioning (presumably of first sets) as four and a quarter years, and they seem to have thought this (and the preceding periods of planning) too long. It is understood, however, that such difficulties as shortage of materials, labour disputes and so on can easily extend the period a further six months or a year. Moreover, in non-nuclear stations it will now take four years to commission the first generating set only. In the post-war years the commissioning of successive sets was often spread over long periods—sometimes a year passing between each. The aim now is to complete a station as quickly as possible, with the intervals between the three to six successive sets varying between four and nine months, according to size. It is also hoped to reduce the period between start on site and first commissioning. The timetable for plant manufacture has to be fitted in with these constructional timetables, the controlling factor being the time for making boilers and turbo-alternators. The Herbert Report said that in 1955 a boiler had to be ordered four years before commissioning (to allow two and a quarter

[3] Report, p. 24, para. 87.

years for manufacture and one and three-quarters for erection on site) and a turbo-alternator three years before (two years for manufacture and one year for erection). These times are still likely to obtain owing to the greater size and complexity of modern generating sets.

In a non-nuclear power station scheme there will be some forty or more main contractors (apart from sub-contractors) providing plant and machinery and civil and other engineering work on site. Most of the plant manufacturers have to do some work on the site, and the largest items of plant—turbo-alternators, the boilers and nuclear reactors—are too large to be completely constructed anywhere else. For the largest stations, both nuclear and non-nuclear, there will be at the peak nearer 2,000 than 1,000 men working on site. So much of the most important work of constructing both nuclear or non-nuclear power stations depends on *manual operations*, despite the very advanced types of plant and the increased mechanisation, particularly in civil engineering, of recent years. One of the most important jobs is the construction of the massive steelwork which encloses the turbine house and encloses and supports the boilers and the nuclear reactors. Despite all the mechanical lifting equipment, this steelwork is actually put together by riveters working very largely individually and climbing about on the girders in mid-air. This work is skilled and highly specialised. At one site a dispute between the contractors and their riveters and other steel erection staff cost the C.E.G.B. a delay of six months. Perhaps even more important, especially at the nuclear stations, is the welding. This is skilled and very arduous work, but very high wages are reported to be earned by men who are prepared to stick to it for long hours. Some may work sixty to seventy hours a week. We have seen how nuclear reactors are enclosed in pressure vessels composed of great spheres of steel. These are far too large to be constructed anywhere but on site, and this is done by high-grade welding. Not more than about sixteen men can work simultaneously on one of these spheres. To counterbalance their high wages is the fact that they are liable to be dismissed from all further work on the site if a fault is detected by the radiographic tests which must be applied to every weld. Any fault, however small, can result in quite large sections of work having all to be done again, with a delay of perhaps a couple of months or more.   At one nuclear station site some months of delay was caused by a dispute between a contractor and his welders.   The welders were said to have wanted certain rates of pay and allowances to continue while there was no welding to be done and to have claimed that the management should have so organised the work that welding was continuous—or else made compensation payments.   The site was fairly remote, and the men would have probably had to travel some considerable distance, perhaps right across the country, to find other comparable work.   This case is not quoted to comment in any way on the merits of the dispute (which may well have involved many other considerations on both sides), but to indicate how much depends on co-ordination of the many groups of men (of many trades and firms) who work together on these remote sites.   Despite all the scientific and engineering complexities, the problems must be basically human and—whatever the responsibilities of the contractors—the C.E.G.B. is bound to be deeply concerned with them.

For instance, because questions of meals, tea breaks and so forth are of such importance in the timing of any organised work and can so easily become the subject of disputes, it is now usual for the Board to provide a canteen for all contractors and other workers on all their power-station sites—except at the nuclear sites, where this is done by the consortium or one of its principal members.   Problems of living accommodation are increasingly important as sites get more remote.   It is usual for a contractor—generally the principal civil engineering contractor—to provide a large camp where the bulk of the men, probably over 1,000, can live.   At a nuclear site the consortium may itself build some hundreds of permanent houses for certain grades of its own employees, and these will later be available for sale to C.E.G.B. staff.   Arrangements also have to be made with Local Authorities for more houses, both for people involved in the construction of the station and for permanent staff afterwards.   Much depends on the goodwill of the Local Authority, and housing problems tend to be more serious for the more senior staff.

As power stations go to more rural areas, relationships with local communities become more important, and might well affect not only the progress of construction of a station but also its efficient working afterwards. These problems may be aggravated by the public controversies that usually precede the selection of a site, and in the case of nuclear stations by fears about radio-activity. Workers on a large power-station site may come in large numbers from any part of the United Kingdom or Ireland, and with no great fault on anybody's part, it is easy to imagine how difficulties could arise. At one nuclear-station site it was said that the good local relationships and avoidance of serious incidents owed a great deal to the personality of the single policeman responsible for law and order throughout the area concerned. But clearly, heavy responsibilities rest on all the C.E.G.B. senior staff concerned with the local side of station construction, and they appear to be well aware that the problems of these vast operations are almost as much human as engineering.

(e) *Some Continuing Problems of Organisation*

While it seems clear that the C.E.G.B. subdivision of generating station planning work between the Planning Department and the Design and Construction Department at Headquarters and the three Project Groups represents an improvement on the C.E.A. system, there are some facts and considerations which make one wonder whether it will still be considered the best form of organisation in a few years time. We have seen[4] that from 1964 onwards there may each year be only two new stations having their first sets commissioned and another three having their last sets commissioned. Allowing two years for planning, three years for construction up to commissioning of the first set and another year for final completion, these figures might suggest that within four or five years there will only be at any given time about four stations in course of detailed planning and eight in course of construction—a dozen in all. This implies each Group working on only about four projects at a time compared with over a dozen when the Groups were first set up. In 1959 C.E.G.B. officers thought that the number of projects per Group might fall below ten in 1963. There seemed to be clear indications of a further fall after that. No decisions had been made in 1959 about allocations to particular

[4] Table X, p. 159.

Groups of the schemes starting in later years, but even if the numbers quoted prove to be under-estimated, the trend of diminishing numbers seems inescapable in the absence of some really sharp increase in the rate of load growth. If no change is made in the organisation there will be working on this diminishing number of schemes not only three complete Project Groups with all their common services but also the Headquarters Branches of the Design and Construction Department and of other Headquarters Departments.

The Project Groups cannot be described as particularly local organisations. Their boundaries are flexible and drawn primarily with a view to equalising loads of work. The area of the Southern Project Group already includes many places which can scarcely be visited without a stay overnight. It would surely only be marginally more inconvenient to visit, say, Trawsfynyd from North London than from Manchester. The reason for setting up three Project Groups originally presumably rested on the belief that if the number was less than three the Group or Groups would be too large and unwieldy. If, however, none of the Groups is unwieldy at the present time while they are handling a dozen or more cases each, surely when the total number is reduced to a dozen a single Group to handle them all should not be unwieldy either.[5]

What would be the other advantages and disadvantages of one Project Group as opposed to three? There would be staff economy in civil engineering, contracts, programming, administration and finance—all now organised as common services outside the Project Teams and together comprising about three-quarters of a Project Group's headquarters staff. The Administrative, Accounting and Finance staff alone comprise about one-third of each total. Amalgamation might mean a loss of the initiative and original ideas which can be presumed to come from a diversity of people and organisations tackling the same problems—but would the price for diversity still be worth paying? Would there be a balance of advantage or disadvantage in the same groups of people always dealing

[5] There seems to be no suggestion of any future station's capacity exceeding 1,300 MW—the maximum now being planned. New types of nuclear stations will bring more complex planning problems no doubt—but surely it will in any case be necessary for such new developments to be centrally controlled.

with the same groups of outside contractors, consultants and so on?

The idea of a single Project Group, however, immediately produces other problems of organisation. There are some lines of division which do not seem very clear between the Project Groups and the Headquarters Departments, particularly the Design and Construction Department and the Purchasing and Contracts Department. For instance, the importance of the efficiency of design of major items of equipment like nuclear reactors, boilers and turbo-generators—*all* of which now always cost over a million pounds *each*—is obviously of such enormous financial consequence that it must be kept under the closest possible study by specialists all the time. These specialists will need to accumulate all the information they can—including the hypothetical costs of alternative designs—for the whole or parts—even when such alternative designs might not be practicable in the particular station under consideration. On the other hand, an organisation like a Project Group, directly responsible for a particular job, does want to feel it is in effective control at all points and able to deal with contractors and other outside interests on that basis. Yet again there are, no doubt, certain commercial and financial principles which the Board as a whole wishes to maintain in its dealings with contractors so that some important point in one set of negotiations has not been prejudiced in advance by concessions which have been made in a former case. Having therefore achieved a single Project Group, would there not then be a case for eventually amalgamating it with the rest of the Design and Construction Department's Branches at Headquarters? Obviously such a proposal would involve considerable internal problems whose seriousness and extent an outsider cannot easily assess. On the other hand, if in any case it had been decided to combine the Project Groups into one, the scope for overlapping and friction between two large central organisations with very similar functions might be very much greater than any scope there may be for overlapping between the Headquarters Departments and Branches and the present Project Groups. The case for one central unit only seems strong. A final solution might partly turn on the extent to which common service staffs and staffs in the Project Groups and at Headquarters carrying out similar or related functions could be combined and assimilated with any overall substantial reduction in numbers. There would also be the question of how far any changes in organisation would make easier any interchanges of staff between different functions and how far such interchanges would be desirable in themselves and helpful in career planning and training for higher management. At present the degree of interchange between different engineering groups and functions seems rather limited.

However all this may be—the C.E.G.B. have clearly in their Project Groups produced a highly original solution to the problem of centralisation versus decentralisation in major capital construction. The basic feature of this solution is the principle confirmed by experience in the Coal Board and other large organisations, *that major capital construction programmes seldom go ahead at a proper speed and in a proper manner unless their supervision is given to strong and distinct Departments with highly qualified staff freed from all other responsibilities.*

(f) *Water-power Stations in North Scotland*

Water-power generating stations are in some ways more distinct from all others, even than nuclear stations. They have certain features which are very interesting from the economic and organisational point of view. The great bulk of British hydro-electric capacity has been created by the North of Scotland Hydro-Electric Board, and was still expanding very substantially at the time of writing.

TABLE XII[6]

WATER GENERATING PLANT IN NORTH SCOTLAND

	Installed capacity (MW)	Average output million units per annum
Taken over in 1947 by the N.S.H.E.B. from former Companies. Commissioned 1944–58. Total in operation in 1958	813	2,293
At constructional stage	169	432
In course of promotion	448	527
Under survey	224	765

Scottish hydro stations are smaller than English steam stations built in recent years. The largest now working is of 130 MW

[6] *North of Scotland Hydro-Electric Board Report and Accounts*, 1958, p. 2.

capacity, and the largest proposed 450 MW. Individual generating sets in stations range from about 40 MW to less than 1 MW, and there may be one, two, three or four sets in a station.

Recent complete schemes have varied in cost between £5 million and £9 million. The proportion of different kinds of work involved in constructing them is indicated by the following table:

TABLE XIII[7]

CAPITAL EXPENDITURE ON HYDRO-ELECTRIC
GENERATION SCHEMES IN THE NORTH OF SCOTLAND

	Expenditure on all schemes during 1958 (£000)	Board's total expenditure up to 1st December 1958 (£000)
Land and compensation . . .	143	966
Building and civil engineering works .	9,196	117,047
Plant and machinery, pipelines, etc. .	2,234	14,578
TOTALS .	11,573	132,591

The great bulk of the cost of the stations goes in the civil engineering work required to collect and canalise the water. When a scheme is being surveyed the problem is to get as large a potential catchment area as possible from which rainfall will drain into one reservoir. The natural catchment area is enlarged by a series of small dams and diversion aqueducts (in tunnels or otherwise), which may total 20 miles or so, and the reservoir is made by the construction of the main dam, which may be 100 or 200 feet high and over 1,000 feet long. From the reservoir the main aqueduct leads to the power station by tunnels through mountain-sides down steel pipelines some 7 feet in diameter and descending perhaps 1,500 feet.

Water generating sets can be brought into operation in a matter of minutes—which makes them particularly suitable for carrying peak loads and for emergencies. They can be installed in the station in successive periods, but relatively little capital expenditure can be thus saved in the first period. The main aqueduct must be complete from the outset and also the

[7] *North of Scotland Hydro-Electric Board Report and Accounts*, 1958, p. 35.

bulk of the main dam, although its height can be raised later. It is very hard to quote typical periods for the planning and construction.   Much depends on the time taken to survey and to acquire various rights in land and water.   Construction work of this kind in any remote mountain area is, of course, particularly vulnerable to the weather and to unforeseen difficulties which may be discovered after work has started—for instance in tunnelling.   It is now considered that hydro-electric schemes should normally be going into commission in about three to five years from the time Parliamentary approval has been obtained.   One could hardly quote any typical overall time for the whole process, including the difficult stages before Parliamentary approval.   In 1957 certain schemes started in 1948 were still under construction.[8]

The North of Scotland Hydro-Electric Board[9] differs from the other Electricity Boards in Great Britain in policy objectives, in its internal organisation, in the equipment with which it works and in the nature of its territory.   It was started in 1944 to help in the general rehabilitation of the Highlands by exploiting their natural water-power resources for electricity generation and using the proceeds to develop rural electricity distribution.   The Board's task contrasts with that of industries which have had to be careful not to lay down more capital than will produce a fair return.   The limit of the Board's production is what the South can take, and does not depend simply on demand in its own District.   Its problems have, perhaps, been like those of the Coal Board's first decade, when the whole country was clamouring for coal and the problem was just how quickly the resources could be opened up.   Of course, the Coal Board had to decide which mines to develop first to get the quickest and most economic results (not always the same thing), and the Hydro-Electric Board also has such priority problems. But the overriding need has been to develop the natural

<hr>

[8] House of Commons, *Report of the Select Committee on Nationalised Industries*, 1957, Q887.

[9] See the articles in *Public Administration*, Vol. XXXI, Autumn 1953, by H. A. Clegg and T. E. Chester; *Scottish Journal of Political Economy*, Vol. III, February 1956, 'Electricity in the North of Scotland', by D. L. Munby, and *ibid.*, Vol. IV, February 1957, 'Electricity in the North of Scotland', by Sir Murdock McDonald and Prof. J. M. Kay; *Report of the Select Committee on Nationalised Industries*, October 1957; and House of Commons Debate, 27th January 1958.

resources as quickly as possible and, for a start (like the Coal Board), to find out just what resources there were.

Both the Coal Board and the Hydro Board started with broad estimates only of their potential resources, and one of the latter's most important tasks was to make meteorological, geological and civil engineering surveys. The Cooper Committee in 1942 put the potential hydro-electric capacity of the Highlands at 4,000 million units[10] annually on the basis of some seventy schemes. The Board first estimated it as about 6,000 million units annually and later increased this estimate to 10,000 million.[11] By the end of 1958 plant with a capacity of 2,293 million units was working in North Scotland and a further 1,724 million units capacity was under construction, promotion or survey—a total of 4,017 million units. Subject to the very important assumption—which is now being questioned—that water power is and will remain cheaper than coal, oil or nuclear power—the Board seem to have no great problem of how much capacity to provide. They could go on for some years till they had developed every potentially economic scheme. The only problem would be which to develop first. The Cooper Committee could not foresee any time when steam would be competitive with water power. Whatever the technical justification of this view in 1944, the position has changed radically since and become much more complex. As we have seen (pp. 145–146), great improvements in efficiency in steam generation have been made and are still continuing, nuclear energy has been applied to steam-raising, and interest rates have risen. These and amortisation periods are particularly important in hydro-electric generation, as the bulk of its cost consists of capital charges. Relatively little maintenance cost is incurred.

How long in future will it still be worthwhile building new hydro-electric stations? It is not sufficient to compare the greatly reduced costs of generation at coal-fired steam stations with the cost of water generation: transmission costs and transmission losses have to be considered. Moreover, so much

[10] This measure has been considered best for hydro-electric schemes rather than kilowatt capacity, because the potential power can be stored, so what matters is how much can be used in a year—not simultaneously. *Report on Hydro-Electric Development in Scotland*, 1942, Cmd. 6406, p. 14, para. 33.

[11] *Report of Select Committee on Nationalized Industries*, 1957, p. 29, Q225.

depends on load factors. On the whole, nuclear stations and the most modern coal- or oil-fired stations should operate on base loads and hydro-electric stations on peak loads. All this makes comparisons extremely complicated. The C.E.G.B. now makes the most complex calculations, with the aid of a staff of mathematicians and a computer, to decide the extent and location of its future generating capacity. It takes into account such things as capital charges, costs of fuel and its transport and the alternative, or supplementary, costs of main transmission. Perhaps some such calculations may be needed to determine future policies and programmes of hydro-electric generation construction. The Select Committee on the Nationalised Industries reported in 1957:

> Your Committee did not attempt to adjudge whether or not the [North of Scotland] Board is placing too much reliance on hydro-electricity; they merely point out that on the weight of the evidence given to them, the question exists.

A new type of hydro-electric scheme has recently been developed—'pumped storage'. Such schemes involve water generating plant worked by a 'head' of water from a very considerable height, but with a relatively small reservoir. This reservoir is filled by water pumped up to it by electric power (from a remote steam station) at night or other off-peak periods, from the level of the generating station. The water is then used to generate electricity in the day or other peak periods. The net effect is, therefore, to enable steam generating stations, particularly nuclear stations, to be used more economically. The pumping may be done by a reversible apparatus which acts as an electric motor and pump when the water is going up at night and as a turbo-alternator when it is coming down by day. This system is most suitable for working in conjunction with nuclear stations, which ought to be worked at high load factors because their fuel 'burns' continuously. Already the C.E.G.B. are building a 300-MW pumped storage scheme at Ffestiniog in North Wales[12] and the North of Scotland Board another at Loch Awe in Argyllshire of 400 MW capacity (greater than that of any of their other stations). This is due to start working in 1965 in conjunction with increases in the

[12] To work in conjunction with the nuclear power station at Trawsfynydd.

generating capacity of the South of Scotland Board (principally their nuclear station at Hunterston). It seems likely that pumped storage schemes will provide the best answer to the problems of the peak loads and of getting the best possible value not only out of nuclear but also out of other steam stations. Pumped storage, however, seems likely to be limited to rather mountainous sites, which are rare in Great Britain. One would expect most of them to be in Wales and Scotland, especially the Highlands. The Select Committee on the Nationalised Industries said:[13]

> they were impressed by an expert's (Professor Kay's) view that the Board's future policy . . . should be directed increasingly towards the construction of large capacity pump storage schemes.

All this would seem to point to the likelihood of closer collaboration and joint forward planning in the future not only between the two Scottish Boards but also between both of them and the C.E.G.B.

The fact that the North Scotland Board have nearly as much generating capacity in course of planning and construction as they have already operating will help us to appreciate certain features of the Board's constitution and organisation, which differ from those of the South Scotland and English Electricity Boards. A very large part of the North Scotland Board's job is to commission and run hydro-electric generation schemes. They are preponderantly civil engineering schemes designed by consultants, built by contractors and requiring very few men to run and maintain them. This may partly explain the relatively small size of the Board's total staff, which is referred to in the article by Messrs. Clegg and Chester, already cited.[14] These authors praise the Board for this in contrast with other nationalised industries, which they say they have themselves previously criticised as too big and over-centralised. We may doubt, however, if they are really comparing like with like. The planning of the Northern Board's new generation capacity involves surveying the resources of the Scottish Highlands as a whole and selecting in reasonable order the most economic and practicable projects. There could therefore be no question of dividing up the Northern Board's District into smaller sub-

[13] *Report*, 1957, para. 42, p. xii.   [14] p. 209 note.

units each working out its own constructional programmes—
even if there were a sufficient load of work for such separate
sub-units.[15]   The preliminary surveying of potential schemes
is carried out by the Board's own staff, but as soon as they are
considered in detail, outside consultants are employed.   The
Board usually employs separate consultants in:

(a) civil and hydraulic work; and
(b) mechanical and electrical work.

Some small schemes have been carried out by the Board's own
staff with no consultants.   For the building work professional
architects are separately commissioned.   The Board's staff
hold regular progress meetings with consultants and contractors
during construction, but not during the planning period.   The
consultants are responsible for providing resident staff to supervise work on site.   It is interesting in this connection to note
that their Report for 1958 says that examination of sites on the
East Coast has continued, so that they can consider the desira-
bility of bringing a nuclear station into use in the late 1960s.
Presumably to do this they would need to draw considerably
on the advice of the C.E.G.B. and the U.K. Atomic Energy
Authority.

The Select Committee noted certain very great differences
between the estimates and the final costs of the first hydro-electric
schemes.   These are shown in Table XIV.

The Secretary of State for Scotland has said that these dis-
crepancies were explained partly by the general rise in prices
and partly because 'the Board agrees that some inaccurate
estimating had taken place in the early days before the necessary experience in post-war conditions had been gained'.   He
said that the Board were confident that the final costs for current
schemes would turn out much closer to the original estimates.[16]
It can be seen that considerable periods—between six and ten
years—elapse between the dates of the estimates and the dates

---

[15] In fact, not only the planning but also the operation of generating stations is
generally controlled direct from the Board's Headquarters. The only degree of
decentralisation on the generating side is that the Area Managers of Aberdeen and
Dundee control the detailed operation of the steam stations there and the super-
intendents of some of the other larger stations control also a group of smaller ones
and are responsible for their maintenance and repairs.
[16] Hansard, Vol. 581, 27th January 1958, cols. 107–108.

of the final completion, and indeed the Select Committee were told in 1957 that work was still in progress on two contracts which had been entered into in 1948.

TABLE XIV

ORIGINAL ESTIMATES AND APPROXIMATE FINAL COSTS OF HYDRO-ELECTRIC SCHEMES OF WHICH THE FINAL COSTS ARE KNOWN WITH REASONABLE ACCURACY[17]

Constructional Scheme	Date on which estimate was made	Published estimate £	Year in which scheme was substantially completed	Approximate Final Cost £
1. Sloy, Lochalsh and Morar	Mid 1944	4,600,000	1951 (Sloy)	8,870,000
3. Fannich	Late 1944	960,000	1955	3,500,000
4. Cowal	Late 1944	570,000	1953	1,680,000
7. Mullardoch–Fasnakyle–Affric	Mid 1946	4,800,000	1952	9,780,000
8. Lussa (generation only)	Mid 1946	358,000	1952	730,000
15. Gaur	Early 1947	650,000	1954	1,040,000
20. Ullapool	Mid 1947	200,000	1955	460,000
22. Sloy Extensions	Late 1947	285,000	1952	560,000
24. Garry	Early 1948	4,850,000	1956	9,060,000
27. Allt-na-Lairige	Early 1948	620,000	1956	1,630,000
61. Kilmelfort	Mid 1950	458,000	1956	790,000

Notes: 1. Scheme 1 includes Lochalsh and Morar, which are small local projects.
2. These approximate final costs do not include Interest During Construction, although about 5½ per cent of the estimate figure represents such interest.

In 1957 the Board had not been successful in arranging contracts on a fixed-price basis—a policy which the Government was then trying to get introduced by public authorities generally.[18]   The Board's General Manager in answer to several questions by Members of the Select Committee said:

We have tried on several occasions to have a fixed contract basis and on each occasion it has been necessary to enter into an adjustment with the contractors, although one is still running where there is no variation on the materials.   It is a very sub-

[17] Annex C to Appendix II of *Report*, p. 197. John Hughes in his pamphlet *Nationalized Industries in a Mixed Economy* (Fabian Society, 1960) analyses the figures quoted in relation to changing money values and calculates that some schemes have, *in real terms*, cost between 20 and 40 per cent above the original estimates.

[18] *Report of Select Committee on Nationalized Industries*, 1957, Evidence, Q884.

stantial contract and I have no doubt in my mind that we will have to come to some arrangements with the contractor about it yet, simply because the increases have far outstripped what he could reasonably have expected to have had to pay on materials in the period.

He added that:

> The Board did not have support from local and other authorities in Scotland in introducing fixed-price contracts as the Secretary of State had asked, and in a few cases where we tried ourselves we have, as I have said, had to make adjustments in the end and go on to a variation contract.   It has been disappointing.

The Board has bought most of its equipment on open competitive tenders, except what are probably the most expensive items—water turbines and water-wheel alternators.   At an early stage the Board encouraged firms which could make water turbines to establish factories in Scotland.   Three firms did so, and the Board allocated its orders between them, using its mechanical engineering consultants to check prices.   Somewhat similar contracts for water-wheel alternators are allocated between the firms considered capable of undertaking the work, but in this case the Board only *take into account* the extent to which the firms manufacture in Scotland, and do not absolutely confine themselves to Scottish-produced equipment. The Select Committee noted this procedure and the conditions under which it had been introduced.   The Board were providing a completely new market for this sort of equipment so far as the United Kingdom was concerned, and special steps had to be taken to get the necessary manufacturing capacity developed.   The Committee, however, considered that this had now been reasonably well done and the Board should put all contracts out to open competitive tender.

(g) *Main Transmission in England and Wales*

The planning and development problems concerned with main transmission equipment are easy for the outsider to overlook—the Herbert Report did not discuss them at all.   Yet although the annual capital investment in main transmission represents only about a seventh of the total annual investment of the C.E.G.B., it is very large indeed in comparison with that

P

of most other concerns—public and private.   For example, it exceeds that of the L.C.C.[19]

TABLE XV[20]

CAPITAL ASSETS:
MAIN TRANSMISSION (ENGLAND AND WALES 1958–59)

	Total Capital Assets 31st March 1959 (depreciation not deducted) (£ million)	Additions during 1958–59 (£ million)
Land and buildings . . .	1·5	0·1
Overhead lines	61·6	10·3
Underground and other cables .	21·7	2·3
Transformer and switching stations and control rooms . . .	123·7	18·0
Miscellaneous	0·8	0·1
TOTAL .	209·3	30·8

Broadly the main transmission network consists of the Supergrid (275 kV) and the Grid (132 kV), with a few lines or cables at 66 kV and even lower voltages.

The 275-kV Grid, including the lines, towers and foundations, now very broadly costs about £25,000 per route mile (double circuit) and the 132-kV Grid about £8,000–£10,000 per route mile.   If, however, there is enough electricity to be transmitted the 275-kV system is very much more economic. Indeed, there is the possibility of transmission at higher voltages.   The C.E.G.B.'s Annual Report for 1958–59 speaks of its predecessor, the C.E.A., having designed the Supergrid towers for possible future operation at 380 kV,[21] and Sir Christopher Hinton recently said that Swedish and Russian lines were being worked at 400 kV and American (experimentally) at 750 kV.   He believed the C.E.G.B. must develop transmission 'around 500 kV' in the future; but conditions in this country were more difficult owing to atmospheric pollution, and the research required might take 7–10 years.[22]   It would be many

[19] L.C.C. Annual Estimates, 1959–60, p. 6.
[20] *Central Electricity Generating Board Report and Accounts*, 1958–59, Statement 13, pp. 122–123.
[21] C.E.G.B. Report and Accounts 1958–59, p. 26, para. 128.
[22] Since this was written the C.E.G.B. have announced in their 1960/61 Report (p. 3, para. 13) that from 1965 they will introduce 400-kV transmission by re-insulating 275-kV lines and operating them with new transformers and switchgear.

times[23] more expensive to provide main transmission cables underground compared with overhead, and normally this is only done in closely built-up areas. As Sir Christopher succinctly put it, 'The overhead transmission line uses air as an insulator and no insulator can be as cheap as air'.[24]

It has for some years been the normal practice to have transformer stations and switching stations in the open[25] and, therefore, they are now largely electrical engineering jobs (apart from foundations and concrete framework). We may take as an example a large combined switching and transformer station, built in recent years, at an intersection point of different 275-kV Supergrid lines, with a connection also with the 132-kV Grid. The site is of about 14 acres, about half for the 275-kV switchgear and the transformers for stepping down from 275 to 132 kV, and the other half for the 132-kV switchgear. The four transformers are enclosed in steel casing about 20 feet high, with oil for insulation and cooling being circulated by pumps. Each weighs about 250 tons, and so needs heavy foundations. The transformers and both sets of switchgear are worked from one small control room on the site.

Such a station would take about two and a half years to complete from start of work on site, but part of the equipment would be working within about eighteen months. The dates of delivery of the equipment from the first year might vary from twelve months to three years according to their size and the state of trade at the time. The cost might be roughly as follows:

Civil engineering	£225,000
Transformers	500,000
275-kV switchgear	660,000
132-kV switchgear	350,000
Cables	60,000
Meters, lighting and heating . .	10,000
	£1,800,000

[23] Very broadly about sixteen times in the case of 275-kV lines.

[24] Sir Christopher Hinton in a paper read to the Royal Society of Arts on 25th November 1959.

[25] But buildings may be necessary if a transformer station has to be sited in a built-up or at least a residential area, in order to prevent people nearby being disturbed by the humming noise most large modern transformers produce.

One contract would cover all civil engineering work—foundations, site works and concrete frames—and possibly another for all electrical equipment—or more probably one for transformers and one for switchgear. A C.E.G.B. site engineer would supervise local construction but not stay permanently on site. He might control one large and one or more smaller schemes simultaneously.

We can take as another example a switching and transformer station taking current from the 132-kV Grid and providing a point of supply to an Area Board (who would themselves take it away from there at 33 kV and 11 kV). The C.E.G.B. would have purchased the whole site—about 3 or 4 acres—and allocated part to the Area Board. The C.E.G.B. would provide the 132-kV switchgear and the transformers for stepping down to 33 kV. The Area Board would have switchgear for distributing the current at 33 kV, and some perhaps at 11 kV— this involving another transformer. The Area Board would also provide a building with remotely operated control equipment. The whole station might cost between £300,000 and £500,000, with the contract arrangements for each part similar to those for the larger station.

The B.E.A. took over the 132-kV Grid and its transformer, switching and control stations from the C.E.B. as a complete system in 1948. Then, and for some years after, the main emphasis was on power stations. When, however, the B.E.A./ C.E.A. had got the measure of its first problems of generation planning it put in hand the first stage of the 275-kV 'Super' Grid. Since then special needs for further links at 275 kV have emerged, partly as a result of the nuclear-power programme and its relatively remote sites. There has been a good deal more emphasis, therefore, in the last few years on main transmission.

The prime function of the main transmission network is to bring a supply of electricity by the most reliable and economic means to the various points where the Area Boards need it. There may be a score, or even two or three score, of such bulk supply points in each Area. As the Area Board has to meet increased demand, it has to reinforce, extend and reshape its local distribution system. This may often involve asking for new bulk supply points or for increase in the capacity of existing bulk supply points.   There may often be a problem of how far and how fast to reinforce, extend and rationalise the electricity supplies of some very extensive district.   This may well involve a choice between two or more alternatives, and in particular a choice between schemes which require most of the extension to be carried out, on the one hand, on the main transmission system or, on the other, mainly on the local distribution network.   These alternatives can normally be costed on both a capital and an annual basis to show both the charges falling on the C.E.G.B. and those falling on the Area Board; but the choice may be fairly evenly balanced, and there may be different ways of doing the calculation.   Up till 1957 the B.E.A./C.E.A. could in the last resort have over-ruled an Area Board in the event of any differences.   In fact, however, it was usual to find not so much a conflict of views as a tendency, in cases of doubt, for work to be done by the C.E.A. because the Area Boards had less money.   It now seems to be more usual to work out the financial effect of any alternative schemes on the electricity supply industry as a whole and then choose the cheapest from that point of view.

New schemes may be roughly divided into four groups:

(a) links from one part of the country to another to provide for major transfers of load (or links outside England and Wales—of which the only cases at present are those with Scotland and France);

(b) links to connect new generating stations into the main system;

(c) projects to reinforce the supply from the national network to a particular district—for instance the whole of a moderate-sized county;

(d) local schemes to provide new points of supply or to increase the capacity of existing points of bulk supply.

Very broadly, (a), (b) and (c) will now involve construction of substantial new links—generally at least two or three score of miles—of Supergrid overhead lines at 275 kV.   (d) will generally mean adapting the Grid (normally 132 kV) and constructing additional lines at 132 kV or lower voltages.   Such schemes will usually be required in towns, where they will involve a complex extension and rearrangement of networks both overhead and underground at different voltages, partly within the main transmission system and partly within the distribution system of the Area Board, and the whole scheme will be a joint effort of the engineers of the C.E.G.B. and the Area Board.

Any one of these four types of scheme will probably involve both transformer and switching stations at two or more terminal points of the new lines and/or increasing the capacity of existing transformer and switching stations.   New transmission schemes are not provided only to meet increased demand—nor have any hitherto been provided *solely* to achieve financial savings—but economic advantages will often form part of the case for carrying out a 'reinforcement' scheme.   So will reduction of risks of accident or failure of supplies.   Some transmission reinforcements, notably in London, are required in consequence of Area Board standardisation schemes.

Schemes in the categories (*a*) and (*b*) are affected by the long-term programmes of 'System Planning' for the country as a whole.   The Supergrid has been a major piece of nationwide planning.   There have, however, not been enough planning staff to meet all the demands for local reinforcements, and much of the design work has therefore, at least until recently, been carried out piecemeal.

Contract arrangements are much less involved than those for power stations.   For most of the equipment there are standard specifications from which the contractors produce their own detailed designs, but there are a number of standard designs for towers.   For 132-kV and 275-kV Grid lines there are single main contracts.   Transformers, ancillary apparatus and civil engineering work are each the subject of separate contracts. The main contractor is responsible for providing (directly or through sub-contractors) all the steel towers and their foundations and the cables and insulators, and for their planning and erection (including surveys of detailed heights and levels). C.E.G.B. officers survey the route, map out and acquire sites and wayleaves and C.E.G.B. site engineers check progress.

Under the B.E.A./C.E.A. virtually every transmission construction job involved both Headquarters and a Generating Division.   Headquarters engineered the work and placed all contracts, and the Division usually supervised construction. This division of functions seems to have been somewhat similar to that in power-station construction under the B.E.A./C.E.A. The C.E.G.B. have devised quite a different system. For major schemes almost all design and control of construction is carried out by Headquarters. (Construction on site is supervised by resident engineers appointed by the Divisions, but responsible to Headquarters.) Regional or local schemes, on the other hand, are the sole responsibility of the Region or Divisions. Thus, as far as possible, one party or the other is fully in charge throughout, but the division of functions is not absolute. All wayleave negotiations for all schemes are carried out by Divisional Wayleave Officers, but in the Headquarters-controlled schemes the planning of the route is done from Headquarters and the Divisional Wayleave Officers simply act on Headquarters instructions. Site supervision is much less complicated than in power-station building, and is normally done by a single engineer. On the request of the Region or Division, Headquarters provide drawing-office facilities and bills of quantities for civil work.

Very broadly, Regional/Divisional schemes are those described in (d) above. The control of each particular scheme will be agreed between Headquarters and the Region and/or Division when the Annual Programme is settled. Regions/Divisions will do about a quarter of all main transmission schemes. All this division of responsibility is quite new, and was only being worked out at the time of writing. It has been decided that the programme of main transmission work should be planned on a long-term basis, but many of the transmission projects are too small to be included in the general 'system planning'. There is to be a series of meetings each autumn between the Transmission and Planning Departments at Headquarters and the Regions, at which long-term programmes can be settled in outline and the following year's programme in detail, and agreements reached as to the allocation of work between Headquarters and the Regions. The long-term programming now proposed seems clearly essential. Sir Christopher Hinton, the Chairman of the Board, has said:

A wise programme for the construction of new transmission lines should allow an overall time of four or even five years, three years or even more of this being spent in negotiating the route.[26]

[26] Paper read to Royal Society of Arts, 25th November 1959.

Regional schemes will often cost over £100,000 each, and may sometimes cost as much as £500,000.   The line of division between Headquarters and the Regions is not determined by the limits of financial powers.   It is intended that the channel of formal submission of Regional schemes will be from the Regional Executive Committee to the Central Executive Committee, but the Headquarters Transmission, Finance and other Departments will have the chance to comment.   It remains to be seen how this will work in detail.[27]

(h) *The Financial Control System of the C.E.G.B.*

The C.E.G.B.'s long-term 'Final', 'Provisional' and 'Tentative' programmes include proposals for the amount of money to be spent both on the total programmes and each individual station.   Before any individual power station (and sometimes a transmission link) is considered the full Board will have approved a long-term programme in which that project is either named or specified in general terms—e.g. 'coal-fired station in the Midlands'.   They will usually also have already considered the case as a site proposal.

When financial estimates[28] are made they see it in outline in a standard form with the chief parts of the station and its equipment set out under standard headings.   The first sheet comprises technical particulars—under some thirty to forty heads—numbers and capacity of sets, steam conditions, particulars of water circulation, switchgear and transformers, etc.   Then, on the other sheets the cost of the work is broken down under civil, mechanical and electrical engineering contracts. There are 11 standard items on the civil sheet, 20 on the mechanical and 20 on the electrical, and further items may sometimes have to be added.   Against each item there is space for a

---

[27] Since this was written, the C.E.G.B. in their *Annual Report* 1960–61 (para. 241, pp. 63–64) have announced the setting up of a Transmission Project Group at Guildford 'organised similarly to the . . . Generation Project Groups' to be 'responsible for the design, execution and commissioning of new primary transmission lines' (i.e. those which form part of the National Grid network), 'assisted in the supervision of the actual construction by Regional transmission engineers'; and also 'Regional transmission construction departments . . . to deal with secondary schemes' (i.e. those 'for the delivery of bulk supplies to the Area Boards').

[28] Estimates of cost are prepared once a station has been included in a 'tentative', 'provisional' or 'final' plant programme. The estimate relating to the latter becomes the first firm budgeting estimate.

figure of total cost and cost per kilowatt. The Project Group prepares the forms. When the 'Final' long-term programme is before the Board there will be submitted for each station in it, not a complete form, but the summary sheet, breaking the cost down into five main heads—Land, Civil, Mechanical, Electrical and 'Engineering'—the last meaning broadly design, etc., costs—C.E.B. engineers' salaries and fees to consultants (each also expressed as £ per kilowatt). The incidence of all this expenditure will also be forecast over the various years. The next stage of working out of the estimate into its full detail normally follows in the same year as that in which the scheme is approved as part of a Final Programme—that is in the fifth year before the first set is due to be commissioned. In each succeeding year until the last unit has been commissioned the estimate is revised and resubmitted—again with an estimate of the incidence of expenditure over successive years.

One may ask at this point how far the C.E.G.B. has, or ought to have, any system comparable with the 'Stage I' and 'Stage II' procedure of the N.C.B. which we have noticed as particularly valuable in getting schemes agreed on the right lines in outline at the earliest stages. There may not be as much scope for fundamentally different solutions to the same problem in power stations as in coal mines. Once a decision in principle has been taken to site a station of a certain capacity in a certain area, and for it to draw its heat from coal, oil or nuclear energy, planning can then proceed on the basis of the latest engineering policy. There will be different methods on which a scheme can be worked out—for instance, as regards grouping and layout on the site—but the adoption of such different methods is not likely to result in fundamentally different types of station. It is important that there should be correct choices at the outset of sites and of types of plant, but this requirement is covered in the long-term programmes. The Board review the subsequent development of individual stations when the estimates and budgets are put before them each year.

There is a somewhat similar procedure for main transmission, but the cost is given under about eight heads—first, all civil engineering taken together and then the different sections of electrical engineering—lines, towers, transformers, switchgear, and metering and control equipment, with possibly one or two more items, including a contingencies item and, as in the generating project form, 'engineering'. A more detailed, standardised procedure for financial approval of transmission schemes was being worked out at the time of writing. There are, of course, various other types of capital project which may be carried out by Project Groups, Headquarter Departments or Regions. Extensions of generating, switching and transformer stations and provision, extension and renewal of engineering plant of all kinds will be classed as 'operational', and workshops, stores, research buildings and offices as 'non-operational'. The limits of financial authority to approve scheme estimates are as follows:

Operational Schemes

Complete Generating Stations	All schemes go to Board level

Main transmission schemes

£250,000 (Regional Schemes)	Regional Executive Committees
£100,000 (Headquarters Schemes)	Chief Transmission Engineer, Headquarters

All other operational expenditure

£50,000 (Regional Schemes)	Regional Executive Committee
£5,000 (Headquarters Schemes)	Headquarter Departments and Project Groups

All non-operational expenditure

£10,000 (Regional Schemes)	Regional Executive Committees
£5,000 (Headquarters Schemes)	Headquarter Departments and Project Groups

Capital scheme estimates of any kind outside the above limits, if they come from Project Groups or Headquarter Departments, may be authorised by the Full-time Members of the C.E.G.B.; if they come from Regions, by the Central Executive Committee (that is the Full-time Members plus the Regional Directors).

There are standard instructions about the submission of all types of capital scheme—applying broadly at whatever level the approval is given.   (The Board look for a specific rate of return on all 'optional or marginal' capital schemes—that is on schemes which they have an effective choice whether to undertake or not.   While this may cover only a relatively small part of the Board's total capital expenditure, they nevertheless consider it a salutary exercise likely to make those concerned think whether a scheme is really worthwhile before it is put forward.) Each scheme must be accompanied by an 'economic appraisal' in a standard form.   Points to be covered include:

(*a*) A classification of the scheme as 'operational' or 'non-operational' and then also whether—

   (i) initiated to secure *compliance with statutory or other obligations*, e.g. the new generating plant to meet the future load. (*Research and development* projects should be included under this head and be specified as such.)
   (ii) *directly revenue-earning or cost reducing*, e.g. . . . new and more efficient generating plant which by replacing old and inefficient plant will either increase the revenue-earning capacity of the industry or lead to a reduction in overall costs, and
   (iii) *indirectly revenue-earning or cost reducing*, e.g. welfare projects which are necessary to bring amenities at a Power Station up to standard—the benefits of which cannot directly be measured in monetary terms.

(*b*) Cost estimate divided between:
   (i) direct labour
   (ii) contract work
   (iii) engineering design costs (consultants, architects, etc.)
   (iv) contingencies.

(*c*) Value of any surplus equipment being used or thrown spare.

(*d*) Probable useful life of the equipment used (and the surplus equipment).   It is noted that this may not coincide with the period over which depreciation is charged.   If uncertain maximum and minimum periods to be quoted.

(*e*) Effect on annual charges of any supersession of any existing arrangements which will result from the new scheme.

(*f*) Any possible alternative schemes and reasons for their rejection.

(*g*) Annual incidence of expenditure.

(*h*) Whether the above is covered by a current budget and if not whether the money is to be found by increase in the budget at next revision or by cancellation or deferment of another scheme.

(*i*) Overall annual saving (or loss) resulting from the scheme and net return on capital invested.

(*j*) Dates for starting and completion of work.

Where any scheme is not started within one year of approval it must be re-submitted for further approval.

In addition to all this there is the C.E.G.B.'s extensive system of budgetary control. Annual budgets have to be submitted for capital schemes. The initial budgets for a financial year are due to be submitted in December of the preceding year and then revised in July/August and again in the following December. These budgets are submitted through the Headquarters Finance Department by each of the bodies incurring expenditure—the Headquarters Departments, the Regions and the Project Groups. The budgets include the latest estimate of total expenditure on all schemes authorised and not yet completed, and estimated incidence of expenditure over successive years. They list individually:

(*a*) operational schemes, costing over £10,000 each, controlled by Regions;

(*b*) other operational schemes costing over £5,000 each; and

(*c*) non-operational schemes, however controlled, costing over £5,000.

Bulk totals are also given for the current and the next two financial years, comprising all expenditure on schemes outside the limits just quoted.

The C.E.G.B. seems to delegate greater powers to committees than to individuals. (The powers of the Chief Transmission Engineer are an exception.) The Project Committee, for instance (which authorises certain *contracts* but not schemes as such), consists of:

> The Chief Project Engineer;
> The Assistant Chief Project Engineer;
> The Project Engineer (for the scheme concerned);
> The Regional Director's representative (from the Region where the generating station is situated);
> The Project Administrative Officer; and
> The Project Contracts Officer.

A quorum for a Project Committee is three, one of whom must be the Chief Project Engineer or an Assistant Chief Project Engineer or the Project Engineer.

There is a separate code for approval of contracts. For generation equipment Chief Project Engineers may authorise the placing of contracts not exceeding £10,000 and their Project Committees contracts not exceeding £100,000, provided (if over £10,000) the tender is the lowest, and contains no special features. All larger contracts go to the Headquarters Contracts Panel, which comprises:

> The Chief Design and Construction Engineer
> The Chief Purchasing and Contracts Officer
> The Chief Financial Officer
> All three Chief Project Engineers

Any of the above may send his Deputy, but the Panel cannot act unless at least one of the Headquarters Chief Officers and the Chief Project Engineer directly responsible is present or represented. The Panel can approve any contract, unless it exceeds £2 million or is in respect of an item in the 'nominated list' (in effect, boilers, turbo-alternators and nuclear reactors) or unless the tender contains special features. All such cases go to a meeting of the Full-time Board Members. The Chief Purchasing and Contracts Officer submits to the Central Executive Committee, for their general review, a monthly list of all capital contracts authorised during the preceding month by the Full-time Members, the Headquarters Contracts Panel, the Project Committee and the Chief Project Engineers.

Within a year of completion of a capital project a report is submitted to the authority that originally approved it, showing details of the probable final cost, a comparison with the *original* estimates under each head and an explanation of any variations. This form of post-mortem report differs somewhat from that of the Coal Board—which is only submitted when a scheme reaches the full level of production expected when it was authorised, or at least when the time has passed when such a level of production should have been reached. It is then possible to make a comparison not only between the estimated and the actual capital costs but also between actual and estimated operating costs and output—and hence a review of the net financial return on the capital invested. The C.E.G.B. had not, at least at the time of writing, considered such reviews practicable, although they were understood not to have come to a final conclusion on the point. The operating costs and output of a power station do not depend only on the way it is planned, built and worked. It forms part of the total pooled generating capacity of the whole country. The relationship between its output of electricity and the capital invested in it will depend very largely on how long it is kept running—whether virtually continuously on 'base load', or for short periods on 'peak load', or for something in between. An efficient station planned to work on base load may in fact work with progressively lesser loads, simply because, after it has been commissioned, other even more efficient stations are one after another brought into commission, or because for some other reasons (for instance, because they are nuclear) it is desirable to keep such new stations running for the maximum time.

All this would at least seem to be a fair reason for the C.E.G.B. practice of making the original full economic appraisal of a power station scheme in relation only to the running costs and economic return in the period of a year or two after it has been brought into commission and not trying to extend it in detail for the whole of the station's economic life. The latest coal- and oil-fired stations now being planned might last into the twenty-first century, or at any rate into a period whose scientific developments are not easy to predict. Nevertheless, the C.E.G.B. do attempt broadly to estimate the economics of the running of their stations in future years and not merely in their opening years. It may be arguable, moreover, that in future they may find it possible and desirable to review the working results of their stations some while after they have come into commission more in the way that the Coal Board do. There is more similarity between the coal and electrical industries in this matter than might at first appear. Although coal mines are not interconnected in the same way as generating stations, many of them are complementary or indeed alternative to one another or exist to serve nationwide markets; and all may be affected by developments in those markets or by other factors not within the control of the people who planned the colliery project. Nevertheless, the Coal Board does attempt these reviews.   The question raised here is an extremely com-plex one and could only be answered after a much closer examination than the present writer has been able to make of the effectiveness of the Coal Board reviews and the various factors affecting the economics of electricity generation and distribution.   The C.E.G.B., however, seem to be developing their management and control systems in general and their financial control system in particular all the time.

CHAPTER VII

CONCLUSIONS

(a) *Varying Composition and Sizes of Capital Programmes*

The purpose of this book has been to place the results of explorations in certain limited fields beside one another so as to suggest some provisional conclusions and further study. This final chapter will simply focus attention on a few outstanding points, and not try to exhaust all the lines of thought along which the facts we have set out may lead.

There are certain basic distinctions among the capital projects and programmes we have described:

(*a*) in the size of projects, both absolute and in relation to total programmes;

(*b*) in the numbers of separate projects in each programme and in the regularity with which they occur;

(*c*) in the similarity of projects to one another or in the extent to which they have to be individually planned.

These points are fundamental. The whole basis of planning, authorising and seeing through to completion any kind of capital projects is utterly different, on the one hand, for a medium-sized manufacturing firm which will only occasionally build a new factory, and on the other hand, for the Coal and Electricity Boards, for whom capital development is a continuous process always calling for a high proportion of the total effort of management. All these Boards each year have to undertake a large number of capital projects, most of them of a basically similar kind to one another (however much detailed, individual planning each may involve). The Coal Board's capital equipment requires, and will go on requiring, continuous renewal, because coal deposits are always being worked out. That of Electricity Boards has hitherto been in process of continuous expansion, and so far there is no sign of the need for this falling off. These industries require a continuous run of projects which are quite new—even though they may replace other old projects elsewhere. It is therefore one of the major functions of the top managements to be continuously planning large new projects—totally new projects and not merely improvements, extensions or alterations. London Transport, on the contrary, serves a large saturated area. Apart from the Victoria Line, there seem no more foreseeable prospects of major new capital development. Individual stations will need improvements—some very large and expensive. Road and rail vehicles must be replaced at the end of their economic lives —if possible with better designs. But there seems no prospect of major expansion of the system or wholesale technical change.

One needs to make these distinctions to appreciate how totally different the problem of capital development is for different types of organisation. For one or two very large concerns, mainly in the public sector, it is a major continuing responsibility. Outstanding examples are the Coal Board and the C.E.G.B. and on a smaller scale the North of Scotland Hydro-Electric Board. The development problems of all these are vastly greater than anything confronting the medium-sized and smaller industries and public services, and one might expect that such problems place great strain on the top managements. On the other hand, for these organisations capital development is a continuous process and accepted as a prime responsibility when each was first set up. So there must be a great deal which they can take in their stride. The start of planning of a new power station, costing £20 million or £30 million or more, or a new coal mine costing £10 million, or a colliery stores of, say, £½ million—all these will now be relatively normal occurrences for the N.C.B. or the C.E.G.B.—to be expected perhaps once a year, perhaps several times in a year. They would be as normal occurrences indeed as the sanctioning of a £50,000 building by London Transport or a £20,000 crane by a big steel company. Any one of these projects in the organisation concerned could by now be compared with others which had gone before, as regards cost and general methods of planning, and the top management could usually have confidence that their staff or consultants or manufacturers had designed and constructed somewhat similar things before. However conscientious top management might be, the bulk of the work could be carried out by middle management.

Q

Now imagine similar-sized projects being carried out by smaller, though not really small, concerns without the special experience and special staff of those we have mentioned—a medium-sized Local Authority faced for the first time with a road or drainage scheme such as the L.C.C. has to contend with every year—a small firm with one works having to order a crane or moderate-sized building of the sort of size which a big steel company may have in nearly every year.   The same also applies when one of the organisations we have described undertakes something of a different type from its usual run of capital projects, even if the cost is comparable or even much less.   A complete new carbonisation plant or brickworks would no doubt very properly involve a great deal of discussion at top levels if the Coal Board decided to undertake such a thing now. So, perhaps, would a new ship for the C.E.G.B., even if one of similar size would present no serious problems to a large shipping company or to the Admiralty.   Many other examples must occur to the mind, but these are sufficient to show that the complexity of management problems in capital development depends less on the cost of the projects than on their nature and the type of organisation which undertakes them.

(b) *The Processes of Design, Manufacture and Construction*

We need to consider now just what is involved in the *process* of different types of capital development.   One broad division is between things constructed mainly on site and things made elsewhere and only assembled on site.   Construction on site involves interest, and usually some participation, in the process by the user organisation—at least to a greater extent than manufacture elsewhere.   The user organisation may or may not do the construction itself with its own labour, or do the design—but at least it must first make the site available, and then one would usually expect it to check the progress of the work through its own site engineers, or clerks of works.   However, practice seems to vary.   Some user organisations leave a good deal of this progress checking to their contractors or consultants.

On the other hand, an organisation with a large programme which involves plant manufacture takes a very close interest not only in the quality but also in the progress of the work in the manufacturers' works. London Transport do this with railway rolling stock, but the process seems to have been taken farther—and perhaps may yet be taken farther still—by the C.E.G.B., especially for very large things of constantly improving design—notably turbo-alternators. Here progress control seems to be very much a matter of joint concern and co-operation between the Board's engineers and those of the firms. This sort of thing would certainly seem essential where the user:

(a) has a closely timed programme;
(b) is closely involved in design work; or
(c) has important things to do at the site before or after the manufacturer completes erection or installation.

A more useful distinction, however, than that between construction on and off site is that between what is designed and/or made by the user concern itself and what is provided by contract. Most (but not all) underground tunnelling in coal mines, and the laying of the lower-voltage electricity cables, is generally done by the Board's own employees directly. In most industries, however, the user organisation neither designs nor constructs its own larger buildings, but is only responsible for stating its requirements and seeing they are met. (Even here there are variations. Some architects complain of having to tell their clients what they want. Other architects seem rather to like doing so.) In between these two opposite types of arrangement there are very many others where the user designs or takes a considerable part in the design, but where an outside organisation manufactures. Sometimes the same type of equipment may be provided by either method. For instance, London Transport now have all their vehicle bodies made by entirely independent firms (to their own detailed designs), but at one time their predecessors had some of these made in their own works or those of their subsidiary or closely linked companies. British Railways, continuing the practice of their predecessors, manufacture most of their own rolling stock and a great deal of other equipment.[1] A smallish

[1] Sir Reginald Wilson, 'Structure and Purpose in Transport Organisation', *Journal of the Institute of Transport*, January 1957, p. 49. Sir Reginald, a Member of the British Transport Commission, after referring to British Railways' principal activities, said:

'As if these purposes were not ambitious enough British Railways also engage

proportion of distribution cabling is laid by contractors subject to the Electricity Boards' supervision and design. The Coal Board has done some of its main underground tunnelling by contract, and at one time employed consulting engineers to supplement the work of its own planning engineers. The South of Scotland Electricity Board—like the C.E.A. and the municipal and company-owned electricity undertakings before it—employs consulting engineers for the main mechanical and electrical design work in its power stations—which the C.E.G.B. does with its own staff.

Can we discern any logical pattern among all these variations, or do things just happen through habit and short-term convenience? Taking design work first, all those concerns which use both their own staff and consultants tend to suggest that their main consideration is keeping an even flow of work for their own staff. For occasional bursts of activity well above this level they will employ consultants. They may also use consultants as a short-term expedient in a period of sustained expansion until they can build up their own staff. The Coal Board did just this. A user concern may not have enough work for a full design staff, but it may need some for preparing at least outline specifications, liaison and co-operation work with manufacturers and so on—like the L.T.E.'s (railway) mechanical engineers or the Coal Board's carbonisation engineers.

This brings us to the further question of how far design work should be divided between independent consultants, on the one hand, and manufacturers or contractors, on the other—assuming it is not to be done by the user. For carbonisation and some other large complete industrial installations, design, manufacture and construction tend to be combined in the same firm. The nuclear power station 'consortia' are an outstanding example. A few of the very large civil engineering contractors have highly qualified professional staff of their own, and would probably claim that they could themselves do everything a consultant could do.

---

a great deal in "self-supply", for they not only provide their own track and lines but they also manufacture most of their own rolling stock.'

After saying that half the staff were engaged in construction, maintenance and functions other than 'traffic work' he concluded:

'Certainly one might say the railways make it difficult for themselves.'

Do the respective advantages of these different agencies—contractors, consultants and internal staff—depend solely on the volume of work and the economics of scale? Or are there considerations of having too few—or too many—independent minds applied to any type of project? Do you get the best ideas and have them most efficiently co-ordinated and put into effect most quickly by having everything unified under the direct control of the user concern? Or is the second opinion and wider experience of contractor or manufacturer worth having—or the third opinion of a consultant? The answers to these questions must depend partly on the extent to which the user concern is the sole or the main user of the equipment, at least within this country. It is very natural that the Coal Board, for its coal-mining activities as distinct from carbonisation, should rely largely on its own staff. It has a monopoly of British coal mining and a sufficiently large and dispersed staff to accumulate every variety of experience and develop alternative ideas. (Coal-mining conditions in other countries are often very different, but there seem to be many interchanges of visits between high-level N.C.B. engineers and those of practically all other coal-mining countries.) Development of mechanical and electrical mining equipment—as distinct from mining processes—seems to be a joint activity between the Board and manufacturing firms. On the other hand, the Board was never the sole British purchaser of carbonisation plant, and is not now even the main British purchaser. However, the North of Scotland Board has been the sole British customer since the War for hydro-electric schemes:[2] yet it relies almost entirely on consultants and manufacturers. Of large steam generating plant the C.E.G.B. is not only the sole purchaser in England and Wales but one of the leading purchasers throughout the world. For nuclear reactors, on the other hand, it apparently relies largely on the design staff of the privately owned 'consortia' and those of another public corporation, the U.K. Atomic Energy Authority. The latter has, of course, many other responsibilities in the nuclear field, including research.

One is left with the feeling that the divisions between inside and outside design work in the industries we have looked at on

[2] Except for one C.E.G.B. pumped storage scheme.

the whole make sense.   The precise lines of division must be fluid as long as the user industry itself and its supplier industries are expanding or contracting to any great extent.   What is not so clear is whether the question of where the dividing line should be drawn is always consciously posed as one of major policy by all concerns—public and private—before they first consider embarking on large capital programmes.   One might indeed add that a reasonable and economic size of capital programme, sufficient to justify special internal design, planning and constructional staffs, might well be one of the factors determining the whole size and constitution of an industrial organisation when it was being first set up or reorganised— whether in the public or private sector.   Wider study of this subject would no doubt be very well worthwhile—but it would come up against difficulties.   In private industry an independent organisation for design or construction or manufacturing may be set up for other reasons than speed or economy.   In a rapidly advancing industry technical 'know how' may be among a firm's most valuable capital assets, and it may be essential to keep it under its own direct control.   In such a case it might scarcely feel it worthwhile to work out the alternative cost of employing outside concerns.   Furthermore, in both the public and the private sectors an organisation may decide to make certain essential parts of its own equipment itself for reasons of continuity and reliability of supply.

We must now look at the special cases of industries with their own constructional labour forces, notably coal and electricity distribution.   None of the organisations we have studied seem anxious to maintain a large labour force solely for capital construction.   The Coal Board, in constructing new mines or extending old ones, is, of course, simply using the same sort of labour and supervision which it maintains primarily for its day-to-day work of coal getting.   Similarly, in electricity distribution new construction, renewal and maintenance all go together.   We have found direct-labour building organisations under the London and other Electricity Boards and the L.T.E., but broadly these only do fairly small jobs or parts of larger schemes.   Much the same can be said of permanent-way work under L.T.E. and presumably that of other railways.   It is significant that none of the organisations we have studied seem to have set up a direct-labour building organisation originally just to save time or money. The Works Department of London Transport originated with a policy that work on or beside railway lines must be done by railway staff under railway supervision, and the organisation, having been set up for this purpose, has been used for others. It seems to have been useful for getting small jobs done quickly, but London Transport are extremely cautious about its costs, and take particular precautions for the control of them. The London Electricity Board also have a fairly large direct-labour Works Department, which originated from the special nature of some of their jobs— e.g. sub-stations in awkward places and underground electrical work—jobs which contractors sometimes would not undertake. Steel companies seem to have had similar difficulties in getting builders to do work which might be interrupted by steel-making operations. Their remedy, however, is not to set up their own building organisation, but to use special forms of contract.

To justify a direct-labour, capital-construction department, without any other functions of either day-to-day production or *maintenance*, or construction for outside concerns, one would need to imagine not only an organisation with a large, continuing and fairly uniform programme of capital development but also possibly one where the equipment was quite different from any being provided in large quantities for any other users.[3]

(c) *Objectives and Long-term Planning*

Most capital development is undertaken either:

(*a*) to meet increased demand; or
(*b*) to replace existing (and still usable) equipment so as to serve existing demands in a more efficient way; or
(*c*) to replace equipment which has become worn out or otherwise reached the end of its economic life.

(The dividing line between (*b*) and (*c*) is not always clear, and a small proportion is in other special categories, such as making

---

[3] The subject of direct-labour building organisations of local authorities is discussed by Elizabeth Layton, *Building by Local Authorities* (Report of Inquiry by Royal Institute of Public Administration) (Geo. Allen & Unwin, 1961), pp. 233–280. She says that four-fifths of the labour of these organisations is employed on maintenance and that the Local Authorities 'stress the importance of continuity of work'.

good war or other exceptional damage, improving working conditions and meeting new legal requirements.) Most of London Transport's capital programme is for replacement, and among the basic considerations in its planning are the original dates of supply. There is a basic difference between capital programmes undertaken mainly for replacement or mainly for expansion. The difference depends not only on whether the industries concerned are expanding but also on whether the equipment is such as to need much replacement. On the whole, in electricity distribution and main transmission new capital equipment is provided primarily for expansion. The Coal Board stands in a midway position. Its total capacity is not increasing, but it is nevertheless undertaking a vast amount of new construction and mechanisation, and relatively probably much less investment in direct replacement of existing equipment.

In capital development planning policy a most important consideration is what period the estimates should cover. Here there is a basic difficulty and a contradiction which affects most industries and services, both public and private, and for which few, if any, seem to see a complete solution. Many major capital programmes, and indeed individual projects, take a longer period to plan and bring to fruition than that for which many people would care to make predictions of demand. And even if one could estimate demand at least as far ahead as the time when a new scheme would be *completed*, there is the further problem of what demand will be throughout the effective life of that equipment. It is easy to be cynical about long-term planning and long-term estimating, and even to say that one cannot estimate most forms of demand farther ahead than about a year. Many people in expanding industries or public services can point to cases where demand estimates have been greatly exceeded and capital provision, land purchase and so on, has been on such a niggardly scale as not only to delay the meeting of demand but also, in the long-term, to waste a great deal of money. It is equally easy to be wise after the event in relation to industries and services which are contracting or where expansion has not kept pace with expectations or has been diverted to other channels by technological change. In either type of case faith in long-term planning is weakened.

The fact remains, however, that anyone who undertakes any

kind of capital development, whether in publicly or privately owned industry, is by that very act committed to some kind of long-term forecast. The business man who invests money, whether in a factory or a small extension to a shop or a garage, is working either on a reasoned forecast or an act of faith that he will have sufficient business, at least to enable him to meet the interest on the capital until such time as he has paid it all off. The exceptional point about the very large-scale industries and services which we have been discussing is that the assumptions need to be made over much longer periods, and the consequences of their being ill-founded would be much more disastrous. The largest types of project we have discussed—large new coal mines and power stations (coal, oil, nuclear or water)—may take seven to ten years to bring to fruition. That is, seven to ten years may be expected to elapse between the decision to go ahead with planning and the time when the project is in full production. One may be tempted to think that these projects are quite exceptional, but in fact there are a good many of their kind—for instance, major railway projects. Indeed, most of the large capital schemes which we have discussed seem to involve at least a five-year preparatory period if one includes both the initial time required to arrive at a firm decision to go ahead and also the period of negotiation about the site. Probably much the same could be said of the major water and trunk roads projects. For all these things five-year estimates of demand would only show at best whether the scheme was going to be adequate for a few months after it was first completed. It would take a very high rate of financial return to pay off all the capital, over and above interest payments, even in four or five years after that. Moreover, most other types of capital equipment which we have discussed would be expected to have at least a further five years of economic life—more likely fifteen to twenty years. All this seems to require something like *twenty-year planning*.

When, however, planning becomes as long-term as this it is impossible to confine it to individual projects. A complete programme for the whole organisation is essential to avoid competition for money, materials and men. All the organisations we have described here, and most others of comparable size, have long-term programmes of some sort. Several in the

Q 2

public sector have published them in outline, while generally having more detailed versions for internal use. Long-term programmes may serve a number of objects, such as:

(a) to settle priorities between competing projects;

(b) to set out a timetable against which progress can be checked;

(c) to determine the needs for finance;

(d) as a public declaration of the objects of the organisation concerned and to help it to deal with public criticisms of excessive or insufficient expansion;

(e) as a basis for various internal discussions, for instance about personnel planning, consultation with trade unions and so forth, and as an aid to morale;

(f) to enable orders and contracts to be placed at the right times and arrangements made with (and by) individual manufacturers or trade associations;

(g) to enable projects to be approved in principle at an early stage before resources are committed to their detailed planning.

Some of the most detailed long-term planning which we have met is that of the Coal Board. The fact that it has had to be varied should not blind us to its value. *Plan for Coal* stated quite clearly that variations might be expected later; but with a programme of such size and complexity, progress surely would have been impossible without some long-term planning from the earliest stages. We have seen how some time after the original main plans had been settled particular specialised types of planning had to be undertaken—for instance, for stores and equipment and for recruitment and training of engineers. Moreover, the Coal Board has needed to set out and revise periodically a comprehensive picture of its future, because both inside and outside the industry there was so much doubt about it. Long-term planning in the electricity industry has been rather different. It was started before the War by the Central Electricity Board, and, although since the War outline plans have been published,[4] the more detailed and technical

[4] British Electricity Authority: *Power and Prosperity*, 1954.
Electricity Council: *Power for the Future*, 1958.
North of Scotland Hydro-Electric Board and South of Scotland Electricity Board (jointly): *Scottish Electricity: Plans for the Future*, 1958.

internal plans may be much more important. The major electricity projects—power stations and grid schemes—seem more closely linked with one another than are most of the main projects in the coal industry. The internal morale factor, however, and even that of public relations, may be somewhat less important than in the coal industry at present. Few people doubt the continued expansion of the electricity industry as a whole. On the distribution side shorter-term programmes have generally sufficed, but the publications in South Scotland about rural development have constituted a rather special and interesting type of long-term plan. The object of these published plans was not only to provide a framework for the detailed planning of the engineers but also to make clear to potential consumers what they could expect and when, and how important it was to get co-operation in good time about wayleaves. London Transport has not had a comprehensive plan going anything like as far ahead as the other organisations, but it has had its long-term plans for particular things, for instance, the dovetailing over a period of about ten years of the replacement and interchanges of railway rolling stock. When particular lines were being improved or electrified, however, London Transport, like British Railways, has given some publicity to its planning.

We have no doubt said enough to make it clear that capital development in these major industries and services is a very *long-term process* which cannot be *turned on and off at short notice*— that is, as regards the really large projects. The smaller and more routine programmes of minor development and re-equipment require less space and less time for planning, manufacture or construction. But even for these minor programmes fairly long periods are needed unless they consist simply of standard plant and machinery or road vehicles. In general, one must assume that *all* substantial capital development programmes will take a long time—sometimes years—to get under way. This is not only because of the time taken in design or even in land acquisition, but because of the even longer, but not necessarily unreasonable, time which is often taken to decide what is wanted.

There has recently been a fashion for 'business games' as a means of training managers. The essence of such a game is a series of decisions as to how the trainees would employ their firms' financial and other resources—for instance, in sales promotion, capital investment, raw materials, running costs and so on. The effects of the imaginary policy decisions are worked out by a computer, and at the end of each part of the game it shows which player has achieved the best financial results. This is followed by an analysis and discussions of what has happened. The kind of lesson supposed to be learnt is that one firm might have allocated too much or too little to capital investment and in the next financial period—apparently six months to one year—they might have to make important changes or even reversals of policy. Such games are apparently played in general terms not much related to particular industries. No doubt they teach some important lessons. Yet one shudders to think of the future of British industry if its top managers are to get their ideas of the planning of capital development from the analogy of pressing buttons on a computer and achieving sudden expansions or contractions over short periods—regardless of the nature of the development work to be done. Presumably most practical managers in publicly and privately owned industry do not really think or work in these abstract terms. Nevertheless, one does still sometimes detect in public discussions of the policies of our major industries and public services some lack of realisation of the enormously long periods required for the building up of sound development programmes and of the great number of different and changing elements—human and material—which go into the making of capital development programmes. People are still apt to think of five-year planning as long-term planning. For the industries and services whose individual projects take well between five and ten years to get *started* in production, five-year plans would be clearly far too short. And there are a good many more industries and services in this category than those mentioned in this book.

In connection with long-term planning we must mention one of the main factors which makes it necessary—land acquisition—a subject which cannot be reduced to any scientific formulae, but which, we have seen, is the source of most serious delays for the Electricity Boards. It is also very important in the capital development planning of most public services and many industries, notably the steel industry, which requires a great deal of space. It was exceptional that under London Transport and the Coal Board we found it of *relatively* little significance—in the first case because relatively little construction requiring new sites has been going on, and in the second because—apart from opencast mining—the coal industry tends to do most of its surface construction in places where few other people want to go.

We have seen how periods of two years and more can be added to the timetable of important projects owing to siting difficulties. When one looks closely at what exactly happens in the periods of delay—the writing of letters, the holding of meetings, the waiting for people to come to decisions—one is tempted to react like the Cooper Committee on hydro-electric development in Scotland and suggest that forceful action could brush difficulties aside. It is interesting to note how this sort of line was taken in relation to road construction by Mr. J. Maurice Laing, Chairman of the Federation of Civil Engineering Contractors, in an article in *The Financial Times* of 28th September 1959:

> There are many difficulties to be overcome in the obtaining of land, but if the country really wants a system of first-class roads as quickly as possible, this problem must be resolved, and it is inevitable that the appropriate authorities must be given greater power than they have at the moment to obtain the right land at the right time and at a fair price.[5] At present the obtaining of land is obviously the main, and I believe the only real, bottleneck to an expanded road programme.

Mr. Laing's main argument was really answered by the then Minister of Transport, Mr. Harold Watkinson, in the same issue:

> A road cannot be bulldozed through in a democratic country, where government respects the rights of individuals.

Does this mean that there is no cure for land delays? Surely one answer lies in longer-term planning. After the South of Scotland Board had had much trouble over their nuclear site at Hunterston they started a long-term site programme, both

[5] Mr. Laing wrote before the passing of the Town and Country Planning Act 1959, but price difficulties do not seem to have been the major trouble for the concerns described in this book.

for power stations and grid lines—running some years ahead of the main engineering programmes and of final decisions about plant types and construction dates. The Board did not seem to be thinking so much of advance purchase as advance planning—the working out of routes where agreement could most easily be obtained and of forward planning to see how transmission routes and power-station sites would affect one another. Speeding up all these processes, or rather starting them earlier, need not mean riding roughshod over people's interests. On the contrary, failure to consult all the parties at the earliest stages usually results in delay rather than time saving. It is really a matter of pressing ahead discussions, between all parties—internal and external—vigorously, but tactfully. Site disputes may seem to arise from a conflict of general principle, but the scope for resolving them in general terms at the national level is in practice very limited. Yet something can be done to clear the ground and remove general misunderstandings. The C.E.G.B., who have probably had more of these difficulties than any other concern, are clearly very conscious of them. They have done what they can by such methods as preliminary public announcements that they are looking for a site in a particular, but very widely defined, area. They have also explained their general plans and policy to the public by such means as the papers read by their Chairman and by Sir William Holford at the Royal Society of Arts in November 1959. They realise that trouble sometimes arises because people do not like public bodies appearing to impose things on them before they have a chance to know what they are all about.

(d) *Financial and Progress Control*

The various instruments of financial control of capital projects normally include detailed calculations of estimated and actual cost and of financial return in the forms both of the direct new revenue earned and other costs saved. We have seen how the Coal Board have detailed systems of estimating return on capital and how they are applied (with modifications) to different types of case, even those where no direct profit is involved. Of course, among those concerns which we have discussed, and probably among all publicly owned concerns, the Coal Board is the closest to manufacturing industry in its ability to make direct assessments of financial return.[6] One project can—up to a point—be assessed separately from others. The C.E.G.B. also make detailed financial appraisements of certain individual projects. At least some Area Electricity Boards try to relate their 'new business' capital expenditure to the additional revenue which it will bring in. But it would be difficult or impossible to apply a system like that of the Coal Board to their reinforcement and standardisation expenditure.

London Transport is similar to the Electricity Boards in coming somewhere between an industrial organisation and public services like those of Local Authorities. It certainly tries to assess its capital expenditure in terms of annual savings or costs —for instance, individual items of improved mechanical equipment, complete vehicles of improved design or electrification schemes. But there are many things it provides for reasons of safety or convenience or relief of traffic congestion. How, for instance, can one measure the financial value of such things as two-pedal control on buses or better indicators at stations? Even where a financial return may be expected, it sometimes cannot be isolated from that due to other causes—for instance, if vehicles are improved in comfort in the hope that more people will travel on them.

Presumably few, if any, organisations would claim to apply a yardstick of profitability to such things as office buildings, common service equipment—workshops, stores and so on. The Coal Board and the C.E.G.B. have probably gone farther than the other organisations we have studied in financial assessment of the value of such projects—that is in calculating the continuing annual costs and charges which they create in comparison with any which they save. London Transport make assessments on similar lines, and it would seem that the Area Electricity Boards might well do so. It would be interesting to know how the practice varies in manufacturing industry.

There are other methods of cost control which can be applied to many types of project and which are especially useful for those which produce no direct return (whether the latter are

---

[6] Dr. Tibor Barna, *Investment and Growth Policies of British Industrial Firms*, 1962, p. 33, doubts whether the financial return on investments is often at all carefully assessed.

subsidiary projects in a primarily commercial organisation or main projects in a public service organisation). One method is to try to reach a standard of what a certain quantity of equipment should cost—so much per yard of underground tunnelling or of electricity cabling, so much per square foot or per cubic foot in a building. The latter has the advantages of making possible comparisons with other industries. Another method is based not on the unit of equipment, but on the unit of the product or service which the equipment provides. It is with this latter method that the Ministry of Education made such a revolutionary advance in building-cost control. Their standards are primarily those of cost per school place and not of cost per square or cubic foot of accommodation. They thus measure economy in the provision of space as well as in specification of materials, methods of construction and so on. Of course, such a system has to be linked to one of minimum standards of space and other facilities if it is not to result in general degradation of service. A school architect has to provide at least so much space for each child and various other minimum facilities, as well as see that he does not spend more than so much on each child. There have to be adjustments of the cost standards in certain cases or types of case—more for a grammar school than for a primary school, more for exceptional sites and so on.

There must surely be a considerable future for cost control on these lines in some types of industry and public services, and it is perhaps remarkable that it has not yet been more widely extended. We have not, for instance, found it used for any of the organisations discussed in this book in quite the same way the Ministry of Education use it. Of course, such simple yardsticks are not practicable for many types of buildings, but cost per kilowatt seems an effective yardstick for power stations. There may be good reasons why one component costs proportionately more in one type of station than another, but the yardstick of comparison with suitable qualifications at least provides the initial basis of challenge of apparently high expenditure. The situation is somewhat similar with substations or electricity distribution networks and some surface buildings at collieries. Presumably the organisations we have studied do not consider they have enough other new buildings of similar types, either to have worked out standards from past experience or to make it worthwhile to apply them in future. One would, however, have thought that they might well apply the more general building-cost standards of the purely dimensional type, which should by now be becoming fairly common knowledge in the architectural world. Of course, any organisation with a number of projects of broadly similar type could make broad comparisons. The Finance Department of London Transport, for instance, would enquire the reason why one garage or a workshop of a similar type cost more than another; but this is not quite the same thing as detailed standard-cost yardsticks.

Such dimensional yardsticks have been introduced on different dates by various Area Electricity Boards—no doubt in different forms—for their distribution networks. The question arises why common standard-cost yardsticks for these networks could not be applied to the whole country—with provision for variations for local labour or materials costs. As most of the materials, however, are manufactured on a national scale by a fairly small number of firms, this does again raise the question of whether bulk-purchase arrangements for the whole electricity supply industry would also be worthwhile.

Another important element in financial control is the degree of independent check and criticism which proposals receive. We have noted the varying practices of the Area Electricity Boards. Under some the Accounting Departments do not see individual capital expenditure proposals at all, and under others they play an important part—although this may still differ between one Area and another. In others again the Commercial Department consider the revenue to be expected from the 'new business' element in an investment project, and to that extent perform a similar function to that performed elsewhere by a Finance Department. Again, Area Engineering Departments have Budgeting Sections which are concerned with figures and costs, and which in fact may be fulfilling functions of financial assessment and criticism. This is not, however, such independent criticism as a separate department can give. Indeed, in many Area Electricity Boards it would seem that the most independent criticism operates not horizontally so to speak, but vertically—when the Area Headquarters applies fresh minds technically and/or financially to Sub-Area or District proposals. (In the United Steel Companies' Branches there are Estimating Sections working under the Chief Engineers, but staffed partly by accountants. The Headquarters organisation of the Group, on the other hand, have a strong Finance Department and examine capital expenditure proposals from Branches from a financial point of view—but without the benefit of any further engineering review at Headquarters level.) Submission of capital expenditure projects from one level to another is also normal under the Coal Board, where there are three levels concerned and under the C.E.G.B. Divisions and Project Groups generally constitute one level below Headquarters. In London Transport, however (and also in the Scottish Electricity Boards so far as generation and main transmission are concerned), there is, for the purpose of capital expenditure, only one level—apart from the distinction between the Departments and their Chief Officers, on the one hand, and the Boards or their Committees, on the other. Therefore, in these organisations the only independent second opinions are those of different Departments—primarily the Finance Departments.

One argument for such review by finance departments is that they possess special experience or expertise or have access to wider information on certain points than the Departments who prepared the proposal originally. People who seek to minimise the value of independent financial examination, however —and they can apparently be found in both private industry and in publicly owned industries and services—may argue that accountants have little knowledge and experience which their colleagues do not possess or cannot readily acquire, and furthermore, that accountants may lack knowledge of technical policy or even of commercial considerations or economics. Part of the answer to such arguments is that they should be trained to acquire such knowledge as well as their own technicalities of rates of interest, depreciation and so on. But to argue like this is really to miss one of the main purposes of independent financial examination, which is to see that all possible points of criticism are raised and the proposals looked at by fresh minds unprejudiced by any particular enthusiasms which may—perhaps quite rightly—have gone into the original preparation of the scheme. If unfortunately any organisation has no independent check of its capital-expenditure proposals by a finance department, one can only hope that there is an independent check by somebody else—for instance, a Sub-Area Engineer looking at a District Engineer's proposals for a cabling scheme, or an Area Board Chairman looking at those of his own Chief Engineer—or the Chairman or Managing Director of a private company, those of his Branch Manager or Works Engineer. In each case the value of such examination will largely depend on the independence and judgement of the person making the second examination. We have seen, however, that the Coal Board do not regard the submission of capital-expenditure projects—usually from an Area to a Division, from Division to Headquarters Department and from Headquarters Department to the Board—as sufficient substitute for full examination by the finance side at each level. The Coal Board system is certainly impressive, and it would be hard to argue that it is over-elaborate for such a complex industry with very large capital schemes. Almost certainly many other organisations in private as well as public ownership could learn a great deal from it.

Most people with practical experience would agree that one of the best ways of keeping the cost of any project within bounds is to announce firmly and unequivocably well in advance that only a certain amount of money is available for it —and to stick to that decision, even if it means modifying the project. Of course, if there is not also a close control on the components that make up the scheme and standards of design there is a danger that this maximum, even if it is not exceeded, will tend to become the minimum. All this applies to time control as well as to cost control. In cost planning a scheme needs to be broken down as far as possible into its components and a cost assigned to each. In time planning and progress control the project is also broken down into its parts—generally the same parts as for cost control—and a period of time assigned to each. It is now fairly common knowledge that detailed advance planning of this kind is the secret of achieving targets both of cost and of time, but probably only a few large and very well-organised concerns apply these techniques completely effectively. They have been worked out and applied in great detail by the Coal Board and the C.E.G.B. with elaborate arrangements of target dates, bar graphs, site supervision and progress meetings. These indeed are the essential elements in any system of progress control, and for the very large and complex projects of these two Boards a considerable expenditure of money and of the time of many highly qualified people is obviously worthwhile. All this clearly provides a further justification for really long-term programming. It takes a very long time, not only to construct power stations and coal mines but also to construct the progress charts and schedules and to make all the arrangements with contractors and so on before construction starts. The longer ahead the work is planned, the quicker it will get done. We have not in this book attempted any analysis of schemes which have suffered delays, but it seems clear that the worst delays have occurred to schemes which were to some degree unprecedented, or which were being started in a hurry by organisations which were relatively new to the job. The Coal Board admittedly failed to use large proportions of the capital allocated to it in its first few years. The earliest schemes of the North of Scotland Hydro-Electric Board appear to have taken a very long time. Serious delays have affected the only nuclear power station so far planned or contemplated by the South Scotland Electricity Board. Only in recent years does it seem to have been realised (and perhaps still only incompletely) what large special internal organisations and how much advance planning are needed before large capital projects can be got under way. Clearly there is an advantage in organisations large enough and old enough to have acquired experience with runs of really big projects of similar kinds.

The timing of progress and cost controls is very important. One of the most valuable features of the Coal Board's financial system is the arrangement for provisional discussion of schemes at 'Stage I', to see if a project would be likely to be acceptable to the higher authorities, before too much time has been expended on it at the lower levels. This procedure must avoid, at a later stage, having to choose between wasting money in order to save time, or vice versa. It is also likely to avoid feelings of frustration in the lower formations. We have not found this kind of procedure quite so formalised as a standard drill anywhere else. No doubt there is often an advance consultation with higher authority, but one would have thought that unless it was made obligatory, it might be neglected in just those cases where it would be most valuable. The forward programming arrangements of the C.E.G.B. and its predecessors have probably served a similar purpose. The Coal Board do not regard their own long-term planning arrangements as a substitute for their 'Stage I' and 'Stage II' procedure, but then these long-term plans are brought out not annually but only every few years. The published versions of these plans do not give detailed individual projects, and even the more detailed internal planning which accompanies them is probably not quite comparable with that of the C.E.G.B. The C.E.G.B.'s long-term plans are brought out annually and are based on much calculation of the economics of placing stations of particular sizes and types at particular spots. This sort of thing can reasonably be regarded as comparable with the Coal Board's 'Stage I' procedure. Moreover, we have seen that the C.E.G.B. has different stages of approval of individual schemes in total and then for the separate main contracts.

The Coal Board seems to be most in advance of other organisations in its detailed reviews of results of capital projects. No other concern we have described seems to have quite such a detailed and rigid system on bringing up, after a scheme is working, the whole financial case that has originally been made out for it, and comparing each estimated figure with what has actually been spent or the return which is actually coming in. Some people doubt the value of such inquests. In other concerns one sometimes hears the comment that they would only waste time and result either in recriminations or futile and overelaborate attempts to justify the *fait accompli*. On the other hand, one has heard of an American organisation with a 'postmortem' system which not only compared predictions with results but attempted to fasten the resulting blame or credit on particular individuals, with the object, partly, of influencing their future careers. One can certainly imagine that such a system might result in excessive caution or self-justification. The object of any sensible inquest should primarily be to prevent accidents in future, and only secondarily to apportion responsibility for past events—although it is valuable to test by experience the soundness of a complete unit of organisation or of a system of working. But the value of inquests also depends on how often similar cases will occur in future. Thus the Coal Board has particular scope for inquests. It has, and will go on having, very many schemes of a basically similar kind involving many different factors—engineering, geology, marketing, labour and so forth—and providing much scope for miscalculations.

The other concerns which we have described are mostly in a different category. There are few cases where there might be substantial differences between estimates and results, not only in capital cost and running expenditure but in the volume and quality of the physical product, and hence of the financial return. Most of the capital equipment of the electricity supply industry is bound to work as predicted. The outstanding exceptions are, of course, nuclear power stations. For them detailed scientific and financial reviews would seem inevitable, both immediately after they have started working and a few years later. There might also, presumably, be scope for a review of the savings produced by road or rail vehicles. There must be many other concerns with a run of capital projects which are intended to yield a financial return and which might be reviewed in a very similar way to those of the coal industry —even though they are smaller and fewer.[7] There seems to be remarkably little reliable quantitive information in any organisation about the maintenance costs of buildings and their relation to changing types of construction and materials. Architects and builders can very often only state in general terms that certain materials will last longer or save maintenance. This is understandable in respect of new materials or types of construction, but even in older types of building the information is scanty. It would seem reasonable for any large organisation proposing to put up a building to make a prediction of its maintenance costs and then review this annually against the actual expenditure. It might take ten or twenty years or longer to build up from this a compendium of all the information needed to make complete assessments of the future commitments involved in building expenditure. But the

[7] See Tibor Barna: *Investment and Growth Policies of British Industrial Firms*, 1962, p. 34: 'Regular scrutinies of the results of investment are few and cursory.'

attempt would still seem to be worth making, and would no doubt yield valuable interim results.

Different types of concern should benefit in the long run by exchanging the fruits of inquests with one another (at least privately), even if the first results were embarrassing. There are, of course, other types of capital project where there is very little to measure in the way of results, even on running costs or maintenance expenditure, but where comparison of estimated and actual capital costs alone will afford scope for enquiry and heart-searching. So will comparisons of construction times and reasons for any delays. No doubt in most cases the speeding up of a programme would save money, and delays would mean waste; but occasionally it will be worth considering whether extra expenditure in order to save time really was, or would have been, fully counter-balanced by savings in other directions—for instance, by the earlier closing of a less-economic installation. Inquests on previous cost planning and the drawing up of timetables should make it possible to draw up more accurate and more helpful cost plans and timetables in future—whether or not the time allowed should have been shortened or lengthened.

(e) *Higher Management and Policy Direction*

Both top-level and departmental organisation are important in capital development. Clearly in both public and private industry and in the public services new capital development is one of the major functions of top management. Indeed, in the organisations we have described probably the bulk of each year's capital development requires at least formal approval— individually, project by project—at the highest level. But the formal process of approval is not the main point. The whole policy of the extent of new capital development and its nature and timing is bound to be one of major policy in any organisation. There are some organisations indeed where most major policy questions at any time concern new capital development and where this subject is the main preoccupation of most of those in the top management. The most outstanding example is now the C.E.G.B., and on a much smaller scale the North of Scotland Hydro-Electric Board. The other organisations we have discussed have all been somewhat different. The Coal Board has had capital development problems, probably as great as those of any other organisation which has ever existed in this country.   Its financial and demand estimating problems have probably also been more difficult even than those of the C.E.G.B. and its predecessors.   Yet we cannot put the Coal Board in quite the same category as the C.E.G.B. and the Hydro-Electric Board, because simultaneously with these problems it has had others of comparable seriousness concerning current production, labour relations and internal organisation.   It has seldom been able to concentrate on capital development before everything else.   London Transport have capital development problems which are large and difficult, but not comparable with those of the Coal Board and the C.E.G.B.—nor always the most serious problems at the highest management levels.   No doubt the balance would be somewhat different in the various London Transport organisations in their major periods of expansion between the Wars.   With the Area Electricity Boards expansion and new capital development have, ever since their creation, been very considerable, but the size and complexity of the individual projects and their variety have hardly been comparable with those of the C.E.G.B., the Coal Board and the Hydro Board.   They have been less affected by technical change.

All this has been reflected in the different organisational structures.   Capital construction, including the problems of nuclear generation, was clearly among the major tasks which the C.E.G.B. was expected to undertake from the outset.   This comes out in the Parliamentary Debate on the Electricity Act 1957.[8]   Likewise it seems clear that the Coal Board did not get its capital development programming going at full momentum until it had built up separate and specialised sections of staff, at least at Area level, to deal with new construction and nothing else.   To organise its capital programme with full effect it needed also its separate Departments for Reconstruction and for Purchasing and Stores, and the support of other organisations, such as the three Research and Development Establishments and the reorganised Staff Department.   The other

[8] An interesting parallel is to be found in the suggestion in the *Report of the Select Committee on the Nationalized Industries*, July 1961, pp. 116–118, paras. 467–475 that the organisation structure of the Gas industry should be changed and a body similar to the C.E.G.B. created in order to deal with the development of major new plant.

organisations we have discussed have rather fewer and less heavily weighted special sections for capital development. The merging of such sections with those for maintenance and current operations is most complete in London Transport, presumably because of the relative volume of the different kinds of work and the extent to which reliance is placed on manufacturers. In the Area Electricity Boards a somewhat similar result is probably due to an opposite cause. While the pressure on the whole organisation is probably less than elsewhere, new development is a major preoccupation, and current operations and maintenance can presumably be made subsidiary to it, at least at the highest levels.

The major responsibilities of higher management in relation to capital development are to provide sustained policy objectives, clear direction on priorities, a continuing supply of money and resources of all kinds, a firm and steady system of control and channels for a regular flow of information between all concerned. Only thus will the higher management create within its organisation that degree of confidence in long-term planning without which no major capital development can go ahead properly. We have kept emphasising the enormous size of the projects in the programmes we have described and the long periods required for planning. Assurances of adequate staff and finance to see programmes through and continuity of policy have therefore been essential to any progress. The question of priorities is crucial. In order to get the internal organisation going on the right lines, not only for planning but for such things as land acquisition, research and development, staff training and so on, it has been necessary to know the relative importance to be attached to such matters as carbonisation within the Coal Board, and nuclear developments within the C.E.A. and the C.E.G.B. In each case continuity of policy over a long period has been essential to progress. The North of Scotland Hydro-Electric Board, for instance, was fortunate to start out with limited and clearly defined objectives and considerable public and Parliamentary support. Its complex programme of construction has in any case taken a long time to realise and has sometimes been controversial, but, as pre-war experience showed, it could hardly have been embarked upon at all, without such backing.

R

(f) *Centralisation and Decentralisation*

One of the basic problems of planning and supervising capital development is whether this should be done at the centre, or by local management, or at some intermediate level of general management, or by some special units set up for this purpose only.   This question of centralisation versus decentralisation is, of course, a very wide one indeed.   One of the characteristics of our age is a feeling of disquiet about large organisations (public and private), while another is that these organisations continue to flourish in response to the demands for their products.   Most people seem to recognise that they cannot be abolished.   So, as the next best thing, there is a constant demand for their structure and methods of working to be decentralised.   Our problem here, however, is not whether decentralisation is a sound principle of management generally, but how far it can be applied to the particular question of capital development—a very different matter.   Moreover, one needs to look at the various forms of capital development and the various functions involved in its planning and control and see where each function can most conveniently be carried out.

Such studies as that of the Acton Society Trust on 'Size and Morale' are sometimes read as if they proved that everything is always done more efficiently in the smallest possible units.   It is wiser to consider first which functions are being studied in each case and whether it is reasonable to draw analogies from them for quite different functions.   The Acton studies were concerned mainly with basic production units, such as factories and mines.   But the fact that a small or medium-sized factory may have better morale than a big one does not prove that a firm which only owns one factory is necessarily more efficient than one which owns ten.   The Fleck and Herbert Reports are sometimes considered the classic contrast between doctrines of centralisation and decentralisation.   They indeed tend to be so treated by Professor R. S. Edwards and Mr. H. Townsend[9]— the former himself a member of the Herbert Committee and now Chairman of the Electricity Council.   These authors, while recognising the differences between the two industries,

[9] R. S. Edwards and H. Townsend, *Business Enterprise*, 1958, p. 504.

nevertheless feel that there is also a basic conflict of principle. A similar view was taken in an article on 'The Organisation of the Nationalised Industries', by Mr. A. E. Thompson:[10]

> Sir Alexander Fleck brought to his investigation an unrivalled knowledge of large scale enterprise gained in his work with I.C.I., Sir Edwin Herbert as a solicitor, a bias in favour of an organisation based on checks and balances, with the right to resist central control built into the structure of lower formations. These principles are the glory of the British Constitution, but they may be less relevant to electricity supply.

While the contrast of personal backgrounds is interesting and indeed illuminating, we need, if we are to understand the two reports, to look at the technical and organisational facts of the situation in each industry at the time it was investigated. It does not by any means follow that either Committee would have made similar recommendations for the other industry.

Moreover, the Fleck and the Herbert Reports are not in conflict all along the line. The Fleck Report did not say that everything should be done at the centre. It, in fact, specifically approved the basic structure of an organisation which delegated considerable powers and functions to its subordinate units—and in particular gave most of the basic project planning work to the forty-eight Area Headquarters. Indeed, the Fleck Report recommended strengthening these Area Headquarters. The Herbert Committee, on the other hand, recognised that the organisations at the centre had most important functions of direction and co-ordination.

Generally the best guide as to what to devolve to any lower management level is whether at that level there will be enough experienced and competent staff to carry the responsibility. This in turn depends on whether there is enough work to devolve and whether it would come in a sufficiently regular flow to allow experience to be accumulated. In capital development it is a matter both of the number and the variety of the projects. The Herbert Committee recognised this in suggesting that the planning of 'advanced' power stations should be reserved to Headquarters and that of 'conventional' ones left to Divisions. Their mistake was in over-estimating

[10] *Scottish Journal of Political Economy*, Vol. IV, June 1957, p. 81.

the number of 'conventional' projects.   In these matters formal rules sometimes matter less than the way in which practice actually develops.   Even when subordinate units in a large organisation are given very wide formal powers, they will nevertheless often have to consult specialists at their Head-quarters if they lack experience or have projects of exceptional size or technical complexity—or if they fail to consult, Head-quarters may need to intervene when things go wrong.   On the other hand, if there has already been a run of successful projects a Headquarters may tend to approve similar projects in future quickly and easily.

In the Coal Board the settlement of the planning function entirely at Area rather than Divisional level seems to have come about finally in the last few years, since Areas have accumu-lated sufficient staff and experience.   The only room for argu-ment about decentralisation of colliery capital development work would seem to be in the level at which approval and authority can be given.   It might be asked why projects have to be submitted successively to two higher levels above those at which they are planned.   In the first place Divisions can them-selves approve schemes costing up to £250,000.   This is the highest authorising power possessed by any subordinate Head-quarters of any of the organisations discussed in this book— almost certainly the highest in any British public body—and probably much higher than in almost any British private industry.   Of course, £250,000 is not relatively a very high figure in the coal industry, but it does reflect the magnitude and complexity of the scheme itself.   It represents the largest type of colliery project which does not add significantly to total productive capacity—as distinct from improvement or replace-ment of wasting assets.   The procedure therefore means that the Board itself and its Headquarter Departments must be consulted about every such addition to capacity.   This is no doubt because the whole coal-producing capacity of the country and the balance of advantage in producing in different coalfields must be considered together.   In the Board's earliest years there was desperate need to enlarge productive capacity as much and as quickly as possible, and at the same time there was a great shortage of resources, both human and material. Naturally the Board would want to consider its strategy as a whole so as to make the best use of these resources. Similarly' at the time of writing there were severe limitations on development—in terms of money, and to prevent excess production—while the capacity for future years had nevertheless to be preserved. All this clearly called for a judicious balancing of the advantages of concentrating a limited amount of new development in one coalfield or another. The other major kind of capital development undertaken by the Coal Board has been carbonisation plant, and, as there is less experience of providing this and probably less need to provide it in the future, it is natural that the discretion given to Divisions should be more limited in terms of money than that for colliery schemes.

In electricity we have found a completely different situation. The basic pattern of centralisation and decentralisation has largely been laid down by statute, and less by managerial direction. The Area Boards in England and Wales have always been legally autonomous bodies, and thus it is natural—but not inevitable—that their capital development has always been controlled, whether by the Government or the B.E.A./C.E.A., or through the Electricity Council, in terms of total programmes or broad categories rather than by individual projects. There never seems to have been any limit on the amount a Board could spend on any individual scheme, nor on the form of such a scheme. This independence of the Electricity Boards is not an automatic result of their having distinct legal status. The L.T.E. as a separate statutory corporation was required to submit to the British Transport Commission any scheme costing more than £100,000. One reason for this relative freedom of the Electricity Boards may be that the bulk of their schemes are technically much more like one another than those of L.T.E. or N.C.B. They are also generally much less expensive.

There may be a case for further standardisation or even bulk supply of equipment for electricity distribution, but not for control of particular distribution schemes at national level. Such schemes will often have gone through two management levels within the Area before approval, and there appears to be a distinct tendency for planning to be done at lower levels as planning staffs are built up and experience accumulated. This trend may well continue as the whole network grows. Quite naturally the degree of devolution of planning, even within particular Areas and particular Sub-Areas, varies according to the nature and density of the networks, and the localities concerned, and the size of the Districts. It is perhaps surprising that so far only two Areas have apparently adopted a suggestion of the Herbert Committee[11] for reducing the number of management levels from three to two.   Perhaps problems of 'span of control' prevent the elimination of the third level in all the electricity Areas, but such problems vary, as everyone with experience knows, according to the complexity of the job to be done.   As the work of electricity Districts grows, there will presumably be fewer new problems to put up to the next management level (Area or Sub-Area) and, therefore, that level might be able to control more Districts.   Possibly as the whole network grows the number of Areas will increase.   One might expect that sooner or later the three levels would somehow be reduced to two.

The C.E.G.B. has a quite different pattern of delegation— parts of it only recently worked out, as the whole organisation is new.   Moreover, most of the schemes are vastly larger and more complex than those of the Area Boards.   For reasons which we have discussed, the C.E.G.B. has not followed the suggestion of the Herbert Committee of handing over any of the main functions of generation construction or planning to its Regions or Divisions.   The only delegation of this work has been to the Project Groups.   Not only complete new power stations but their major components are so large and their designs are developing so fast that Headquarters Branches must be deeply involved on the technical, financial and contractual sides.   The financial powers of the Project Groups to place contracts were larger than those of the subordinate units of probably any other organisation except the N.C.B. Divisions and the C.E.G.B.'s own Regions (on the transmission side), but nevertheless they were not large relative to the enormous total cost of power stations.   Moreover, they were, understandably, conditional on consultation with Headquarters on technical and scientific matters, and on contract policies.   On the main

[11] *Report of the Committee of Enquiry into the Electricity Supply Industry*, Cmd. 9672, 1956, p. 77, para, 291. and p. 142, Summary 25 (b). (The latter is more explicit than the former.)

transmission side the C.E.G.B.'s Regional Executive Committees had power to authorise schemes up to the same total limits as the N.C.B.'s Divisional Boards—£250,000, but it is significant that before delegating these powers, the Board set up the Regions above the Divisions.

Decentralisation on any scale is scarcely possible in London Transport. Much centralisation seems inevitable in any London organisation, and perhaps in any transport organisation. Spheres of railway operating management are naturally divided by lines rather than by areas. The road and rail vehicles are highly standardised and to a large extent interchangeable, and their replacement is planned as a whole. Major civil engineering works are clearly too large and too few to be distributed between separate units.

We can sum up on the question of decentralisation by saying that there are few general principles, and it is a question of finding within each organisation the right places where each kind of work can most effectively be done. This will differ according to its volume, continuity and variety, its technical complexity, the nature of the outside organisations which are concerned in doing it, how well established the main organisation itself is, and how stable its policies. The management of capital development involves very special kinds of function to which one must not apply, without most careful question and reserve, any general principles which may have been worked out and proved sound in other management fields. There must be many other industries besides those discussed here where it is usual and indeed right to leave day-to-day operations largely to the discretion of local managers, while concentrating the planning and production of new capital equipment as quite a separate function at the centre. This does not mean that all sides of capital development work must always be centralised. It is vitally important for much of it to be decentralised. But decentralisation must be to the right sort of subordinate units—generally units or parts of units set up for this purpose alone, quite separate from the operating units.

(g) *Conclusion*

Finally, we must remember that capital development is not simply an economic or financial abstraction. It consists of complex pieces of machinery—steel structures, lumps of concrete, holes in the ground and ideas which can never be realised without taking other people's dearly cherished land, creating dirt and confusion, and perhaps making people change their jobs and move about the country. Capital development, above all, involves people, miners and cable jointers, unskilled labourers and skilled welders, planning engineers and architects, accountants, solicitors, estate surveyors, and—not necessarily above all, but among all these—people skilled in the indefinable arts of very large scale general management and administration—people who can think in terms of years and decades and tens of millions of pounds. But, above all, these people, and indeed everyone concerned, must be capable of thinking and feeling at the same time in much simpler human terms and of understanding the perfectly obvious, but often disregarded, fact that you cannot get large projects carried out without persuading large numbers of extremely different sorts of people to understand the importance of what is being done and to work together.

INDEX

263